THOUGHTS
ON
ZECHARIAH

The Restoration of Israel and the
Millennial Reign

RSI
PUBLISHING

Kenneth Giesman

RSI
PUBLISHING

Kenneth Giesman

ISBN: 9781960641915
Printed in the United States of America
Edition Date: October 2025

Disclaimer

Disclaimer Statement:

This book contains general Biblical and personal information based on the author's knowledge and experiences from God's Word and his Christian walk. It is published for general reference purposes to bless others only.

The publisher and the author disclaim any personal liability, either directly or indirectly, for the information contained within this Bible study. Although the publisher and the author have made every effort to ensure the accuracy and completeness of the information contained within this Bible study, we assume no responsibility for errors, inaccuracies, omissions, and inconsistencies.

Contents

Preface

Writing this commentary on Zechariah has been a journey for me. I did not start out to write a commentary. I started journaling my thoughts on a book of the Bible, just as I've done with many other books of the Bible in the past. The Prophets, though, are different for me. They are mysterious, and their truths are like nuggets of gold that just draw me in and motivate me to find more nuggets. I am not a scholar; I am just a lover of the Word. I love reading the Prophets and understanding what they are saying. Typically, when I read anything in the Prophets, I pull out a commentary and read both the scripture and the commentary to gain a deeper understanding of what I am reading. And that is how I started reading Zechariah, by reading commentaries and listening to pastors preach on Zechariah via YouTube. Somewhere in the middle of Zechariah, I went on a fast, praying for my family. Shortly after the fast ended, the LORD began to show me how to view the second coming of Jesus Christ through the teachings of Joel Richardson, and the LORD started leading me to scriptures that helped me understand Zechariah better.

He also showed me that the vast majority of prophetic scriptures discuss either the first coming of Jesus Christ or the second coming of Jesus Christ. I don't have conclusive figures, but it appears to me that the Old Testament discusses the second coming of Christ more than the first coming of Christ, and many scriptures point to both the first and second coming of Jesus Christ in the same passage. When you begin to understand the events surrounding the return of Jesus Christ, you start to see it everywhere in the Prophets. Understanding the events surrounding the return of Christ brings the prophets to life, and it becomes clear that they build upon each other, offering additional details concerning the return of Christ. It is like the four gospels. Many of them discuss the same event with just a slight variation, because they are telling us about the event from their perspective, yet it remains the same event. None of the gospels is wrong, but when you put their writings regarding one event together, you have a clearer picture of what happened. That is what you have with the Prophets. The Prophets are all writing concerning the return to the land, the first coming of Christ, and/or the second coming of Christ. They continue to discuss the events that will surround these three occasions repeatedly. Each prophet tells us a portion of the event that God assigned to them.

What helped me tremendously to understand the book of Zechariah is the work of Joel Richardson. Joel's knowledge of and interpretation of scripture led me to think differently, and his understanding of the return of Christ makes the most sense and is the most biblically sound. Understanding how the scripture reveals the return of Christ helped me tremendously when reading Zechariah. Joel's knowledge of the Old Testament, the major prophets, and the minor prophets helped show me how all these scriptures build upon each other. I don't agree with Joel's interpretation of events because he is the first one I've heard. I agree with his interpretation of the scripture because I am well aware of the other views, and they left me with too many questions. Even before discovering the teachings of Joel Richardson, I was leaning toward a post-tribulation rapture because the argument for a pre-tribulation rapture is like trying to put a jigsaw puzzle together where the pieces don't all fit together quite right, so we try to force them together. Nowhere does scripture directly tell us of a pre-tribulation rapture. You must piece it together, and you are still left with parts that don't fit together well. Joel's knowledge of the scriptures and his interpretation of events left my spirit in agreement with him. As you look through the scriptures, there are too many scriptures saying the same thing to ignore the reality of Jesus' triumphant march through the desert, including those here in Zechariah. I highly recommend Joel's book, "From Sinai to Zion", for anyone who wants to understand the second coming of Jesus Christ.

In His teaching, Joel points out that Israel is the true Bride of Christ, and we, the Gentiles, comprise a portion of the bride because we are grafted into the root. The end times are all about God bringing His bride back to Him once and for all time. Never again will His bride stray from His love. The Antichrist will be Islamic and will come against Israel, but before he comes against Israel, he will come against Saudi Arabia and Egypt. Once he subdues the nations of the King of the South, these nations join his coalition. The Antichrist and his coalition will be winning this war, and Israel will be on the brink of extinction, with most of the population hiding in refuge, killed, or taken captive. Many of the prison camps will be in the desert south of Jerusalem.

When Jesus returns, He will first gather His host of angels and saints and will march and/or ride through the sky from Egypt, following the route of the first Exodus. As he marches through the desert, He frees the people in the prison camps, and they will continue with Him as He marches to Jerusalem. On this march, He destroys the forces of the Antichrist, and when He gets to Jerusalem, He leads the people in final victory at the battle of Armageddon. If I understand correctly, the time between his return and the final triumph will be approximately 30 days. This 30-day period corresponds to the time difference between Daniel and Revelation, as given for the final three and a half years of the Great Tribulation, also known as The Time of Jacob's Trouble. Once the final victory is won, the reign of Jesus in the Millennial Kingdom begins. This understanding helped tremendously as I attempted to understand what Zechariah is telling us.

I consider myself to be a student of Joel Richardson. I believe that Jesus will return after the tribulation, and His victory will mark the beginning of the Millennial Kingdom. I believe that Jerusalem, Israel, and the Middle East are central to the end times. Europe, Asia, and the Americas are part of the world that will be judged and will play a role in the story, but are not central to it. As you read the Book of Zechariah and the other Prophets, you begin to see that the end times center around Israel and its neighbors. You can't read the book of Zechariah without understanding the love of God for the people of Israel and the land of Israel, particularly the city of Jerusalem. You can't read the book of Zechariah without understanding that the end times are all about Israel.

I believe that the war of Gog and Magog is the same war that the Antichrist prosecutes against Israel, and Gog is the Antichrist. Joel Richardson has an excellent article on his website, joelstrumpet.com/gogandmagog/, explaining why the Battle of Gog and Magog is the same as the battle that the Antichrist wages against Israel and why Gog is identified as the Antichrist.

I consulted a variety of sources to gain a deeper understanding of Zechariah. I started by reading commentaries from EnduringWord.com, BibleHub.com, Explainingthebook.com, and Studylight.com. I listened to Chuck Missler's entire YouTube Series on Zechariah. I listened to many of Joel Richardson's YouTube sessions on the end times, including his series on Revelation, Daniel, the Return of Jesus, and Fulfilled, as well as several of his individual YouTube videos on the end times. I listened to my own pastor, Ryan Brennan, preach a series on Revelation, as well as Matt Chandler's series on Revelation on YouTube. I also used the NASB Lexicon and the Strong's Concordance on Biblehub.com.

It seemed to me that many of the commentaries agreed, with slight differences, but still did not provide me with a clear understanding of what Zechariah is trying to convey.

Many of these commentaries were written in the 1800s, and the writers did not believe that the people of Israel would ever be restored to the land. I read the commentaries found on Biblehub. I read some more thoroughly than others, including the Benson Commentary, Gill's Exposition of the Entire Bible, and the Pulpit Commentary. To a lesser extent, I also utilized commentaries available on StudyLight.org. However, the key for me to understand what Zechariah was saying was Joel Richardson's work on the end times and his sequence of events for Jesus Christ's second coming.

I found the first six chapters of Zechariah to be frustrating because they appear to be a series of random visions intended to encourage the Israelites to complete the temple. I went through them several times before I began to realize that they, too, pointed to the Day of the LORD. These visions portray a God who is on the side of Israel, who is doing a work in Israel, and who will punish those who've persecuted Israel. But the visions are vague. You must review these visions in conjunction with the scriptures written by other prophets to understand where these visions are pointing. It is as if God was developing Zechariah as a prophet with these visions before He communicated the more specific prophecies concerning the first and second coming of Jesus Christ.

As you read the Old Testament, you are left with sadness and an empathy for the Jewish people. I would tell any Jewish person that I take no joy in your suffering and the suffering that is to come. The nation of Israel suffered so much persecution and pain because it bears the responsibility of being the people God chose as His bride. They also suffer because of their rebellion against God and their rejection of Jesus Christ. It seems to me to be too much. I have no idea where the judgment of God stops and where the persecution by Satan starts. In Revelation 12, we see that the woman, Israel, gives birth to a Son, Jesus Christ, and the great Red Dragon wants to devour the Son. The Woman then flees to safety away from the Dragon. If Satan cannot have the child, he wants the Woman (Israel). Satan has been after Israel throughout all of history to make God out to be a liar and to appear weak. Being the people of God hasn't been easy for Israel; it carries a great responsibility and burden.

Much of Israel today is very secular. Without understanding the modern state of Israel, you may think that their only sin is that they still do not recognize Jesus as the Messiah. However, the music festival that was attacked is indicative of modern Israel, chasing other gods or no god at all. The young people at the festival were dancing around a large statue of Buddha. I'm sure that most of these young people were not Buddhist, but they also did not object. The point that I am making is that just because the Jews are back in the land, it does not mean that they are restored to their God. They are chasing other gods or no god at all. The middle of Zechariah discusses a people rejecting their God, and the end of Zechariah focuses on the extreme measures that God takes to restore His people to Himself.

I write this not because I have some great perspective that others do not, but because I want to share what I've learned with others. I am not a scholar. In fact, sometimes I think that scholars get lost in the minutiae and forget about the larger picture of what is happening or what the writer is trying to convey. Scholars attend our esteemed institutions of theology and study orthodox doctrine, which is a highly beneficial practice. However, they are also taught a theory of eschatology based on the view to which that school subscribes. Therefore, the prominent thoughts in Christianity today are amillennialism, postmillennialism, or dispensational premillennialism. Very few teachers are proponents of historic premillennialism. For many years, I subscribed to the teaching of a premillennial pretribulation return of Christ. I knew little about dispensationalism, and I did not realize that the theory behind dispensationalism is what drives the theory of a pretribulation return of Christ. However, when I study the scripture, it is difficult to see a direct passage pointing to the pretribulation return of Jesus.

What I've come to believe is a simple, direct understanding of eschatology, which tells me that Jesus is coming back for His Church and for His bride, Israel. Israel will recognize their Messiah and will repent of their rejection of Him. Together, the Church and Israel will eat the marriage supper of the Lamb and will be served by the Bridegroom, Jesus Christ.

Acknowledgments

Without the invaluable support of Pastor Charles Morris, this work would not have reached its final form as a book. Pastor Charles encouraged me to undertake the task of writing my own book, even though I had never intended to do so. His guidance extended far beyond encouragement; he also served as my advisor, editor, and publisher. I am deeply indebted to him for his dedicated efforts, particularly in helping to add the finishing touches to this book.

Although I've never had the opportunity to meet Joel Richardson in person, I am profoundly grateful for his teaching ministry. Joel possesses an extensive understanding of the Old Testament, with particular expertise in the prophetic books and passages. By learning from Joel's YouTube teachings, I discovered many key passages that reveal the connections between Zechariah and other prophetic books of the Bible. Without his insights, these important links might have remained unnoticed in my work.

Introduction To Zechariah

Zechariah is a priest from a priestly family. His father, Berechiah, and grandfather, Iddo, were priests. One of my favorite nuggets of information I discovered in studying Zechariah is the meaning of their names in Hebrew and what they say when you string them all together. Zechariah means "The LORD remembers," Berechiah means "The LORD blesses, and Iddo means "The appointed time." When we put this phrase together, it means the LORD remembers and blesses in His appointed time. This theme permeates the entire Book. In the early chapters of Zechariah, his messages are intended to encourage the people to finish the Temple. In the latter chapters of Zechariah, he encourages today's readers with the promise of the Millennial Kingdom.

This message was essential to the people of Zechariah's day because the return from exile was not an easy life. Zechariah's family returned from Babylon with Zerubbabel around 538 BC, bringing great enthusiasm to rebuild the Temple. However, after a strong start, the Temple lay unfinished for 16 years (Ezra 4:23-24). The people of the land were very discouraged during this time. Zechariah began his ministry in 520 BC, encouraging the people to complete what God had called them to do. They laid the foundation of the Temple, and then they stopped building for 16 years because of local opposition that did not want to see a restoration of Israel. Zechariah was writing to encourage the people that

God had not forgotten them and that they should be obedient to finish the Temple and not forget God.

Life was difficult for the people in Judah, trying to restart a life in a country destroyed by war, surrounded by people who wanted to claim ownership of the land and not share it with the exiles. It was easier for the people to focus on their daily existence than to pursue obedience to God and take on the cause of building the Temple. The LORD wanted to encourage the people and let them know He remembered them and would bless them. The LORD also wanted to convey a much larger message to Israel and the Church about the first and second coming of the Messiah, as well as the future reconciliation of Israel with their God. The Book's central message is that the LORD remembers His people and will bless them at the appointed time, whether in Zechariah's day or at the second coming.

The Book of Zechariah is split into three sub-themes: 1) a series of visions to encourage the people of Zechariah's day to finish the Temple; 2) the first coming of Jesus Christ and the people's rejection of Him and His rejection of them for a time; and 3) The second coming of Jesus Christ, His judgment of the nations, and the reconciliation of the Jewish people to Jesus Christ through some challenging circumstances.

You have a series of seemingly disjointed visions in the first theme and the first section of Zechariah. Zechariah is writing to remind the people that God sees them and is their protector and provider. As I've tried to understand these visions I began to see the Millennium in them. Although they may seem to be a series of random visions to encourage the people of Israel. These visions point to the Millennial Kingdom more than the reader sees in the initial reading.

Chapters 7 & 8 are a transition from Zechariah's day to the future. Chapter 7 begins with a question about whether the people should continue fasting as they did when they were in exile. In Chapter 7, God tells us why He scattered the people from the land. However, chapter 8 tells us of God's favor for the people and the land during the Millennial Kingdom, when the people will live in peace, and the land will yield an abundance of produce. Chapter 8 begins with future prophecies, and Chapter 9 continues with the foretelling of Alexander the Great's coming to judge those who've been Israel's enemies. Chapter 9 concludes with a depiction of the impending war between Gog and Magog and Christ's triumph over the armies of the Antichrist. Chapters 10 through 14 point to the second coming of Jesus Christ, when He will make Israel His people again and restore the Kingdom of Israel, from which the Messiah will rule the world. Chapter 11 is an interlude that covers prophecies of the Messiah's first coming as the Good Shepherd and the people's rejection of the Good Shepherd. This rejection leads the Good Shepherd to abandon the flock and leave them to be slaughtered on their own. Chapters 12-14 continue with the Messiah's second coming to save the people of Israel from annihilation and restore the Kingdom of Israel during the Millennial Kingdom.

Because it foretells the first and second coming of Jesus Christ, the Book of Zechariah is often quoted in the New Testament. It is estimated that the Book of Zechariah is cited 67 times in the New Testament from 54 passages in Zechariah.

I was excited to study this Book and reach the ultimate state of humanity. A world with Jesus as the King reigning from Jerusalem. My wife and I wanted to go to Israel in 2023, but we decided it wasn't God's timing for us at that time; hopefully, it will be soon. Pilgrimages will be a regular occurrence when Jesus is in charge. At that time, you will be blessed to be chosen to live in Jerusalem. This study made me both sad and excited. It is heartbreaking to see the rejection of the Good Shepherd by the flock of Israel and His rejection of the flock of Israel, giving them over to be slaughtered. I am excited because it doesn't end there. We are so near the second coming of Jesus as the Messiah and the reconciliation of the flock of Israel to their Good Shepherd.

Jesus Christ does not reject His people forever; He rejects them only until the fullness of the Gentiles is complete. Zechariah chapter 11 tells us that He annuls the covenant He made with the children of Israel at Mount Sinai, but He is not done with Israel. He replaces a conditional covenant with an unconditional covenant, the New Covenant. Although the nation did not fulfill its part of the Mosaic covenant, God made two unconditional covenants with individuals: the Abrahamic Covenant with Abraham and the Davidic Covenant with David. The Abrahamic covenant includes the promise of specific land, descendants as numerous as the stars in the sky, and kings that would come from Abraham. Abraham was promised that he would become a great nation, possess the land, and the whole world would be blessed through him. The David Covenant is an extension of the Abrahamic Covenant, but it adds that a descendant of David would sit on the throne of David forever.

While God annuls the Mosaic covenant, or I would say He replaces it with a New Covenant, God does not forget Israel. In the last days, He renews His commitment to them as His bride, but at a steep price. The New Covenant was initially made for Israel (Jeremiah 31 and Matthew 15:21-28); however, it extends to anyone who will accept Jesus as their Savior. In the last days, all of Israel will be saved under this New Covenant. We tend to think of the New Covenant as being intended for the Church, but Romans 11 says we who believe in Jesus as the Christ are grafted into the family of God as spiritual children of Abraham. Israel has been set aside for a time to allow the Gentiles to take part in this New Covenant, but Israel hasn't been replaced.

Zechariah 12:10 says,

"And I will pour out on the house of David and on the inhabitants of Jerusalem the Spirit of grace and of pleading, so that they will look at Me whom they pierced; and they will mourn for Him, like one mourning for an only son, and they will weep bitterly over Him like the bitter weeping over a firstborn (NASB).

Romans 11:26-27 says,

"and so all Israel will be saved; just as it is written: "THE DELIVERER WILL COME FROM ZION, HE WILL REMOVE UNGODLINESS FROM JACOB"; "THIS IS MY COVENANT WITH THEM, WHEN I TAKE AWAY THEIR SINS" (NASB).

Zechariah 13:9 tells us,

"And I will bring the third part through the fire, Refine them as silver is refined, and test them as gold is tested." They will call on My name, And I will answer them; I will say, 'They are My people,' And they will say, 'The LORD is my God.'"

"As Paul tells us in Romans 11:11, God is not finished with Israel; they have stumbled but not fallen. God is very clear about this in Romans 11:1-2, where Paul writes,

"I say then, God has not rejected His people, has He? Far from it! For I too am an Israelite, a descendant of Abraham, of the tribe of Benjamin. God has not rejected His people whom He foreknew. "(NASB)

You can't read the Book of Zechariah and think that the Church has replaced Israel. Israel is central in the last-day plan of God, and all the remnants of Israel will be saved. The Church has not replaced Israel but has been added to Israel.

Zechariah 1
A Jealous God

The prophet Zechariah prophesied alongside Haggai. His first prophecy is two months after Haggai's first prophecy. Haggai's prophecy centers on God's concern for the Temple and is much more direct in his language. Zechariah focuses on God's care for the people of Israel and uses more visions, pictures, and symbols in the language.

Zechariah tells us when he began writing this book by using the date of the King who controlled the land. There was no king in Israel at that time, therefore, Zechariah cited the reign of Darius, ruler of the Medes and the Persians. He started writing in the eighth month of the second year of Darius' reign.

Zechariah tells us who is writing this Book, and to ensure accuracy, he provides the names of his father and grandfather. Zechariah is also mentioned in Ezra 5:1-2 and Ezra 6:14. These passages mention that Haggai and Zechariah were prophesying and assisting the leaders of the people in rebuilding the city, specifically the Temple. The name Zechariah means "the LORD remembers," which fits perfectly. This book is all about the fact that God remembers and has a plan for His people. Zechariah encouraged them indirectly by telling them about God's love for them and by keeping the presence of the Messiah very much in their minds.

> *Zechariah 1:1 (NASB) In the eighth month of the second year of Darius, the word of the LORD came to Zechariah the prophet, the son of Berechiah, the son of Iddo saying,*

Twice in the first chapter, we read "Zechariah, the son of Berechiah, son of Iddo." While we are being told who wrote the book, God also provides us with a message about Himself and His love for His people and the land of Israel. As stated in the Introduction, Zechariah means "The LORD remembers." However, Berechiah means "The LORD blesses, and Iddo means "The appointed time." When we put these names together, they mean "The LORD remembers and blesses in His appointed time." This one phrase, taken from the names of Zechariah's father, Berechiah, and his grandfather, Iddo, summarizes the message of this book. God gives us a message even from the names of the author, his father, and his grandfather.

We also see here that true prophets are called, and Zechariah did not overstep his authority. The Word says, "The word of the LORD came to Zechariah the prophet." (NASB) Zechariah was not proclaiming his own words; he was proclaiming the Word of the LORD. Before Zechariah began to speak and write, the LORD spoke to him.

> *Zechariah 1:2 (NASB) "The LORD was very angry with your fathers.*

Verse 2 reminds the people of something that they knew very well, "The LORD was very angry with your fathers." (NASB) Even though they might have known this, they needed the prophets to remind them that God was still in control and had a plan for them. They just spent 70 years in captivity, and now they have come back to the land. Initially, upon returning to the land, everything was new and exciting; however, as time wore on, things became difficult, and opposition arose to their rebuilding efforts. As the Introduction to Zechariah reminds us, the people had become discouraged, faced opposition, and just wanted to live their lives. When offered the opportunity to return to the land, most Jews preferred to stay in Babylon and maintain the lives they had created for themselves.

Being on a mission for God was hard, and where was God? Why wasn't He making this mission easy? This is an excellent reminder for us. Being on a mission for God is not always easy and not always exciting. The details of life must still be dealt with; you still have to figure out how to provide for your family and handle all of life's difficulties. After being there for 30 years, the people just wanted to live their lives in the most comfortable manner possible. They had grown tired of sacrifice. The prophets reminded them that they were there for something more important. They had a God who loved them and who jealously regarded their worship. This one small sentence reminds them that they were not just any nation; they were the people of the one true God, and their God wanted their worship.

Zechariah 1:3 (NASB) "Therefore say to them, 'This is what the LORD of armies says: "Return to Me," declares the LORD of armies, "that I may return to you," says the LORD of armies.

Verse 3 is very much like James 4:8, "Come close to God and He will come close to you. Cleanse your hands, you sinners; and purify your hearts, you double-minded" (NASB). Zechariah is reminding the people that because of their fathers' sins, they were taken out of the land and into captivity. The LORD urges them to return to the LORD, and the LORD will return to them. God is calling them back into fellowship. God is a lover wooing back His beloved. It very much reminds me of the book of Hosea. Hosea's wife is unfaithful to him (as a prostitute), and yet he continues to go after her and bring her back. That is the picture we are given of God in relation to the nation of Israel. They have been unfaithful, and He wants and desires to restore His relationship with them.

That is the same thing God does with each of us. He does not care what you have done. He pleads with us to turn away from our sins and return to Him. When we turn from God to chase other "gods" and sins, God compares that infidelity in sexual terms to help us understand the severity of our actions. See Ezekiel 23 to understand how God sees our rebellion against Him. He compares us to whores. You may say He is talking about Israel in Ezekiel 23, and yes, He is talking about Israel, but what makes you think we are any different than Israel? Consider the second half of James 4:8, which reads, "Cleanse your hands, you sinners; and purify your hearts, you double-minded" (NASB). I know my own selfish, lustful heart, and I know my times of rebellion where I think I make a better god than God. The enemy has come to steal, kill, and destroy, and when he is not doing his job, our sinful nature pulls us into sin. God is pleading with us to return to Him to cleanse our hands, purify our hearts, and be faithful to Him. If we do that, He will draw near to us.

I said in the Introduction that the people were discouraged. Enduring Word Commentary reminds us that the land was still desolate after 70 years of neglect; the work to rebuild and restore the land was difficult; they didn't have a lot of money (Haggai 1:6) or manpower; they suffered crop failures and drought (Haggai 1:10-11); hostile enemies resisted their work (Ezra 4:1-5); and they remembered easier times in Babylon. The people were discouraged, and they needed to draw near to God. However, these issues made them feel further away from God. God tells them and us that He is not the one who moved away. All we need to do is return to Him. The beautiful thing about God is that He will always take us back if we just return to Him.

Zechariah 1:4-5 (NASB) "Do not be like your fathers, to whom the former prophets proclaimed, saying, 'This is what the LORD of armies says: "Return now from your evil ways and from your evil deeds."' But they did not listen or pay attention to Me," declares the LORD. 5 "Your fathers, where are they? And the prophets, do they live forever?

Verses 4 and 5 are a reminder of their fathers' past. God says He sent out the same message to their fathers, but their fathers did not heed the call and did not turn from their evil ways. Where are their fathers now, and where are the prophets now? God reminds us that we do not live forever. Our time to repent is now because we do not always have more time. He also reminds us that He is eternal, and we have a limited time here on this earth. It reminds me of what Matt Chandler said, which I will paraphrase here. Who are we to think that we make a better god than God when God is eternal? When we live our lives the way that we want to, in disobedience to God's Word, we are telling God that we are a better god than God.

> Zechariah 1:6 (NASB) "But did My words and My statutes, which I commanded My servants the prophets, not overtake your fathers? Then they repented and said, 'Just as the LORD of armies planned to do to us in accordance with our ways and our deeds, so He has dealt with us.'"

Verse 6 tells us that God is eternal, and His Words, commands, and statutes live forever. God doesn't change. He is not learning as He goes and evolving based on what He has learned. He is all-knowing and all-wise, and His statutes are right and good for mankind to follow.

The latter half of verse 6 says, "Just as the LORD of armies planned to do to us, in accordance with our ways, and our deeds, so He has dealt with us." (NASB). The more I read the Bible, the more I see the sovereignty of God and the faithfulness of His Word. Once a Word comes out of the LORD's mouth, it is true and will happen. We cannot run from His Word or His statutes. They are true, and no matter how far we try to run from them, we can't outrun them. This truth breaks my heart for all my loved ones running from God's Word. Reading the Book of Zechariah will convince you of one thing: God is God, and His plan will be established. God will let you run from Him. He will even allow you to believe you are in control, but He will have the final say over your life. Job asked,

> *"Why do the wicked still live, Grow old, and also become very powerful?" (NASB) in Job 21:7.*

Asaph said in Psalm 73:3,

> *"For I was envious of the arrogant As I saw the prosperity of the wicked." (NASB)*

But Asaph answers the question for Job in Psalm 73:27,

> *"For, behold, those who are far from You will perish; You have destroyed all those who are unfaithful to You." (NASB)*

We really need to get to the place where we can say, as Asaph said in Psalm 73:28,

> *"But as for me, the nearness of God is good for me; I have made the LORD God my refuge, So that I may tell of all Your works." (NASB)*

Next, we come to what will be eight visions in one night. Each vision provides a different message. This vision appears to be what it is: a message to the people that God loves Jerusalem and Israel and will help them rebuild. However, with verses 16 and 17, I believe we catch a glimpse of the future of Jerusalem and Zion in the Millennial Kingdom, one overflowing with prosperity. These eight visions are vague regarding their timing and our ability to connect them with other passages and events. These visions somehow point to the "Day of the LORD," or the Millennial Kingdom. However, it is not as easy to see the more specific meaning of these visions in the first half of the Book as the prophecies in the second half. We can see that God wants to encourage those who are discouraged and let them know they are His beloved. They do not feel loved as they walk around a once proud Jerusalem that has been left in ruin. Cleaning it up and rebuilding the city is hard, and the people feel discouraged and unloved. The opposition, encouraged by demonic voices, is trying to slow and stop the rebuilding.

I would say the people of Israel today are discouraged and need this word from the LORD. On the outside, we see tough people who endure everything the Devil throws at them. They puff up their chests and stick out their chins, but they are tired of fighting so hard to survive and desire to live a normal, everyday life. Inside, they ask, "Why have I been so fortunate to be one of God's people?" They wonder where God is and why he has allowed the persecution of His people to go on for so long. They are approaching a point where they will be ready to see Jesus as their Messiah.

Zechariah 1:7-12 (NASB) On the twenty-fourth day of the eleventh month, that is, the month Shebat, in the second year of Darius, the word of the LORD came to Zechariah the prophet, the son of Berechiah, the son of Iddo, as follows: 8 I saw at night, and behold, a man was riding on a red horse, and he was standing among the myrtle trees which were in the ravine, with red, sorrel, and white horses behind him. 9 Then I said, "What are these, my lord?" And the angel who was speaking with me said to me, "I will show you what these are." 10 And the man who was standing among the myrtle trees responded and said, "These are the ones whom the LORD has sent to patrol the earth." 11 So they responded to the angel of the LORD who was standing among the myrtle trees and said, "We have patrolled the earth, and behold, all the earth is still and quiet." 12 Then the angel of the LORD said, "LORD of armies, how long will You take no pity on Jerusalem and the cities of Judah, with which You have been indignant for these seventy years?"

Verses 7 through 17 present us with a vision of horsemen. This vision appears to be what it is: a message to the people that God loves Jerusalem and Israel and will help them rebuild and restore their fortunes. The vision concludes in verses 16 and 17: "Therefore the LORD says this: I will return to Jerusalem with compassion; My house will be built in it, declares the LORD of armies, and a measuring line will be stretched over Jerusalem. Again, proclaim, saying, This is what the LORD of armies says: My cities will again overflow with prosperity, and the LORD will again comfort Zion and again choose Jerusalem." (NASB)

It is a prophecy of good welfare for the people of Jerusalem and Israel. God encouraged His people in Zechariah's day and will do so on the Day of the LORD. He was letting them know He was for them then and will be for them in the future. The Enduring Word Commentary informs us that the Temple was completed four years after this prophecy was made. The mercy of God was truly on his people, helping them to rebuild the Temple and the nation. In Chapters 4 and 6, I discuss a Temple that will be built at the beginning of the Millennial Kingdom.

What do we see in this prophecy? First, we see a rider on a red horse standing among the Myrtle trees in a ravine or a narrow valley. With him were riders on other horses that were red, sorrel (chestnut), and white. The passage does not mention the other riders, only the horses, but we assume there were riders on the other horses because verse 10 tells us that these are the ones sent to patrol the earth, and verse 11 tells us that they answered the Angel of the LORD. I believe these colors have meaning, but for this mission, they are on patrol. It is unclear if the meaning is the same as in Revelation 6:1-8. In fact, the horses in the two passages are slightly different. The passage in Revelation describes four horses: white, red, black, and pale (which is described in the original language as having a greenish-yellow hue). The four horsemen of Revelation represent Conquest, War, Famine, and Death. This passage in Zechariah has three colors: red, sorrel, and white. We are not told there is a meaning to their color, but we can assume there is. I believe the functions are consistent with the color found in Revelation, but this mission was just to observe and report on the nations. They were on patrol.

Some believe that the Myrtle Tree in this passage is a symbol of Israel. However, my understanding is that the Fig Tree represents the physical nation of Israel, and the Olive Tree represents the spiritual nation of Israel. Some say that the Myrtle Tree was a symbol of peace. Symbolsage.com states, "The myrtle is a symbol of wealth and prosperity." All these meanings fit into this picture. God was concerned with Judah and Jerusalem, and at the same time, our Lord was telling the prophet that He would have compassion on Jerusalem, rebuild the Temple and the City, and provide prosperity to the people.

The angel of the LORD here is the pre-incarnate Jesus Christ. Notice that He is standing among the myrtle trees. If the myrtle trees symbolize Israel, God is trying to tell Israel that He is there for them. He is not absent, but He is there in their midst. Yesterday, I listened to a professor break down the book of Zechariah. One of the beautiful aspects of the book of Zechariah is that it reveals what is happening in the spiritual world and how it is reflected in the natural world. While outside in the natural world, people are discouraged by the stoppages in the building of the Temple and the city, along with the harshness of life; God is telling them, 'I am here in your midst, and I am directing your restoration and prosperity.' How often do we feel discouraged when God is walking beside us? Unfortunately, we focus on our problem instead of focusing on Him.

*Zechariah 1:13-17 (NASB) And the LORD responded
to the angel who was speaking with me with gracious
words, comforting words. 14 So the angel who was
speaking with me said to me, "Proclaim, saying, 'This
is what the LORD of armies says: "I am exceedingly
jealous for Jerusalem and Zion. 15 "But I am very angry
with the nations who are carefree; for while I was only
a little angry, they furthered the disaster." 16 'Therefore
the LORD says this: "I will return to Jerusalem with
compassion; My house will be built in it," declares the
LORD of armies, "and a measuring line will be
stretched over Jerusalem."' 17 "Again, proclaim,
saying, 'This is what the LORD of armies says: "My
cities will again overflow with prosperity, and the LORD
will again comfort Zion and again choose Jerusalem."'"*

The angel reports back to the pre-incarnate Christ that the earth is at rest. For a time, the earth was not at war. The understanding here is that the countries primarily dealing with the Jewish nation, the Persian Empire, were at peace.

What we have next is what I consider to be an early glimpse into a picture of two parts of the Trinity. You have the pre-incarnate Christ asking the LORD of armies, "How long will You take no pity on Jerusalem and the cities of Judah, with which You have been indignant for these seventy years?" (NASB). Jesus Christ is speaking to God the Father. Just as Jesus intercedes on behalf of the Church, we see Him interceding on behalf of Israel.

Verse 14 tells us that the Father answers with gracious and comforting words. The angel speaking with Zechariah tells Zechariah to "Proclaim, saying, This is what the LORD of armies says: I am exceedingly jealous for Jerusalem and Zion. But I am very angry with the nations who are carefree; for while I was only a little angry, they furthered the disaster." (NASB). First, God reminds us that He loves His people and His land. He is exceedingly jealous. It is challenging for us to understand God's jealousy because we typically associate jealousy with negative connotations. This jealousy is akin to that of a husband for his wife's affection. He wants to see her cared for properly, and when someone mistreats her, his anger wells up. The Father delivered Israel over to the nations for punishment, and the nations executed that punishment with cruel and perverse intention.

We come to the end of the vision, and God declares what He is doing and will do for Judah. "I will return to Jerusalem with compassion; My house will be built in it," declares the LORD of armies, "and a measuring line will be stretched over Jerusalem." (A measuring line as a contractor uses for building). "This is what the LORD of armies says: My cities will again overflow with prosperity, and the LORD will again comfort Zion and again choose Jerusalem." (NASB). He is for His people and His land, and He will rebuild and restore. This is meant to be a message of great encouragement for the people of Israel. One thing you take away from the book of Zechariah is that God has a love for the Jewish people and the land He has given them. Some say that these visions are in the past and have been fulfilled. I say no! Most of these visions have interim fulfillment and final fulfillment, which point to a wonderful future for Israel.

Zechariah 1:18-21 (NASB) Then I raised my eyes and looked, and behold, there were four horns. 19 So I said to the angel who was speaking with me, "What are these?" And he said to me, "These are the horns that have scattered Judah, Israel, and Jerusalem." 20 Then the LORD showed me four craftsmen. 21 And I said, "What are these coming to do?" And he said, "These are the horns that have scattered Judah so that no one lifts up his head; but these craftsmen have come to frighten them, to throw down the horns of the nations who have lifted up their horns against the land of Judah in order to scatter it."

The second vision is a vision of Horns and Craftsman. The Word tells us that there are four horns that scatter Judah, Israel, and Jerusalem. In the Bible, the horns represent power and authority. Strong animals had horns; if you could take them, you prevailed over them. The prevailing thought, including that of the ancient Jews, was that the four empires were Babylon, the Medo-Persian Empire, Greece, and Rome. This would indicate that this is a past and future vision showing what was to come. These empires eventually faded and were replaced by others. There are two other thoughts on who these horns represent. The first of these two thoughts is that these horns represent the empires of Egypt, Assyria, Babylon, and the Medo-Persian. Another thought was that the four horns represented four cardinal points on the horizon. Wherever God's people turned, there were foes to encounter. We are told that these four horns scattered Judah, so no one raised his head. In other words, they oppressed the nation.

Next, we see four craftsmen or carpenters, essentially skilled workers. And what are these craftsmen here to do? We are told that these have come to terrify the horns, to cast down the horns of the nations who lifted their horns against the land of Judah, Israel, and Jerusalem to scatter it.

The point here is the same that God made in Genesis 12:3, "And I will bless those who bless you, And the one who curses you I will curse" (NASB). Anyone who lifts his hand against God's people, against the land of Judah, Israel, and Jerusalem, will be cast down.

Again, this is an encouragement to the people. You may not see it, but behind the scenes, God is at work to punish those who oppress His people. God is patient with His judgment, but His judgment is sure. You may not see it as you go through the daily struggles of life, but God is at work and cares for His people. God is also watching us as we go through these struggles and looking to see if we have faith in Him. James 1:2-4 says, "Consider it all joy, my brothers and sisters, when you encounter various trials, knowing that the testing of your faith produces endurance. And let endurance have its perfect result, so that you may be perfect and complete, lacking in nothing." (NASB) Do we trust Him and believe He knows and cares for us? Or do we get discouraged and begin to wonder where God is? We start asking, Does God love us? Is there a God?

Zechariah 2
The Glory in Your Midst

My initial thoughts upon reading Chapter 2 are that it is intended for both the people of Zechariah's day to encourage them and for the Jews in Israel in our day. It speaks to both the historical events that occurred in Zechariah's day and to events that are happening today and are yet to come. In Zechariah's day, Jerusalem was a city surrounded by walls, and part of their mission was to rebuild the city's walls. Understanding that it was approximately 71 years after the Temple was completed, Nehemiah came to build the walls. God is telling them about another day when there will be no need for walls. The Lord Jesus Christ will be their protector, and He will be as a wall of fire around the city and its inhabitants.

The following section talks about fleeing from the land of the North, and I can't help but think about all of the Jews who went from Europe to Israel after WWII. The verse also says, "Because I have spread you out like the four winds of the heavens" (NASB). That does not sound like their Babylonian captivity, but it sounds like how they were scattered after the death of Jesus Christ. Additionally, there is the coming war of Gog and Magog, a war with the Antichrist that will scatter the Jews during the time of Jacob's trouble, as many are captured and led away, and some run for refuge and hiding. When Jesus Christ returns, He will set the captives free and call those who are hiding to be brought back to their own land. However, the following sentence makes it clear that the angel is also speaking of the Babylonian captivity when it says, "You, Zion! Escape, you who are living with the daughter of Babylon." (NASB). The verse also uses Babylon as a symbol of Jews living comfortably in a foreign land.

The one clear thought that comes to mind when I read Zechariah is the love that God has for His people and the land. I don't understand why, but God has chosen the land of Israel, in particular the city of Jerusalem, to favor in a special way, just as He has chosen the Jewish people to favor in a special way. Verses 1 through 5 demonstrate this love for the land, and the remainder of the chapter reflects His love for the Jewish people. He has given the Jewish people the land. The land is their birthright, and He will bring them back to their birthright to be with Him.

> *Zechariah 2:1-5 (NASB) Then I raised my eyes and looked, and behold, there was a man with a measuring line in his hand. 2 So I said, "Where are you going?" And he said to me, "To measure Jerusalem, to see how wide it is and how long it is." 3 And behold, the angel who had been speaking with me was going out, and another angel was going out to meet him. 4 And he said to him, "Run, speak to that young man there, saying, 'Jerusalem will be inhabited as open country because of the multitude of people and cattle within it. 5 'But I,' declares the LORD, 'will be a wall of fire to her on all sides, and I will be the glory in her midst.'"*

As we read verses 1 through 5, we may tend to think that this measuring and building is all about the return from exile in Babylon because that is precisely what the Jews were doing at that time. They were rebuilding the Temple, the walls, and rebuilding Jerusalem. God wanted to encourage the people of Zechariah's day to continue building; therefore, Zechariah wrote about the building of Jerusalem. Whenever you see a man or an angel with a measuring line, it is always about building. However, the Jews would have understood it was also about building for the time of the Messiah's coming. Unfortunately, they did not understand that the Messiah would have a first and a second coming. They were seeking a Messiah to restore the Kingdom of Israel and establish Israel as a global power. This building is about the Second Coming of Jesus Christ as the Messiah. When viewed in the larger context, Jerusalem is being rebuilt to house the glory and majesty of Jesus Christ. Verse 5 tells us clearly that Jesus will be Jerusalem's protector and her glory. The picture here is of the millennial Kingdom.

It should also be noted that Israel and Jerusalem will need to be rebuilt because of the war with the forces of the Antichrist. When Jesus returns the 2nd time, it will be to rescue His people from the Antichrist. The land will be a mess after three and a half years of war. Ezekiel 39 tells us that Israel will burn the weapons of their enemies for seven years, and they will be burying the dead for seven months. Jerusalem will also be a mess. Zechariah Chapters 12 and 14 tell us that Jerusalem will be the scene of the final battle and the destruction that this entails. While it is evident that

Jerusalem was rebuilt in Zechariah's and Nehemiah's day, it will also need to be rebuilt after the second coming of Jesus Christ.

The first part of this chapter seems somewhat unusual to readers in Zechariah's day. It is of a man measuring Jerusalem to see if it will be large enough for all the people the LORD would bring to Jerusalem. In Zechariah's day, that would have been laughable. Only a few of the Jews had immigrated back to Jerusalem.

> *Zechariah 2:6-7 (NASB) "You there! Flee from the land of the north," declares the LORD, "because I have spread you out like the four winds of the heavens," declares the LORD. 7 "You, Zion! Escape, you who are living with the daughter of Babylon."*

In verses 6 and 7, the LORD calls back the Jews from all over the world, and specifically from Babylon. Many of the Jews had become comfortable living in exile, and they did not want to leave their comfortable lives for a difficult life of sacrifice and rebuilding. The idea of Jerusalem with multitudes returning would have encouraged the people of Zechariah's day.

Though the city had not reached the glory of the times of David and Solomon, these verses give the people hope for what is to come. These verses speak to the future of the city under the reign of Jesus Christ in the Millennial Kingdom. Verse 5 totally speaks to the Millennial Kingdom when it says, "And I will be to her a wall of fire all around, declares the

LORD, and I will be the glory in her midst." I can't think of another time when you would say that Jesus was a wall of fire around Jerusalem or that Jesus was the glory in her midst. What a day that will be!

In verse 4, the angel tells Zechariah, "Jerusalem will be inhabited as an open country because of the multitude of people and cattle within it" (NASB). Zechariah 10:10 tells us, "I will bring them back from the land of Egypt and gather them from Assyria; and I will bring them into the land of Gilead and Lebanon until no room can be found for them." (NASB). The entire land of Israel will be full, and they will also inhabit Lebanon because there will be so many Jews returning to the land. Everyone will want to live in the land to be close to the King. Reading Zechariah and understanding the special significance of the people and land to the King of Kings prompted me to take a DNA test, in the hope of discovering some Jewish ancestry in my DNA. I wanted to be among the people chosen to live in Jerusalem during the Millennial Kingdom. Jerusalem will be the place to be, a special city. Zechariah 14:16 says," Then it will come about that any who are left of all the nations that came against Jerusalem will go up from year to year to worship the King, the LORD of armies, and to celebrate the Feast of Booths." (NASB) Jerusalem will be the capital city of the world during the Millennial Kingdom, and all people are to make a pilgrimage to worship the King every year. It will be more popular than New York, Tokyo, or London.

Jesus will literally be a wall of fire of protection for Jerusalem. Revelation 20 tells us that after 1,000 years, at the end of the Millennial Kingdom, Satan will be released from his prison and gather those who still have rebellion in their hearts to march against Jerusalem and the King of Glory. Imagine these foolish people thinking they can rebel against the King, wanting to rebel against King Jesus. But Satan will deceive many of the nations of the Earth, and they will rebel. Revelation 20:9 tells us what will happen to them. It says, "And they came up on the broad plain of the earth and surrounded the camp of the saints and the beloved city, and fire came down from heaven and devoured them." (NASB) Zechariah tells us that Jesus will be a wall of fire on all sides of Jerusalem, and Revelation tells us that this fire will be used to protect the city and the people during the last battle.

Verses 6 & 7 remind us that God is sovereign. When He calls his people back to the land, they will come. He called them back to the land after the Babylonian captivity, and they came. He called them back to the land after World War II, and they came. In the late 1800s, Mark Twain visited the Land of Israel and described it as desolate. Today, people would say that it bears a striking resemblance to Isaiah 35:1-2.

> *"The wilderness and the desert will rejoice, And the desert will shout for joy and blossom; Like the crocus It will blossom profusely And rejoice with joy and jubilation. The glory of Lebanon will be given to it, The majesty of Carmel and Sharon. They will see the glory of the Lord, The majesty of our God." (NASB).*

This is a Scripture about the Millennial Kingdom, but it has already begun to happen. God has already begun to draw His people, Israel, back to the land, and they have already transformed it from a desolate place to one where flowers bloom in the desert. Today, Israel ranks in the top 10 flower exporters in the world. He will call all Jewish people back to the land after his return at the second coming at the beginning of the Millennial Kingdom. His ways are higher than our ways, and to God, this land is indeed holy. He has set it apart to be His land and the land for His people. It should be noted that although the land blossoms today, during the Great Tribulation, it shall come under great destruction and be a picture of a land scarred by war. However, after Jesus returns, the land will be restored to a land flowing with milk and honey.

> *Zechariah 2:8-9 (NASB) For the LORD of armies says this: "After glory He has sent me against the nations that plunder you, for the one who touches you, touches the apple of His eye. 9 "For behold, I am going to wave My hand over them so that they will be plunder for their slaves. Then you will know that the LORD of armies has sent Me.*

Verses 8 & 9 remind us that you do not want to be used as an instrument of judgment over God's people. You do not want to be seen dealing unfairly with Israel. God uses both the good and the bad nations and rules as He wills. He used Babylon to punish Israel and bring them to their senses to see Him as their God. Now, in verses 8 & 9, what does He say? "For the LORD of armies says this: "After glory He has sent me against the nations that plunder you, for the one who touches you, touches the apple of His eye. For behold, I am going to wave My hand over them so that they will be plunder for their slaves. Then you will know that the LORD of armies has sent Me." (NASB) With all their sin and rebellion, the God of this universe still sees Israel as the apple of His eye. Even today, He has not changed His mind. God made a covenant with Abraham and David, and He will not break His covenant.

Something that God has been showing me lately that seems so simple, but it is one of those things that we get but don't get. Words have power, and His Words contain ultimate power. Once something comes out of God's mouth, it is a fact. Write it down, it will come to pass. He made a covenant with Abraham and Israel, and He will uphold every clause of that covenant. Not only did He make a covenant with Israel, but He loved them and cherished them. Loving Israel and caring for Israel does not mean He does not love and care for the Church. He is big enough to love both Israel and the Church. Just as He planned to graft the Church into Abraham's spiritual line, He intends to graft Israel into the Church. We will see this later in Zechariah. God is saying, "Be patient." Those who plundered Israel and made Israel their slaves will also be plundered. This will ultimately be fulfilled at the Second Coming and in the Millennium Kingdom.

> Zechariah 2:10-12 (NASB) "Shout for joy and rejoice, daughter of Zion; for behold I am coming and I will dwell in your midst," declares the LORD. 11 "And many nations will join themselves to the LORD on that day

and will become My people. Then I will dwell in your midst, and you will know that the LORD of armies has sent Me to you. 12 "And the LORD will possess Judah as His portion in the holy land, and will again choose Jerusalem.

Verses 10 through 12 are again a great encouragement to the people of Israel. Jesus will dwell in their midst in Jerusalem, establish His throne in the Temple, and rule from Jerusalem (Isaiah 2:2-5).

Now it will come about that In the last days the mountain of the house of the LORD will be established as the chief of the mountains, and will be raised above the hills; And all the nations will stream to it. And many peoples will come and say, "Come, let's go up to the mountain of the LORD, to the house of the God of Jacob; So that He may teach us about His ways, and that we may walk in His paths." For the law will go out from Zion and the word of the LORD from Jerusalem. And He will judge between the nations, and will mediate for many peoples; And they will beat their swords into plowshares, and their spears into pruning knives. Nation will not lift up a sword against nation, and never again will they learn war. Come, house of Jacob, and let's walk in the light of the LORD. (NASB)

This encouragement is not only for Israel but for us in the Church. Verse 11 says, "And many nations will join themselves to the LORD on that day and will become My people." (NASB) Zechariah 2:11 reminds me of the Church and how we have already joined ourselves to the LORD (Romans 11:17-24). But there will be many more who survive the Tribulation, who will come to call Jesus LORD with sincerity. Israel and the nations will be His people, joined together in Him. Instead of being despised around the world, the Jews will be favored among the people of the world. This will be after Jesus Christ has defeated the Antichrist and has established Himself as the ultimate power and ruler of the world. The majority of people who remain alive will bow their knee and their hearts to Him. All will bow their knee, but not all will bow their heart. More about this is in Chapter 14. Zechariah 8:23 tells us, "The LORD of armies says this: 'In those days ten people from all the nations will grasp the garment of a Jew, saying, "Let us go with you, for we have heard that God is with you."'" (NASB)

Verse 12 tells us of His love for the Jewish people, the land of Israel, and Jerusalem, in particular. He has not abandoned His people, nor has he abandoned His land. He has turned away from them for a time because of their rebellion, but He will bring them back to Himself, but at a significant cost to Israel. If you truly belong to Him, He will discipline you as a father disciplines a child to restore the relationship and fellowship. Ultimately, that is the story of the Book of Zechariah: His love for His people, their broken relationship, the restoration of that relationship, and the glory of the Kingdom after the restoration. The people and the land will be His prized possession!

If someone were to conduct a study of the land and God's words about the land, one would find enough material to write an entire book. I don't understand it, but the land of

Israel and the city of Jerusalem hold a special place in God's heart. This is truly a holy land. I think about going to Israel and landing in Jerusalem, and the first thing I will do is bow down and kiss the ground! Why? Because if God loves this land so much and declares it holy ground, then I should love it too. The same goes for the Jewish people. However, not just the Jewish people. We should love all people. This chapter is about what is to come, the glory of the land and the people.

Zechariah 2:13 (NASB) "Be silent, all mankind, before the LORD; for He has roused Himself from His holy dwelling."

Verse 13 offers a glimpse into God's greatness. We like to think of God as our friend, which is sometimes too casual. We must remember that He is God and far superior and greater than us. We must never become so familiar with God that we forget He is the Ruler and the Creator of all, and we are the creation. Like so many prophetic Scriptures I have read, this verse reminds me of the time just before the second coming of Jesus Christ. I can see Him standing up from His throne in heaven to begin the journey of His second coming. It will be a terrible day for those on Earth. Truly terrible for His enemies, but glorious and still terrible for His followers. The Father's loving and holy patience has finally ended, and it is time for judgment. Verse 13 reminds me so much of Psalm 46:8-11.

"Come, behold the works of the LORD, Who has inflicted horrific events on the Earth. He makes wars to cease to the end of the Earth; He breaks the bow and

cuts the spear in two; He burns the chariots with fire. Stop striving and know that I am God; I will be exalted among the nations, I will be exalted on the Earth." The LORD of armies is with us; The God of Jacob is our stronghold. Selah (NASB)

This passage of Scripture, found in Psalms and Zechariah 2:13, speaks of the same event. This event will display the power and authority of Jesus Christ. He will be exalted on the Earth, and no one will be able to resist Him. His advice to you is to stop fighting with Him and submit to His rule. We are foolish to think we can resist Him. Until I began studying Zechariah, I had no idea how much the Psalms and the Old Testament, in general, spoke to the coming Millennial Kingdom.

Zechariah 3
Removal of Guilt

Again, this Chapter speaks to both the time of Zechariah and the time of the Day of the LORD. God often gives us prophecies that will fit two periods. It's called double fulfillment. Typically, the first fulfillment occurs relatively soon after the prophecy is given, and the second fulfillment is usually more expansive and literal in nature. The second fulfillment often concerns the Second Coming, the Day of the LORD, and we are still awaiting its fulfillment. Many theologians are preterists. They believe that all the prophecies about the end times have already come to pass, and there will be no second fulfillment. They reject the idea that these prophecies are still awaiting ultimate fulfillment. Preterists often hold to amillennialism, the view that the millennium is not a literal 1,000-year period but rather represents a long span of time. They believe the millennium started at Pentecost, and we are currently in the millennium.

I reject the belief that the prophecies concerning the end times have been fulfilled, and we are already in the millennium. First, I believe that most of the Bible should be taken literally. While some areas are symbolic or poetic, if we spiritualize passages dealing with the end times, we could understand the Bible to mean anything we want it to mean. What parts do we spiritualize, and what parts do we take literally? Second, reading the Book of Zechariah and the other prophets convinces me of double fulfillment. They quite literally tell a story of God choosing a people for Himself. Those people repeatedly sinned and worshiped other gods, and instead of telling the nations about the God of Abraham, Isaac, and Jacob, Israel worshipped the gods of the nations. They missed the first coming of their Messiah, and their Messiah offered Himself to the Gentile nations. The Messiah will return, establish a kingdom on earth, and ensure that a remnant of His people, the Jewish people, are at the center of this Kingdom. The entire Bible is screaming this narrative, and once you begin to see it, it makes a great deal of sense.

> *Zechariah 3:1 (NASB) Then he showed me Joshua the high priest standing before the angel of the LORD, and Satan standing at his right to accuse him.*

As we turn back to Chapter 3, Satan wants so badly to accuse us before the Father. He hates us for following Jesus, for loving God. He hates us for being created in God's image and for being loved by God. He is jealous that he can't be God, and he wants us to worship him or anything other than God. Revelation 12:10 tells us, "For the accuser of our brothers and sisters has been thrown down, the one who accuses them before our God day and night." (NASB). Just as he accused Joshua, the High Priest, before God in Zechariah 3:1, he accuses us day and night. He constantly accuses us before the Father, yet Jesus continually intercedes for us, reminding Satan and the Father that He paid for us with His blood. In verse 1, Satan is accusing Joshua and the nation of not being worthy of God's help or love.

Let the scene that we see here be forever etched in your mind. Yes, we have a sinful nature and would sin all on our own, but we constantly have the push from Satan and his demonic horde to jump headlong into sin. Once they have accomplished their mission, or once they see us fall on our own accord, they run to God to accuse us. The word accuse in the Bible can also be translated as "resist or oppose." Satan works against us; he works for our demise. Satan and his demonic horde work so hard to replace God's truth with their lies, to tell us it is good to put our sinful wants and desires ahead of God's commands. However, as soon as we listen to those lies, as soon as we fall into sin, he just loves to run to God to accuse us and tell the Father and Jesus how dirty and undeserving we are. He is a liar and a deceiver, and we must realize that he only means for us to be judged as he is judged. He is the person who wants everyone else to share his misery. This is his tactic: tempt us to fall, and when we fall, he is right there to accuse us to the Father.

When the Apostle Paul tells us to be aware of the schemes of our adversary, this is one of the tactics to which he is speaking. Just as he lied to Eve, he lies to us and gets us to believe things that are not true, which in turn leads us into a life of sin and ruin. He will tell you that God made you this way, that you can't help yourself, that God understands, and that you don't have to change, or that God didn't really say that.

If Satan loves to accuse us believers, he really loves to accuse the Jewish people. They were called to be a holy nation, a nation of priests. They were, and are, central to God's plan and purpose for this earth and the nations. In Genesis 3:15, we are told of One who would be born of a woman who would crush the serpent's head. Genesis 22:18 tells us that this One would come through the seed of Abraham, and the nations of the earth will be blessed through Him. Through the line of Abraham, the Savior of the world has come. Satan tried to stop it and couldn't. He tried to wipe Israel out as a people and to take them out of the land and keep them out of the land, but he couldn't. Their very existence and presence in the land testify to the God of the Bible. Not only was Satan accusing Joshua, the high priest, but he was also accusing the entire nation.

He didn't believe that his accusations would change the Father's mind, but he couldn't help himself, as that is his character. In English, for the Hebrew word sahtan, Satan means opponent, adversary, and enemy. When scribes had to translate sahtan into Greek, they chose the word diabolos, meaning "devil" in English. Diabolos means one who throws across or casts through. It means accuser and slanderer. These words were not meant to be a name, but because they fit his character so well, Lucifer has come to be called Satan or the Devil.

Satan not only hated the people of God, but he also wanted to take anything that God owned. He tried to take over Jerusalem and see it remain a heap of rubble. He attempts to stop God from reestablishing His Temple in Jerusalem by putting the Dome of the Rock on the Temple

Mount. He comes, and he accuses Israel and wants so badly for God to forsake Israel, but God will never abandon Israel.

> *Zechariah 3:2 (NASB) And the LORD said to Satan, "The LORD rebuke you, Satan! Indeed, the LORD who has chosen Jerusalem rebuke you! Is this not a log snatched from the fire?"*

Verse 2 explicitly states that the LORD has chosen Jerusalem. This is added for the time of Zechariah because God wants the people of Israel to know He is with them in the restoration of Jerusalem. It is also a statement of God's plans for Jerusalem as His holy and eternal city. He is declaring that Jerusalem will be His forever. As we see from other passages in the Scriptures, including Zechariah, Jesus Christ will reign for 1,000 years from Jerusalem. Additionally, once he brings forth the new heaven and earth, He will also bring forth the new Jerusalem (See Revelation 21:1-4).

> *Zechariah 3:3-4 (NASB) Now Joshua was clothed in filthy garments and was standing before the angel. 4 And he responded and said to those who were standing before him, saying, "Remove the filthy garments from him." Again he said to him, "See, I have taken your guilt away from you and will clothe you with festive robes."*

Why is the LORD showing us this picture? He wants us to know that while Satan desires to destroy Israel and steal the land, God will not allow it. The people are His beloved, the apple of His eye, and so is the land. His plan for these people and this land is far from complete. God is saying that these are His people, and He will remove their guilt from them.

> *Zechariah 3:5-7 (NASB) Then I said, "Have them put a clean headband on his head." So they put the clean headband on his head and clothed him with garments, while the angel of the LORD was standing by. 6 And the angel of the LORD admonished Joshua, saying, 7 "The LORD of armies says this: 'If you walk in My ways and perform My service, then you will both govern My house and be in charge of My courtyards, and I will grant you free access among these who are standing here.*

This Chapter is mainly about removing guilt from the people. Why does the LORD even mention Jerusalem? It is as if the LORD is pounding His chest at Satan: this is My city and will always be My city. I will inhabit Jerusalem and make it the most important city on the face of the earth. People will have to look up to it and make pilgrimages to Jerusalem. Jerusalem will be lifted up and possibly become the highest point on the face of the earth, according to Isaiah 2:1-5 and Micah 4:1. We know that Jerusalem is lifted up and shall be on the top of a mountain. The Scriptures indicate it is either the highest mountain on earth, or the most important mountain, or both.

The same can be said for the people. These are His people. "Is this not a log snatched from the fire?" (NASB) While mankind deserves the fires of hell, the Father chose Israel to be a log saved from the fire. Not only to be saved from the fire but also to be a source of salvation for all mankind.

When Israel sinned and God punished them for their sin, He still brought them back to restore them and to rebuild the Temple and Jerusalem. No matter what Satan does or says, God will redeem His people. He has redeemed many of the saints of old, and He will redeem a remnant of His people, Israel, in the future. While it may appear to many that God is done with Israel, He is not; they are His beloved, and He will fulfill all that He promised. Though He hid His face from them for a time, He will have compassion on them with everlasting favor (See Isaiah 54).

> *Zechariah 3:8-10 (NASB) 'Now listen, Joshua, you high priest, you and your friends who are sitting in front of you—indeed they are men who are a sign: for behold, I am going to bring in My servant the Branch. 9 'For behold, the stone that I have put before Joshua; on one stone are seven eyes. Behold, I am going to engrave an inscription on it,' declares the LORD of armies, 'and I will remove the guilt of that land in one day. 10 'On that day,' declares the LORD of armies, 'every one of you will invite his neighbor to sit under his vine and under his fig tree.'"*

You go through this entire Chapter, and it appears that the Scripture only deals with the time at hand, but then you come to verses 8 through 10, and we see both the first coming of Jesus Christ and the second coming of Jesus Christ. We see the first coming in verse 8 and the second coming in verses 9 and 10. The Chapter starts with Satan accusing Israel of their sin, and it ends with God removing the sin from the nation of Israel in one day!

In this Chapter, we see Joshua, the high priest of Israel at that time, standing before Jesus Christ. Standing at the right hand of Joshua is Satan, who is there to accuse Joshua. Joshua is chosen in this vision to represent the entire nation of Israel. He stands there as the High Priest representing the people. We are not told what Satan says. It is not essential. We are only told that he is accusing Joshua and the nation regarding their sin. Remember, the word for accuse can also be translated as resist or oppose, and Satan opposes Israel with everything that he has at his disposal.

Verse 3 tells us that Joshua was clothed with filthy garments. These filthy garments represent the sin of the nation. Satan and his demonic horde were oh so glad to lead the nation into idol worship by telling them lies that worshipping other gods would lead to higher crop yields and more rain or whatever other thing the people wanted. Once he led the nation into idol worship, he ran to God and accused them of their sin. As soon as God leads Israel out of their judgment, the enemy runs to God to remind God of their sin. God's plan of redemption is a beautiful thing. God already knows that He wants to restore these people. Nothing Satan says will change His mind!

There are two points of illustration here connected with the filthy garments. The Hebrew word used here for filth is excrement. The garments were covered with excrement, and Joshua would have been foul-smelling as he stood there before the LORD. The other is the critical nature of the garments. The garments represented your rank in society, and the hem of your garments carried this rank. The rank, in turn, was representative of your lineage. At that time, most people followed in their father's footsteps. The garments stood for Israel's past. Israel was to be a nation of priests and a holy nation. Instead of being a witness to the nations around them, they followed the path of their neighbors and the gods of the nations around them. God chose them, yet they abandoned their calling and chose to play in the pig sty.

Verses 2, 4, and 5 are beautiful verses of redemption. The LORD will hear nothing of Satan's accusation. He says to Satan, "The LORD rebuke you, Satan!" (NASB). The beautiful part comes next: the LORD says, "The LORD who has chosen Jerusalem rebuke you!" Is this not a log snatched from the fire?" (NASB). He says that these people and this land were destined for destruction before I rescued them from the fire! He chose these people and this land and will not allow them to return to the fire! God made a promise to Israel, a covenant, and He will not go back on His Word. God is not a man that He should lie. He takes the filthy clothes off Joshua and puts on new, festive garments for him. "Again, He said to him, "See, I have taken your guilt away from you, and will clothe you with festive robes." (NASB).

To be a child of God, to be the apple of God's eye, is a marvelous thing. He paid for our sins, and He is our defender! God takes us out of our sins, cleans us up, and puts new clothes on us and a new turban (mitre) on our heads. How foolish we are when we take our new clothes and return again to play in the excrement of sin. We must continue to read God's Word to remind ourselves of the crippling effects of sin once we are saved. It affects everything in our lives. Once you have excrement on your hands, everything you touch becomes contaminated with it. Only Jesus can wash you clean, and once He washes you clean, you need to stay out of the pig sty.

Jesus is on our side. When Satan comes to accuse us, Jesus is both our defense attorney and our judge. It is a beautiful thing to have your defense attorney also be your judge. However, Jesus is not your defense attorney until you give your life to Him and follow Him. Otherwise, He is only your judge, and it will not go well for you.

This office of high priest was vacant while Israel was in captivity. Now that they are back in the land and building the Temple, God restores the priestly function to the people. The last thing they put on Joshua is the turban, also called a fair mitre. This was the last of the priestly garments, and it had a gold plate on it that sat on the High Priest's forehead. The inscription on the gold plate is "Holiness to the LORD." God was cleansing and consecrating the priests so that they could once again lead the people in fellowship with Him through their worship. This signifies a restoration of the priestly function.

The angel of the LORD, who is Jesus, assures Joshua that he will maintain his office as high priest and have access to God in that office. However, it is contingent upon Joshua walking in God's ways and commands. God wants a consecrated priesthood that follows Him and His ways, and they must lead the people toward God. He does not want the priesthood to be compromised with sin. A compromised priesthood leads people into sin.

Men, we are the priests of our family. We must also walk in the ways of God. When we don't walk in the ways of God, when we compromise and sin because no one will know, we invite the enemy to sit at our dinner table with us and our family. As priests and protectors of our family, we must be mindful of where we walk. Psalm 1 tells us we will be blessed if we do not walk in the way of sinners.

Additionally, we will be like a tree planted by streams of water, yielding fruit in its proper season, when we delight in the law of the LORD. I want to emphasize the importance of this for men, as we lead our families. Read about the life of Jehosaphat, a godly king (See 2 Chronicles 16 through 20 and 1 Kings 22). He compromised in one area of his life, costing him his legacy. He was a friend of Ahab, and he arranged the marriage of his son to Ahab's daughter. This compromise led to wicked kings following his rule and the destruction of his legacy.

The next thing that the LORD Jesus says is that Joshua and those who sit in front of him are a sign of the coming of the Messiah. There are three possible groups of people to which the passage could be referring: the high priests who came after Joshua, those who also served as priests in the temple under Joshua, or He could be referring to those who worked with Joshua during Zechariah's day to lead the nation. I believe Jesus is referring to those who are priests working with Joshua. Just as God kept His Word and brought the nation out of captivity, bringing them to this place in the rebuilding of the Temple, specifically restoring the priestly office, He will keep His Word and send the Messiah. The pre-incarnate Jesus is prophesying about the incarnate Jesus to come. He uses the term "the Branch," an official name often used by the prophets. It means that the Messiah will come out of the house of David, an offshoot of David. David was promised that his descendants would sit on the throne forever, and Jesus would fulfill that promise. Jesus came for the first time as the Messiah, but the nation of Israel did not recognize him because He came as a suffering servant.

Next, we see a stone with seven eyes. This stone is Jesus. Throughout the Bible, Jesus is represented by a stone or a rock. The rock that Moses was told to strike represented Jesus. He was only supposed to hit it once, but he hit it twice, and because he hit the rock twice instead of once, he was not allowed to enter the Promised Land. Here, we see that a stone once again represents Christ. This time, the stone is most likely reminiscent of a cornerstone, as in the cornerstone they used to build the Temple. He is our cornerstone, the cornerstone of both Israel and the Church.

This stone also features seven eyes. The seven eyes represent the Messiah in His perfect wisdom and knowledge. The number seven represents the completion of perfection. The people could not control much or see trouble beyond the horizon, but the Messiah missed nothing. This also alludes to Revelation 5, where the Lamb represents Jesus with seven horns and seven eyes, all-powerful and all-knowing. The LORD of armies says He will engrave an inscription on the stone, and He will remove the guilt of the land in a single day. I believe the inscription will be a name or title, such as "King of Kings and LORD of Lords" (Revelation 19:16). Although I have no evidence to support this, it makes more sense that it would be a majestic title.

The LORD also says that He will remove the guilt of the land in a single day. Zechariah goes from speaking of the Messiah's first coming in verse 8 to the next verse, speaking of the Messiah's second coming. Zechariah uses the term "on that day." "On that day" refers to the second coming of Jesus Christ. The iniquity of the land has not yet been removed. Still, when Jesus returns, Zechariah 12:10 says, "And I will pour out on the house of David and on the inhabitants of Jerusalem the Spirit of grace and of pleading, so that they will look at Me whom they pierced; and they will mourn for Him, like one mourning for an only son, and they will weep bitterly over Him like the bitter weeping over a firstborn." (NASB). Follow that up with Zechariah 8:8 which says, "and I will bring them back and they will live in the midst of Jerusalem; and they shall be My people, and I will be their God in truth and righteousness." Zechariah 13:9 says, "They will call on My name, and I will answer them; I will say, They are my people, and they will say, The LORD is my God." (NASB). This is the removal of iniquity in a single day. They will see Jesus, whom they have pierced, recognize Him as their Messiah, and mourn for Him.

Further, we see in Zechariah 13:1, "On that day a fountain will be opened for the house of David and for the inhabitants of Jerusalem, for sin and for defilement." (NASB). I believe they will bathe in the waters of that fountain, just like they take their ceremonial cleansing in the mikvah. After they recognize Jesus as the Son of God, they will wash in the mikvah, a practice similar to the one Christians observe through baptism today. What a day that will be for the Jewish people and the nation of Israel.

The LORD of armies tells the people that "on that day," the second coming of Jesus Christ, everyone will invite their neighbor to come and sit under their vine and fig tree. The idea is that everyone will live in peace and prosperity. It harkened back to the height of the nation under Solomon, when the nation had expanded its borders the furthest, was the most prosperous, and the most secure. We see this in both 1 Kings 4:25, during a past time, and Micah 4:4, at a future time, the same time spoken of here in Zechariah. 1 Kings 4:25 says, "So Judah and Israel lived securely, everyone under his vine and his fig tree, from Dan even to Beersheba, all the days of Solomon." (NASB) Micah 4:4 says,

> *"Instead, each of them will sit under his vine And under his fig tree, With no one to make them afraid, Because*

the mouth of the LORD of armies has spoken."
(NASB).

This is the peace and prosperity promised in the Millennial Kingdom.

Zechariah 4
A New, More Glorious Temple

The rebuilding of the Temple was of utmost importance to God. God was to be the King of the nation of Israel until they wanted a king like other nations. The Temple was His palace, His dwelling place on the earth. It was foremost in His plans that the Temple be rebuilt. Read Haggai 1 and you will see how important the building of the Temple was to God. He was withholding His blessings from the people because they were slow to respond to His call to rebuild the Temple.

We have another very encouraging vision here from the LORD. I'm accustomed to most prophets speaking harsh words to the people of Israel. God gives Zechariah encouraging words, at least here in the first part of the book. God continues to encourage the people throughout the book of Zechariah, but later in the book, harsh words are directed at them.

The Book of Haggai deals explicitly with the rebuilding of the Temple, and Haggai is much more direct in his approach with the people. Through Haggai, the LORD tells the people that they are busy fixing up their own homes while His house remains desolate. This is why they plant a great deal but harvest little, and consequently lack food, drink, and clothing. While much of Zechariah deals with the end times, it also serves to encourage the people to rebuild the Temple. While it may seem that rebuilding the Temple is a large undertaking and is all in the hands of the people, God uses this vision to tell the people that He will see the reconstruction through to completion by His Spirit. If a mountain appears to be standing in the way, the LORD will flatten it.

This chapter has a key verse, which could be the key verse for the entire book. Zechariah 4:6 is the key verse, and it says, "Then he said to me, "This is the word of the LORD to Zerubbabel, saying, 'Not by might nor by power, but by My Spirit,' says the LORD of armies." (NASB). I believe every Christian has heard this verse at some point in their life. We must remember that the project of rebuilding the Temple, and indeed the entire story of God and His relationship with humanity, is according to His plans. God is telling Zerubbabel and the people that although He needs their hands and labor, this entire project is in His hands. There is truth to the fact that God needs His people's hands, feet, and voice to be His hands, feet, and voice. However, God will find others if we don't accept the call. His plans will not be stopped. In this case, He is encouraging Zerubbabel, letting Zerubbabel know that Zerubbabel will finish the job.

We are now at Zechariah's fifth vision on the same night. The previous vision concerned the restoration of Joshua as the high priest and the restoration of the priestly office to the nation. This vision concerns Zerubbabel and the completion of the Temple building. God tells Zerubbabel that although the rebuilding of the Temple appears to be a project similar in size to the moving of a mountain, it is in the hands of the LORD. Before Zerubbabel, this project will become plain and easy. In other words, God will move that mountain if they just complete one small task at a time.

What encouragement for the Jews of that day and the Jews and Christians today, knowing that God is working all things out according to His plan. For those who are in need and have brought their request before the LORD, remember the theme of this book: The LORD remembers and blesses in His time! Waiting can be frustrating, but when the LORD answers, it will be sweeter.

> Romans 8:28 (NASB) And we know that God causes all things to work together for good to those who love God, to those who are called according to His purpose.

In this vision, we see a golden lampstand with a bowl that serves as a reservoir for the oil pipes, which carry the oil from the bowl to the lampstand.

> Zechariah 4:1-2 (NASB) Then the angel who had been speaking with me returned and woke me, like a person who is awakened from his sleep. 2 And he said to me, "What do you see?" And I said, "I see, and behold, a lampstand all of gold with its bowl on the top of it, and its seven lamps on it with seven spouts belonging to each of the lamps which are on the top of it;

On each side of the lampstand are two olive trees and two branches that feed the reservoir. This lampstand differs from the lampstands in the Temple that must be attended to by priests who regularly refill the oil. This lampstand is supplied with oil directly from the olive trees, ensuring a continuous supply and keeping the lamps constantly lit. While in the physical world, a significant amount of work went into operating the Temple, in the spiritual realm, God is at work reconciling humanity to Himself.

The golden lampstand we see is a menorah. It has been the symbol of Israel for much longer, even more so than the Star of David. According to templeinstitute.org, depictions of the menorah have been discovered in numerous ancient archaeological digs throughout Israel and elsewhere where Jews have lived. Before the Star of David, the menorah was the symbol of Israel. In Exodus 19:5, the LORD tells the nation of Israel that they would be His possession among all the peoples of the earth. In Exodus 19:6, He further tells them, "And you shall be to Me a kingdom of priests and a holy nation." (NASB). In their article "The Meaning Behind the Menorah," OneforIsrael.org states that the menorah symbolizes God's light and holiness in a dark world. Jewish tradition holds that it is to remind the people of Israel that they are to be a light to the nations. Isaiah 42:6-7 says,

> *"I am the LORD, I have called You in righteousness, I will also hold You by the hand and watch over You, And I will appoint You as a covenant to the people, As a light to the nations, To open blind eyes, To bring out prisoners from the dungeon And those who dwell in darkness from the prison. (NASB).*

The nation of Israel was to be a light to the nations, testifying to the one true God. They were to open eyes blind to spiritual truth and free those who Satan and his demonic horde had taken prisoner. All of this is demonstrated in the image of the menorah.

When Jesus came, He told us that He was the light of the world. In John 8:12, Jesus says, "I am the Light of the world; the one who follows Me will not walk in the darkness, but will have the Light of life." (NASB). John 8:20 tells us that Jesus said these words as He stood in the Temple's treasury area. OneforIsrael.org says, "He was standing close to the huge temple menorah declaring Himself to the ultimate light and witness." When Jesus comes to rule and reign at His second coming, He literally becomes the light of the world. When Jesus returns on that day, there will be no need for light, for He will be the light. Zechariah 14:6-7 says, "On that day there will be no light; the luminaries will die out. For it will be a unique day known to the LORD, neither day nor night, but it will come about that at the time of evening there will be light." (NASB) The Scriptures also tell us that the Son will be our light in the New Jerusalem. Revelation 22:5 says, "And there will no longer be any night; and they will not have need of the light of a lamp nor the light of the sun, because the Lord God will illuminate them; and they will reign forever and ever." (NASB).

As Jesus is the light of the world, we, His followers, are to be a light. Matthew 5:14-16 says, "You are the light of the world. A city set on a hill cannot be hidden; nor do people light a lamp and put it under a basket, but on the lampstand, and it gives light to all who are in the house. Your light must shine before people in such a way that they may see your good works, and glorify your Father who is in heaven." (NASB). We are called Christians because the world saw "little Christs" in the early church believers. As Jesus is the source of light, we are also to shine as a candle lit by the ultimate source of light. Jesus is the sun, and we are to be the moon, reflecting His light.

Thus far, we see that Israel was to be a light to the world, that Jesus is the ultimate light of the world, and that followers of Jesus Christ, the Church, are to be a light to the world. All of this is represented in the one little image of the menorah. Furthermore, Zechariah 4, like all of Zechariah, points us to a time when both Israel and the Church will be a light, pointing to the ultimate light, Jesus. This will occur in the Millennial Kingdom.

> *Zechariah 4:3 (NASB) also two olive trees by it, one on the right side of the bowl and the other on its left side."*

We don't just see the menorah in this passage, but what else do we see? There are two olive trees. One thought is that these two olive trees represent the two covenant people of the LORD, Israel, and the Church. In Romans 11:17-24, Paul describes two olive trees: Israel, the cultivated olive tree, and the Gentile believers, the wild olive tree. Paul tells us that these two trees become one in Jesus Christ. Romans 11:24 says, "For if you were cut off from what is by nature a wild olive tree, and contrary to nature were grafted into a cultivated olive tree, how much more will these who are the natural branches be grafted into their own olive tree?" (NASB).

In Ephesians 2:11-22, Paul further clarifies that in Christ, Jews and Gentiles are one people. Ephesians 2:11-14 says, "Therefore remember that previously you, the Gentiles in the flesh, who are called "Uncircumcision" by the so-called "Circumcision" which is performed in the flesh by human hands— remember that you were at that time separate from Christ, excluded from the people of Israel, and strangers to the covenants of the promise, having no hope and without God in the world. But now in Christ Jesus, you who previously were far away have been brought near by the blood of Christ. For He Himself is our peace, who made both groups into one and broke down the barrier of the dividing wall." (NASB). During the Millennial Reign, Israel and the Church, full of the Holy Spirit, will be a light to the nations, testifying to the ultimate light.

I've spent time explaining how these two olive trees are actually one in the LORD. However, as you read the book of Zechariah, you come to understand that though we are one in Christ, we are separate. Zechariah clarifies that the land of Israel will be for Jews in the Millennial Kingdom. Zechariah 10:10 states that the LORD will bring the Jews back to the land until there is no more room for them in the land. I've come to understand that Israel will be for the Jews, and the Gentiles will continue to live outside of Israel in their own nations. Although we are one in Christ, we are still separate. I liken it to the Trinity, one God, yet three persons of God. One bride, with two covenant people coming together under the New Covenant. I could quite possibly be wrong, and the two olive trees and the two branches at the end of chapter 4 could be the same and refer only to the two anointed ones.

> *Zechariah 4:4-7 (NASB) Then I said to the angel who was speaking with me, saying, "What are these, my lord?" 5 So the angel who was speaking with me answered and said to me, "Do you not know what these are?" And I said, "No, my lord." 6 Then he said to me, "This is the word of the LORD to Zerubbabel, saying, 'Not by might nor by power, but by My Spirit,' says the LORD of armies. 7 'What are you, you great mountain? Before Zerubbabel you will become a plain; and he will bring out the top stone with shouts of "Grace, grace to it!"""*

In Zechariah 4:3, we see two olive trees standing near, from which oil is being poured into the seven lamps to keep them burning without the need for human intervention. The simple meaning explained in the passage is that the LORD, through His Spirit, helps Zerubbabel see the completion of the Temple. What looks like a mountain will be brought low before the LORD and made into a plain. The Temple will be complete, and the Light of the World will once again reside in the Holy of Holies. Israel will again be the light, pointing the nations to the One True God.

This is a divine supply of oil. The symbolism of the Temple lamp represents the true office of Israel. Israel was to be a light to the world. For them to be a light, they must first be consecrated to their God. Oil symbolizes the Holy Spirit, not in a personal sense as in the New Testament, but in His role of watching over the nation and preparing prophets, priests, and kings for their service to the LORD. It is by the Spirit that all this work is being done, not by the might nor by the power of the people, for in truth, the people were very weak. What encouragement for a small band of people with a seemingly insurmountable task. God was there to see that this task would be completed.

God then gives a personal message to Zerubbabel. You will finish this task and put the last stone in place. The last stone will be laid with shouts of "Grace, grace to it." The word "grace" in Hebrew can also be translated as favor. The favor of the LORD is there to help the people, particularly Zerubbabel, in completing the Temple.

Additionally, the favor of the LORD is there for the people who complete the Temple. The angel tells Zechariah that he would know the LORD of armies had sent him by the completion of the Temple by Zerubbabel. Many were discouraged by the sheer enormity of the project and struggled to complete the numerous small tasks required to accomplish the larger task. However, God says that when they see the completion of the Temple, they shall rejoice. Even an enormous task like building the Temple starts with small things. God is watching. Put your hand to the plow and complete the small tasks.

Zechariah 4:8-9 (NASB) Also the word of the LORD came to me, saying, 9 "The hands of Zerubbabel have laid the foundation of this house, and his hands will finish it. Then you will know that the LORD of armies has sent me to you.

Again, what we see here is another double fulfillment. While Zechariah is speaking to Zerubbabel to complete the Temple, Zerubbabel is a type of Christ. Not only is he a type of Christ, but he is a direct descendant of King David and is in the lineage of Jesus Christ (Matthew 1:12-13 and Luke 3:27). While we plainly see that Zerubbabel started and will finish this Temple in Zechariah's day, this is a foreshadowing of a day in which Jesus Christ will return and rebuild the Temple. This is not immediately evident from reading Zechariah 4 alone, but when reading Zechariah 6:11-15, it becomes very apparent.

Zechariah 6:12-13 says, "Then say to him, 'The LORD of armies says this: "Behold, there is a Man whose name is Branch, for He will branch out from where He is; and He will build the Temple of the LORD. Yes, it is He who will build the Temple of the LORD, and He who will bear the majesty and sit and rule on His throne. So He will be a priest on His throne, and the counsel of peace will be between the two offices." (NASB). We see the term "Branch" used in Zechariah 3:8 and again in Zechariah 6:12. Branch is an official name often used by the prophets. It means that the Messiah will come out of the house of David, an offshoot of David. David was promised that his descendants would sit on the throne forever, and Jesus would fulfill that promise. In Zechariah 6:12-13, we see that Jesus will build the fourth Temple and sit on "His throne," reconciling the offices of both Priest and

King. Zechariah 6:15 tells us that people will come from far away to help with the building of the Temple.

What a beautiful picture! I'm eager for that day! I picture Jesus with white hair, eyes of fire, a white robe with a red sash, sitting on his throne in the Holy of Holies. He sits on a throne of gold, and the Holy of Holies is all overlaid with gold. From under His throne originates the river of life, which brings healing to all who partake in it, whether by swimming in it or drinking from it. Throughout the Book of Zechariah, we are pointed to the Millennium Kingdom.

Furthermore, when we look beyond Zechariah, we see that Jesus will rebuild the Temple when He returns. Knowing that Zerubbabel is a type of Christ helps us to connect the dots from other passages to Zechariah 4. In Haggai 1, the prophet Haggai commands the people to rebuild the Temple, telling them that they are suffering because they are making their homes more comfortable and not completing the house of God. Haggai 2 then turns to rebuilding the Temple during the Millennial Kingdom. Haggai 2:6-9 says, "For this is what the LORD of armies says: 'Once more in a little while, I am going to shake the heavens and the earth, the sea also and the dry land. I will shake all the nations; and they will come with the wealth of all nations, and I will fill this house with glory,' says the LORD of armies. 'The silver is Mine and the gold is Mine,' declares the LORD of armies. 'The latter glory of this house will be greater than the former,' says the LORD of armies, 'and in this place I will give peace,' declares the LORD of armies."

Haggai 2:3 makes it plain that this Temple, built by Zerubbabel, paled in comparison to the former Temple built by Solomon. Haggai 2:6-9 tells us of a Temple that will be even more glorious than the Temple built by Solomon. We also see the nations bringing wealth, gold, and silver to build this future Temple. Haggai refers to the Temple that will be built at the start of the Millennial Kingdom by Jesus Christ.

Haggai 2:20-23 draws a direct comparison between Zerubbabel and Christ in typology. The passage describes the shaking of the heavens and the earth, as well as the overthrow of kingdoms. Then verse 23 is the crown jewel, and it says, "'On that day,' declares the LORD of armies, 'I will take you, Zerubbabel, son of Shealtiel, My servant,' declares the LORD, 'and I will make you like a signet ring, for I have chosen you,'" declares the LORD of armies." It starts by saying, "On that day." This refers to the day of the LORD! He uses the name Zerubbabel, but Haggai is speaking about Jesus Christ. Who else would be His signet ring?

The Bible tells us that there will be a third Temple built in Jerusalem and that the Antichrist will desecrate the Temple. He will proclaim himself to be God and sit in the Holy of Holies (Daniel 9:27; Matthew 24:15; and 2 Thessalonians 2:4). I believe this third Temple will be destroyed by the war that wages across Israel and Jerusalem before Jesus comes to save them. If we just look at the war between Israel and Hamas and Israel and Hezbollah, the land is a wasteland. When total war is fought, nothing is left unscathed. This will lead Jesus to build a fourth Temple, as we see in Haggai 2:6-9. Even if the Temple is not destroyed, it is defiled, and Jesus will want to rebuild it and purify it.

2 Samuel 7:10-16 is God's covenant with David and is a fascinating passage filled with double meaning. At times, the passage applies to Jesus Christ, at times, the passage applies to Solomon, and at times the passage applies to both Solomon and Jesus Christ. 2 Samuel 7:10-14 says, "And I will establish a place for My people Israel, and will plant them, so that they may live in their own place and not be disturbed again, nor will malicious people oppress them anymore as previously, even from the day that I appointed judges over My people Israel; and I will give you rest from all your enemies. The LORD also declares to you that the LORD will make a house for you. When your days are finished and you lie down with your fathers, I will raise up your descendant after you, who will come from you, and I will establish his kingdom. He shall build a house for My name, and I will establish the throne of his kingdom forever. I will be a father to him, and he will be a son to Me; when he does wrong, I will discipline him with a rod of men and with strokes of sons of mankind, but My favor shall not depart from him, as I took it away from Saul, whom I removed from you. Your house and your kingdom shall endure before Me forever; your throne shall be established forever." (NASB).

2 Samuel 7:10 points us toward the Millennial Kingdom when Israel will be planted in the land, never disturbed again, and not have the wicked afflict them any

longer. This will only happen once Jesus Christ returns and rules from Jerusalem. Verse 12 says that when David's days are finished, and he lies down with his fathers, God will raise a descendant of David and establish His Kingdom. This must point to Jesus Christ because Solomon was established on David's throne before David died. The passage states that the descendant will be established on David's throne after his death. Verse 13 says, "He shall build a house for My name, and I will establish the throne of his kingdom forever." The only one who will have a kingdom established forever is Jesus Christ. 2 Samuel 7 confirms what Haggai 2 infers: a new Temple built by Jesus Christ at the start of the Millennial Kingdom. This will be a Temple whose glory shall be greater than even Solomon's Temple.

Although the primary connection with this line of thinking in Zechariah 4 is the building of the Temple by Zerubbabel as a type of Christ, I find the connection with Zechariah 6, Haggai 2, and 2 Samuel 7 fitting. Further, in Ezekiel chapters 40 through 43, you see a man whose appearance is like bronze directing the building of a new Temple, the fourth Temple. The dimensions of this Temple are larger and different from those of the previous temples. This Temple will be built by Jesus Christ at the start of the Millennial Kingdom and will be more glorious than Solomon's Temple.

> *Zechariah 4:10-14 (NASB) "For who has shown contempt for the day of small things? But these seven will rejoice when they see the plumb line in the hand of Zerubbabel—they are the eyes of the LORD roaming*

throughout the earth." 11 Then I said to him, "What are
these two olive trees on the right of the lampstand and
on its left?" 12 And I responded the second time and
said to him, "What are the two olive branches which are
beside the two golden pipes, which empty the golden
oil from themselves?" 13 So he answered me, saying,
"Do you not know what these are?" And I said, "No, my
lord." 14 Then he said, "These are the two anointed
ones, who are standing by the Lord of the whole earth."

Zechariah 4:10 sends us back to Zechariah 3:9 and the image of a stone with seven eyes. I said that this stone represents Jesus Christ, the Chief Cornerstone, and the seven eyes represent the Messiah in His perfect wisdom and knowledge. In verse 10, we see that these eyes rejoice when they see Zerubbabel at work constructing the Temple. Verse 10 also tells us that these eyes roam the entire earth. This is a symbolic way of reminding us that God is all-knowing and sees everything in every corner and cave of the earth. He sees and rejoices when we follow Him and obey Him. He sees all the wrongs we do and that are done to us. He has His eyes on Israel because He has a plan for Israel. He will reconcile a remnant of the Jewish people to Himself, and He will judge those who persecute Israel and those who rebel against His rule.

Finally, Zechariah asks about the two olive trees and asks, "What are these two olive trees?" The angel is shocked that Zechariah does not know. It is as if he expects everyone to know. Zechariah does not record the answer to this question for us, but the passage states that Zechariah asked the question again and changed it slightly to ask, "What are these two olive branches?" This is not a different interpretation of the same word. The word used for "olive tree" is "zayith," and the predominant meaning is the olive tree, the fruit of the olive tree, and the oil derived from the fruit. The word used for "olive branch" is "shibbol" or "shibboleth," and the predominant meaning is an ear of grain, a flowing stream, or a branch. (biblehub.org – Strong's Lexicon) I take the usage of the word branch to mean a smaller, identifiable portion of the tree from which oil is flowing extremely well.

The Angel tells him, "These are the two anointed ones, who are standing by the LORD of the whole earth." (NASB). "Anointed ones" means "sons of oil" in the original language. To the most immediate audience of the vision, these two are Joshua and Zerubbabel, who were anointed to do this work. God used these two men to bring His people and blessings back to the land. They represent the priestly and kingly offices of the land.

The "two anointed ones" in Zechariah 4:14 also employ language and symbolism that are very similar to those found in Revelation. The two witnesses of Revelation are reminiscent of the two branches in Zechariah. Revelation 11:4 uses very similar wording as Zechariah 4:14. Zechariah 4:14 says, "These are the two anointed ones, who are standing by the LORD of the whole earth" (NASB). Revelation 11:4 says, "These are the two olive trees and the two lampstands that stand before the LORD of the earth" (NASB).

Thoughts On Zechariah

Although no one knows for sure who the two witnesses in Revelation are. God will use these two individuals to convey a message to Israel. Based on Revelation 11, these two men will warn Israel that they have made a covenant with the devil and will call the people back to God. Unfortunately, the people of Israel will not want to hear this message because they will have peace and security for the first three and a half years, and peace and security are all that they desire after years of persecution and war. The two witnesses will be a source of irritation and pain to the people of Israel and the Antichrist. The end of the age will be about the judgment of the unrighteous. It is also about reconciling a remnant of the Jewish people to their God and fulfilling God's promises to Abraham and David.

Zechariah 5
The Woman in the Basket

There are two visions in Chapter 5. The first vision is of a flying scroll. Before this vision, the visions were extremely encouraging, meant to let the people know that God remembered and blessed them in His time. Zechariah's day was a significant time for the people of Israel, as God restored what had been taken away from them. Although they could not see it, these were small beginnings to greater things. Zechariah 4:10 tells the people, "Do not despise these small beginnings, for the LORD rejoices to see the work begin, to see the plumb line in Zerubbabel's hand." (New Living Translation). This vision, however, serves as a reminder of God's holiness and the destruction that awaits those who violate His commands. Since God is patient, He gives us time to repent and get right with Him. Unfortunately, we often overlook His warnings of judgment.

Zechariah 5:1-2 (NASB) Then I raised my eyes again and looked, and behold, there was a flying scroll. 2 And he said to me, "What do you see?" And I said, "I see a flying scroll; its length is twenty cubits, and its width ten cubits."

Zechariah opens his eyes and sees a flying scroll; this scroll represents the Word of God. The fact that it is flying signifies the swiftness of the action that it takes. The scroll is 30 feet (20 cubits) by 15 feet (10 cubits), which is the exact same dimensions as the Holy Place in the Tabernacle. The meaning here is that the scroll is holy.

The angel tells us that this scroll contains curses or judgments upon those who violate the commands written on it. It states that the scroll extends to the entire land, referring to the land of Israel. It is particularly meant for the Jews. It is also the Jews who have been favored with greater light than the rest of the world. In Luke 12:48, Jesus says, "From everyone who has been given much, much will be demanded; and to whom they entrusted much, of him they will ask all the more." (NASB). When I was at Cedarville College, they put on the chapel wall, "To whom much is given, much is required." The Jews were given the Words of eternal life and held to a higher standard. They were to take the Word and share it with the whole world.

Zechariah 5:3-4 (NASB) Then he said to me, "This is the curse that is going forth over the face of the entire land; everyone who steals certainly will be purged away according to the writing on one side, and everyone who swears falsely will be purged away according to the writing on the other side. 4 "I will make it go forth," declares the LORD of armies, "and it will enter the house of the thief and the house of the one who swears falsely by My name; and it will spend the night within that house and destroy it with its timber and stones."

Zechariah 5:3 tells us, "Then he said to me, "This is the curse that is going forth over the face of the entire land; everyone who steals certainly will be purged away according to the writing on one side, and everyone who swears falsely will be purged away according to the writing on the other side." (NASB). The Bible tells us that sin becomes bondage to us. It leads us to destruction. Sin also carries with it curses, which we might also call judgments. Exodus 34:6-7 says, "Then the LORD passed by in front of him and proclaimed, The LORD, the LORD God, compassionate and merciful, slow to anger, and abounding in faithfulness and truth; who keeps faithfulness for thousands, who forgives wrongdoing, violation of His Law, and sin; yet He will by no means leave the guilty unpunished, inflicting the punishment of fathers on the children and on the grandchildren to the third and fourth generations." (NASB). Fathers, we are responsible to our families to live a life of obedience and righteousness. What father wants their children to pay for their sins? As much as we would like to sin with no consequences, there are consequences. There are spiritual laws in place in our world that are more consequential than most of us understand.

One side of the scroll deals with sins against man, those who steal. The other side of the scroll addresses sins against God, specifically those who swear falsely by the name of God. Benson, in his commentary, states, "According to Calmet, under the two names of theft and false swearing, the Hebrews and Chaldeans included all other crimes; theft denoting every injustice and violence executed against men, and perjury all crimes committed against God." The idea is that men were stealing, then going to court and claiming innocence.

Thoughts On Zechariah

When I first read this prophecy, it seemed out of place. God is encouraging His people, and then suddenly, you have this prophecy about judgment for stealing and false swearing. It seems highly probable that some individuals defrauded the rebuilding effort by misappropriating items dedicated to rebuilding the Temple. To cover their guilt, they would swear by the name of God that they had done nothing wrong. The land was accusing those who were committing these offenses. The Temple was being built to reconcile the land and the people to God. You may ask why, the land? There is something about this land that is special to God, and He cleanses the land and the people.

The words "purged" or "cleaned out" used in verse 3 refer to being punished or judged. God will judge those who have stolen and gotten away with it because they have lied and failed to admit their guilt. Verse 4 tells us that God distinguishes between the guilty and the innocent. They are stealing from God, from what God wants to do for the people and the land. A reading of verse 4 tells you that the judgment will be severe. Verse 4 reads, "I will make it go forth," declares the LORD of armies, "and it will enter the house of the thief and the house of the one who swears falsely by My name; and it will spend the night within that house and destroy it with its timber and stones." (NASB).

Prophecies are not limited to one time period. This prophecy is meant for Zechariah's day and the end of the Age. The more I read Zechariah, the more I see the Millennial Kingdom, and this vision is no different. A broader interpretation of this vision is that the stealing and swearing falsely by God are representative of the entire Ten Commandments. Stealing involves our sins against people, and swearing falsely by God involves our sins against God. In other words, these two sins represent sin in general. This passage tells us that when Jesus rules in the Millennial Kingdom, He will deal with individual sin swiftly, not just national sin. God will cleanse the land of sin and deal swiftly with contaminating agents, so they will not contaminate the entire nation. This vision will apply to the nation of Israel and the world as a whole.

> *Zechariah 5:5-11 (NASB) Then the angel who had been speaking with me went out and said to me, "Now raise your eyes and see what this is that is going forth." 6 And I said, "What is it?" Then he said, "This is the ephah going forth." Again he said, "This is their appearance in all the land. 7 And behold, a lead cover was lifted up." He continued, "And this is a woman sitting inside the ephah." 8 Then he said, "This is Wickedness!" And he thrust her into the middle of the ephah and threw the lead weight on its opening. 9 Then I raised my eyes and looked, and there two women were coming out with the wind in their wings; and they had wings like the wings of the stork, and they lifted up the ephah between the earth and the heavens. 10 So I said to the angel who was speaking with me, "Where are they taking the ephah?" 11 Then he said to me, "To build a temple for her in the land of Shinar; and when it is prepared, she will be set there on her own pedestal."*

I spent significant time studying and reading what I could to help me understand this vision in Zechariah 5: 5-11.

I prayed and asked God to reveal the truth to me from this vision. Much of what I have written here comes from study resources, which include the Pulpit Commentary, The New Unger's Bible Dictionary, gotquestions.org, and a key piece from explainingthebook.com. Much of what I see can be understood in the context of history. However, what God is trying to tell the Israelites is the same message God is trying to convey to us today. Is it as simple as expressing the evil of worshipping anything that is not the One True God?

Some commentators seek to link the vision in the first four verses of Chapter 5 to evil in general and the Millennial Kingdom, and I can see the connection there. However, I believe Zechariah 5:5-11 relates to the Great Harlot of Babylon, which is relevant up to the second coming of Jesus Christ. I do not see this vision in Zechariah 5:5-11, dealing with the Millennial Kingdom, because the basket and the idol are taken to the plains of Shinar, and a house is built for the idol. That will not happen in the Millennium. There will be no temples set up for false gods in that day. Furthermore, Isaiah 13:19-22 and Jeremiah 50-51 inform us that Babylon will not be inhabited by people again in the Millennial Kingdom and that God will judge Babylon.

We know that Babylon is a symbol of the opposition to God. The Great Harlot of Babylon leads people away from God through commerce and the desire for profit above all else. Everywhere Babylon is mentioned in the Scriptures, it is also a symbol of rebellion. I see in this vision that God has driven the idols out of the land with the discipling of Israel and Judah by exiling them to Assyria and Babylon. The focus here seems to be on Babylon since that is where the people have just returned, and it symbolizes all that opposes God. As we transition from Zechariah's day to the time of Jesus, we do not see a problem with idol worship as it was before the exile and captivity. The problem going forward will be the rejection of their Messiah.

As mentioned above, it appears that the woman in the vision of verses 5 through 11 has some connection with the Great Prostitute of Revelation 17. Prophecy is always difficult because it can point to two events simultaneously. The LORD can be speaking to the Israelites in Zechariah's day to encourage them, while also foretelling events that will occur far into the future.

The first thing we see is a basket described in some versions of the Bible as an ephah. What is an ephah? It is a basket thought to hold between 6 and 7 gallons in capacity, used to measure dry goods such as wheat, grain, or barley. The angel says, "This is the ephah going forth." (NASB). As we read on, we see the connection between this ephah (commerce) and the idol.

The translation appears to be a little off for the second half of verse 6, "This is their appearance in all the land." (NASB). The King James Version translates it, "This is their resemblance." The NASB translates it as "This is their appearance," and the ESV translates it as "This is their iniquity." Per explainingthebook.com, the Hebrew word used here for "resemblance," "appearance," or "iniquity" is usually translated as "eye." However, in the KJV, this word is translated as "fountain" eleven times. When you are learning Hebrew, elementary Hebrew flashcards give two meanings for this word: "eye" and "fountain." If we look at this word as a "fountain," we see the source of wickedness in the land. I agree with explainingtheword.com; translating this word as fountain provides us with better context here for the source of evil in the land. "This is their fountain in all the land." The source of wickedness in the land is idol worship, and it is like a fountain that continues to spread evil as long as it remains.

The next thing we see is that the KJV translates the next part as "through all of the earth," while the ESV and NASB translate it as "in all the land." Zechariah, in this sense, is primarily dealing with the land of Israel, so I believe we are referring to the land of Israel. While it is true that worshipping anything other than God is the source of wickedness throughout the whole earth, the Book of Zechariah concerns the people of Israel, their restoration, and their reconciliation with God. Verse 6 tells us that the basket being sent out contains the source of iniquity or wickedness in the land of Israel.

The woman is further identified as the source of evil in the land in Verse 7. Zechariah 5:7 tells us that there was a round cover on the mouth of the basket, made of lead and weighing approximately 75 to 105 pounds. The pulpit commentary tells us, "When the leaden lid was raised, one woman (mulier una, γυνὴ μία) was seen in the measure. She is called "one," as uniting and concentrating in her person all sinners and all sins. This woman is the personification of wickedness. It is very common to find backsliding Israel represented as a faithless and adulterous woman (See Isaiah 1:21; Jeremiah 2:20; Hosea 2:5; and the parable of the two women in Ezekiel 23)."

How is it, though, that we have a woman who can fit into a basket that is no larger than 6 or 7 gallons? We are all familiar with a 5-gallon bucket. Think of a woman trying to fit into something slightly larger than a 5-gallon bucket. It is because she represents an idol. Notice also that she is being hidden in an ephah, which is a measure typically of grain, barley, or another crop. Being hidden in this basket represents that this was a secret sin of Israel.

God told them early on that they should not have any idols, but what do we find at the end of Joshua and Ezekiel? What did Joshua tell the Israelites in his last speech to them? Joshua 24:14-15 says, "Now, therefore, fear the LORD and serve Him in sincerity and truth; and do away with the gods which your fathers served beyond the Euphrates River and in Egypt, and serve the LORD. But if it is disagreeable in your sight to serve the LORD, choose for yourselves today whom you will serve: whether the gods which your fathers served, which were beyond the Euphrates River, or the gods of the Amorites in whose land you are living; but as for me and my house, we will serve the LORD." (NASB).

Thoughts On Zechariah

The people answered that they would serve God, but what do we find again in Ezekiel 20? God was chastising the people for worshiping idols. Ezekiel 20:30-32 says, "Therefore, say to the house of Israel, 'This is what the LORD God says: "Will you defile yourselves in the way of your fathers and adulterously pursue their detestable things? And when you offer your gifts, when you make your sons pass through the fire, you are defiling yourselves with all your idols to this day. So shall I be inquired of by you, house of Israel? As I live," declares the LORD God, "I certainly will not be inquired of by you. And whatever comes into your mind certainly will not come about, when you say: 'We will be like the nations, like the families of the lands, serving wood and stone." (NASB). God is getting to the root of the sin that has plagued Israel since they were in Egypt and has continued up to the captivity in Babylon, idol worship. It is the fountain (source) of all wickedness in the land of Israel.

It is as if this idol is being hidden in the basket. They had to open the lid to see what was inside. While you may be able to conceal your idol from your neighbor, you can never hide your idol from God. Further, the idol is hidden in an ephah, representing the land's produce. One of the reasons they worshipped false idols was that they adopted the belief from their neighbors in the surrounding lands, which held that these false idols were gods of fertility, capable of making the land fertile and bringing prosperity. They failed to understand that God was the source of their prosperity. Instead of turning to God for their provision, they turned to idols, bringing judgment upon the land.

They would have been more prosperous if they had obeyed God and allowed the land to rest every seven years as God instructed. The reason they spent 70 years in captivity is that they went 490 years without letting the land rest. They spent one year in captivity for every year that they missed in allowing the land to rest.

Notice that when the leaden lid is lifted from the basket, the woman attempts to escape it. She does not want to leave the land. Why a leaden weight for a cover? It is used to keep the woman in the basket. When the woman tries to get out of the basket, the angel forces her back and thrusts down the leaden weight onto the basket's opening. Satan does not want the land to be free of idol worship.

God, through the punishment of Judah into captivity, has removed idol worship from the land. The Jews were so determined never to go back to captivity that they learned their lesson, maybe a little too well. After the captivity, they created many man-made laws and traditions to ensure they never again ran afoul of God's law. They also established a court system to govern the land, as seen in Jesus' day, which they did not have before their captivity. They transitioned from worshipping other gods to the legalism that Jesus had to confront during His time on earth.

The basket is removed from the land by two women with wings like the wings of a stork. I believe these two women support the woman in the basket, the idol. They have wings like those of a stork, which is considered an unclean bird in some cultures. This situation is similar to the situation when Jesus cast the legion of demons out of the young man, and they asked if they could go into the herd of pigs. God wants idol worship removed from the land of Israel, but it is not yet time for it to be removed from the earth. Therefore, He allows the idol to be transported back to its birthplace, the plains of Shinar.

They pick the basket up and transport it to the plains of Shinar. Babel, or Babylon, is on the plains of Shinar. I think it is significant that they set her up with a house. This house is more like a Temple in Babylon. What does the worship of this idol in this Temple stand for? It stands for the worship of anything but God, but more specifically, it is the worship of man and self.

The tower of Babel was built on the plains of Shinar. This is where man thought they could build a tower to reach heaven. Shinar and Babylon are symbolic of man's rebellion against God. Babylon is the center of man's rebellion against God. Why else would the iniquity, the sin of the land, be flown off to Babylon to set up in a Temple prepared for it? It is not an accident that the basket of wickedness is carried off to Shinar.

The fact that commerce is displayed here as a measure of dry goods symbolizes the idea of where all sin originates. All sin has its beginnings in our self-centered and selfish wills. In business, you are trying to make a sale and increase your profit. This is the arena of commerce; you are always trying to increase your revenue and profit so you can become rich and prosperous. In an agricultural society, it is about improving your crop yield to become more prosperous.

The woman in the basket symbolizes humanity's worship of idols and our genuine desire for them to fulfill our wants. Babylon represents all that this woman is. Israel often turned to the idols of their neighbors, the fertility gods, to ask for a more bountiful harvest. This is one of the many reasons Israel fell into idol worship; they believed these gods would bring them greater prosperity than what God would give. They failed to follow God's precepts and trust Him for their sustenance.

The New Unger's Bible Dictionary says that the woman in the basket symbolizes "the spirit of godless commercialism." In his commentary on Revelation, George Eldon Ladd discusses the Great Prostitute of Revelation 17, stating that the kings of the earth enter into contracts with Babylon to share in her wealth and prosperity. In doing so, they share in her vices and immoralities.

The Tower of Babel symbolized the people's defiance of God and pride just two generations after the flood. The plains of Shinar are where Nimrod established his kingdom. Genesis 10:8-12 tells us, "Now Cush fathered Nimrod; he became a mighty one on the earth. He was a mighty hunter before the LORD; therefore it is said, "Like Nimrod a mighty hunter before the LORD." And the beginning of his kingdom was Babel, Erech, Accad, and Calneh, in the land of Shinar. From that land he went to Assyria, and built Nineveh, Rehoboth-Ir, Calah, and Resen between Nineveh and Calah; that is the great city." (NASB). The New Unger's Bible Dictionary informs us that Nimrod is evil, and this can be observed from several perspectives.

He is considered a great leader of his time, and earthly kingship initially emerged among the Hamitic peoples. The people threw off God and wanted their own king. The Bible tells us that Nimrod founded Babylon (Genesis 10:8-10), and Babylon is presented in Scripture as both a prophetic and typological symbol of a religious and immoral system. (See Isaiah 21:9; Jeremiah 50:24; Jeremiah 51:64; Revelation 16:19; Revelation 17:5; and Revelation 18:2-3). Unger says that this name, Nimrod, means "against God." Definitions found on the internet said the name Nimrod means "to rebel" or "we will rebel."

Gotquetions.org says this of Nimrod, "According to the historian Josephus, Nimrod said he would be revenged on God if he should have a mind to drown the world again; for that, he would build a tower too high for the waters to reach. And that he would avenge himself on God for destroying their forefathers" (Antiquities of the Jews, Book 1, Chapter 4). According to Josephus, the motive for building the Tower of Babel was to protect humanity against another flood. But the reason for the first flood was humanity's wickedness and rebellion (Genesis 6:5-6), from which humanity refused to repent. Nimrod was rebellious against God, just like his antediluvian forebears, and, according to Josephus, he "persuaded [his subjects] not to ascribe [their strength] to God, as if it were through His means they were happy, but to believe that it was their own courage which procured that happiness" (op. cit.)." Notice the focus on man being his own god. That somehow man could compete with God.

The plains of Shinar are the birthplace of rebellion after the flood. Even congregating on the plains of Shinar was a rebellion of sorts. The people were to "Be fruitful and multiply, and fill the earth," Genesis 1:28 (NASB). Instead, they congregated at Babel and said, "Come, let's make bricks and fire them thoroughly." And they used brick for stone, and they used tar for mortar. And they said, "Come, let's build ourselves a city, and a tower whose top will reach into heaven, and let's make a name for ourselves; otherwise we will be scattered abroad over the face of all the earth." (Genesis 11:3-4 NASB).

It is fitting that this source of wickedness would be flown off to Babylon to have a Temple prepared for it. I believe that this woman, or idol, is of the same evil spirit as the Great Prostitute of Babylon that we see in Revelation 17. She seduces mankind with her charms and promise of prosperity and whatever else is in man's heart to desire. She is evil, and her purpose is to get mankind to worship anything but the One True God. She desires mankind to feed the selfish, self-centered nature that runs contrary to the ways of God and leads us away from God.

The fountain or source of Israel's rebellion against God is sent off to Babylon, and from this time forward, it is not idols that lead Israel astray from God. Israel sets up a rigid legal system to ensure that they never again follow false gods and never again forget the laws of God. The Jews of Zechariah's day, and up through the time of Jesus, learned this lesson regarding idol worship and ignoring God's laws. As we see later in the Book of Zechariah, the next great downfall for the people of Israel is that they fail to recognize the Messiah they have been looking for and hoping for, not understanding that He will first appear as a suffering servant.

Zechariah 6
The Four Horses of the Apocalypse

Two things I noticed at first glance. First, even though God is all-knowing and all-powerful, He sends riders out to go around the entire world, scouting or performing tasks for Him. This is what we would expect from an earthly king. Second, He has a court with His officials that stand before Him regularly. We see them "take their stand by (or before) the LORD of all the earth," also in Zechariah 4 and Revelation 11.

Zechariah 6:1-8 (NASB) Now I raised my eyes again and looked, and behold, four chariots were going out from between the two mountains; and the mountains were bronze mountains. 2 With the first chariot were red horses, with the second chariot black horses, 3 with the third chariot white horses, and with the fourth chariot strong spotted horses. 4 So I responded and said to the angel who was speaking with me, "What are these, my lord?" 5 The angel replied to me, "These are the four spirits of heaven, going out after taking their stand before the Lord of all the earth, 6 with one of which the black horses are going out to the north country; and the white ones are to go out after them, while the spotted ones are to go out to the south country." 7 When the strong ones went out, they were eager to go to patrol the earth. And He said, "Go, patrol the earth." So they patrolled the earth. 8 Then He called out to me and spoke to me, saying, "See, those who are going to the land of the north have appeased My wrath in the land of the north."

After reading verses 1 through 8 of chapter 6, another verse came to my mind. Galatians 6:7 says, "Do not be deceived, God is not mocked; for whatever a person sows, this he will also reap." (NASB) The point of this vision is that God will judge the nations for what they have done to Israel in the past and how they treat the Jews in the future. We return to Zechariah 1 and find God is angry with the nations He sent to discipline Israel. They have gone further than was fitting. In the second vision of Chapter 1, we see that God was going to use four craftsmen to terrorize the four nations that oppressed Israel. God allowed them to become rich and powerful, and they used their power to oppress Israel and other nations. But God is a God of righteousness and justice. Therefore, "Do not be deceived: God is not mocked, for whatever a person sows, this he will also reap." (NASB).

The picture of these horses and chariots is the picture of God's power. They are very much like the horses and riders we see in the Book of Revelation. They represent God's power and judgment. Where are these chariots coming from? They come from between the mountains of brass. Brass is often used as a symbol of judgment in the Scriptures because it was the metal that held the highest temperature before melting, and thus, it played a crucial role in the sacrificial system. In Habakkuk 3:8, we see God's horses and chariots, which are a sign of God's power and strength. In Habakkuk, this power and strength are employed during the Day of the LORD to deliver the nation of Israel and bring judgment upon the people of Cush.

Mountains are symbolic of kingdoms. Therefore, it appears that the chariots come from between two kingdoms. Throughout its history, Israel has always been sandwiched between two kingdoms: Egypt in the south and Babylon or Assyria in the north. These chariots are coming from Israel to the lands in the north and the lands in the south. Typically, we see visions as a means of predicting the future. In this case, it helps us see something in the spiritual realm that affected recent past events in the natural realm. Zechariah experienced this vision in approximately 520 BC. However, we can see an interim fulfillment of this vision with the Medes and the Persians conquering Babylon in 539 BC. We also know that in 525 BC, the Persians conquered Egypt. Both empires saw their defeat just before the exiles were permitted to return to the land of Israel. In fact, the defeat of the Babylonian Empire allowed the Jews to return to Israel. The defeat of the Egyptian kingdom ensured that Israel would have peace from the south.

We will see the final and complete fulfillment of this vision on the Day of the LORD. We know that in the last days, the Antichrist will come from the north and have allies in the south. In Ezekiel 38, we see the following countries included in attacks on Israel: Turkey, Iran, Sudan, Libya, Ethiopia, and Yemen. The Antichrist will have nations in his coalition from the north and the south of Israel. Furthermore, the Antichrist will conquer Jordan, Saudi Arabia, and Egypt, compelling their people to join his coalition (Daniel 11:40-42). Although these are nations that have made peace with Israel today, I do not believe it will be hard to compel the people of these nations to join the coalition because many of the citizens are radical Islamists who still hate Israel, even if their countries are at peace with Israel.

The issue of timing is crucial because, at the time of writing this vision, Babylon had already been defeated and conquered by the Medes and the Persians. I believe this passage refers to a future period when the king of the north and his alliance will be judged. In the first half of the book of Zechariah, these visions can be brief and lack sufficient detail to connect them with other Scriptures, which would provide a clearer picture of precisely what Zechariah is prophesying. Instead, we get a vision of judgment coming against the northern and southern countries. However, we don't know when or if this vision refers to a time in the near or distant future. We know from Daniel 11 and Ezekiel 38 that the Antichrist will come from the north. We know from Habakkuk 3:13 that the Antichrist will be killed by Jesus Christ, who will slice him open from thigh to neck. This vision speaks of the Day of the LORD when Jesus defeats the Antichrist and judges the people who followed him. This includes the people of the North Country and the people of the South Country.

Regarding the judgment of the southern country, Ezekiel 29-32 recounts the judgment of Egypt for its actions against Israel and for Israel's reliance on Egypt for protection instead of its God. But their judgment will only last for 40 years (Ezekiel 29:8-16). The northern country will face the judgment of two horses: conquest and famine, while the southern country faces the horse that represents death and devastation by war, famine, plagues, disease, and wild animals. When you read Ezekiel 29, Ezekiel 38, and Zechariah 14, you see that God will put hooks in the jaws of these nations to bring them into war so that He may judge them. These chariots are going out from Israel in the last days when Jesus Christ returns, and He sends these Spirits to bring judgment to the lands and people that have attacked Israel. This judgment will satisfy the LORD's wrath before He brings peace to the world and begins to rebuild and restore the earth.

What I see in Zechariah are two of these horses going toward the north country, toward those who have historically invaded Israel, and to those who will invade Israel in the last days. Historically, although Babylon was located to the east, it was referred to as the "North Country" because the invaders came from the north, and to reach it, one had to travel north to stay near the water sources. To the east was a desert, and you couldn't make it through the desert without water sources. In the future, we see that the core of the coalition will be Turkey, Syria, Iran, and Iraq. Iraq was formerly known as Babylon. Primarily, these countries are to the north of Israel. In Zechariah 6:8, we read, "See, those who are going to the land of the north have appeased My wrath in the land of the north." (NASB). A quick overview of this passage reveals that God has sent His riders out in judgment over the nations, particularly toward the land of the north.

Many commentators argue that we can't compare these horses and chariots to the riders in Revelation, but it doesn't make sense that God would reveal the colors of the horses if these colors hold no meaning in the vision. I believe that the color of these horses lines up with the horses of Revelation. The colors of the four horses of Revelation 6 represent the following: the white horse conquers; the red horse makes war; the black horse brings both famine and inflation; and the pale horse brings death and devastation through war, famine, pestilence, and wild beasts. Ezekiel talks not of the horses but of the judgments. Ezekiel 14:21 says, "For this is what the LORD God says: "How much more when I send My four severe judgments against Jerusalem: sword, famine, vicious animals, and plague to eliminate human and animal life from it!" (NASB). These are the ways in which God brings judgment, and they are consistent throughout the Word. Yes, I believe these colors have meaning, and I believe that the meaning of the colors is consistent throughout the Scriptures.

These horses and chariots are also referred to as the "four spirits/winds of heaven" that have presented themselves before the LORD. The ESV does a poor job of translating the passage here, translating it as "These are going out to the four winds of heaven, after having presented themselves to the LORD of all the earth." The NASB does a better job, translating the passage as "These are the four spirits of heaven, going out after taking their stand before the LORD of all the earth." The term "four spirits" is used in

Scripture to refer to the scattering of nations as a punishment from God. There are four spirits, but the Prophet sees them as chariots pulled by these colored horses. This is the picture and symbol of judgment and power. The chariot represents power in antiquity, much like a tank today. The Prophet sees these four spirits going out, and they represent power. They are told to go out, and we see that each horse and chariot takes a direction. Verse 7 tells us that they are patrolling the earth. These horses are delivering judgment from the LORD. It is interesting to note that both the black and white horses go towards the north. The spotted horses go towards the south. It does not mention which direction the red horses take.

If I am correct and these horses go out at the time Jesus is fighting the army of the Antichrist, there should be no more war until Satan is released for one last time at the end of the Millennial Kingdom. Therefore, it is likely that the red horse, which makes war, patrols without any specific task once victory over the Antichrist and Satan has been achieved. Zechariah 6:1-8 reinforces the idea that God will bless those who bless Israel and curse those who curse Israel (Genesis 12:3). In this vision, we see that God brings judgment on those who have cursed Israel or those who will curse Israel in the future.

Zechariah 6:9-15 (NASB) The word of the LORD also came to me, saying, 10 "Take an offering from the exiles, from Heldai, Tobijah, and Jedaiah; and you shall go the same day and enter the house of Josiah the son of Zephaniah, where they have arrived from Babylon. 11 "Also take silver and gold, make an ornate crown, and set it on the head of Joshua the son of Jehozadak, the high priest. 12 "Then say to him, 'The LORD of armies says this: "Behold, there is a Man whose name is Branch, for He will branch out from where He is; and He will build the temple of the LORD. 13 "Yes, it is He who will build the temple of the LORD, and He who will bear the majesty and sit and rule on His throne. So He will be a priest on His throne, and the counsel of peace will be between the two offices."' 14 "Now the crown will become a reminder in the temple of the LORD to Helem, Tobijah, Jedaiah, and Hen the son of Zephaniah. 15 "Those who are far away will come and build the temple of the LORD." Then you will know that the LORD of armies has sent me to you. And it will take place if you completely obey the LORD your God.

Many commentators believe that in verses 9 through 15, Zechariah describes an actual event that took place. A crown was made and placed in the Temple to remind everyone that the Messiah was coming. I do not. I believe that this is another vision. I believe this is another vision because they are making a crown and placing it on the head of Joshua, the high priest. This would have been taboo in Jewish society. They were well-versed in the fact that these two offices were separate. King Uzziah was struck with leprosy for disobeying God and performing priestly duties. Second, nowhere else in Scripture do we read about this crown being stored in the Temple waiting for the Messiah. If this symbolic crown was made and sitting in the Temple, why was there never any mention of it after Zechariah chapter 6?

Explainingthebook.com believes that this passage is a vision for several reasons. First, the phrase in verse 9, "The word of the LORD also came to me, saying. " This exact phrase is used in Zechariah 4:8, which the writer of explainingthebook.com believes is a continuation of the vision of the olive trees and the menorah. Therefore, he believes that this phrase would lead one to believe that this is a continuation of the visions that Zechariah has been given. Second, there are time references in the Book of Zechariah that divide the material. We see the first one in Zechariah 1:1 (the eighth month of King Darius' second year) and the second time reference in Zechariah 1:7 (the twenty-fourth day of the eleventh month of King Darius' second year). The third and final time reference in the book of Zechariah is chapter 7, verse 1 (the fourth day of the ninth month of Darius' fourth year), immediately following this passage. The time reference indicates that we are in a new section of the book of Zechariah. This may be one of the more critical visions in the first half of the book of Zechariah, as it foretells the coming of one who will be both a priest and a king. It also tells of the building of the fourth Temple by the LORD Jesus Christ, as we discussed in the fourth chapter. This will occur at the beginning of the Millennium Kingdom.

The vision starts by telling Zechariah to take an offering from the exiles returning from Babylon. It specifically mentions Heldai, Tobijah, and Jedaiah. The thought here is that Josiah was hosting these specific men, and Zechariah was to go to Josiah's to meet these men and receive the offering of silver and gold. They were to take the offering of silver and gold and have a crown made for them. The original language refers to crowns, but it is thought that the plural form was used to indicate "a noble crown." Since we come to understand that this is a symbolic crown for the Messiah, it can also be understood as representing many crowns. In Revelation 4:10-11, the twenty-four elders cast their crowns at the feet of Jesus Christ.

Next comes the importance of the entire symbolic act. They were to set the crown on the head of Joshua, the high priest. The name Joshua is the name for Jesus. Jesus is the Greek translation of Joshua. God is amazing. Given the numerous visions and symbolism that occurred during Zechariah's time, it is fitting that the high priest of that era would be named Joshua. Joshua here is a type or representation of Jesus Christ, the Messiah. Verses 12 and 13 say, "Then say to him, 'The LORD of armies says this: "Behold, there is a Man whose name is Branch, for He will branch out from where He is; and He will build the temple of the Lord. Yes, it is He who will build the temple of the LORD, and He who will bear the majesty and sit and rule on His throne. So He will be a priest on His throne, and the counsel of peace will be between the two offices."'" (NASB).

It is clear that this vision refers to the second coming of Jesus Christ, when He will establish His earthly Kingdom and literally direct the construction of the Temple on earth. I spoke in depth in Chapter 4 of Jesus building the fourth Temple at the beginning of the Millennial Kingdom. Read the dedication of Solomon's Temple (II Chronicles 6-7). You think the Temple of Solomon was something to see. The presence of God filled the Temple and was observable as smoke. Imagine the beginning of the Millennial Kingdom, when Jesus directs the building of the Temple. Imagine that dedication!!!!! I want to be there! Most likely, Jesus will destroy the Temple that the Antichrist defiles and rebuild it as the most magnificent of all the Temples built for Yahweh. This will be where Jesus Christ sets up His throne, and the Holy of Holies will be His throne room.

Not only will He be King, but He will also be the High Priest. There is only one man who can fulfill both duties, and that is Jesus Christ. Verse 12 tells us that He is the "Branch." This word "Branch" is translated in Greek as "Anatole." That's the word Zachariah, John the Baptist's father, uses in Luke 1:78 to describe the one for whom John was to prepare the way. "Anatole" is defined in Strong's Lexicon as Rising, East, Dawn, or Branch. Its meaning is to rise or to spring up. In Luke 1:78, it is translated as Sunrise because it describes the Branch who will be a light to the Jewish people. I could not help but think of the Book of Zechariah when I read the prophecy of John the Baptist's father, Zechariah. Also note. John the Baptist's father is called Zacharias in the King James Version, but in the NASB, the ESV, and the Tree of Life Version, John's father is called Zechariah.

When you read what John's father prophesied in Luke 1:67-79, your thoughts turn to the Messiah during the Millennium. The beginning of the prophecy speaks of the Messiah, who will defeat Israel's enemies and let them live in peace and safety. The latter portion of the prophecy points to the Messiah, who came the first time to make a way for the forgiveness of sin and who will shine light in the darkness. It is as if Zechariah is summarizing Zechariah! It is worth quoting the entire prophecy here to understand how the Word of God fits together perfectly. Luke 1:67-79 states,

> *"And his father Zechariah was filled with the Holy Spirit and prophesied, saying: "Blessed be the Lord God of Israel, For He has visited us and accomplished redemption for His people, And has raised up a horn of salvation for us In the house of His servant David— Just as He spoke by the mouth of His holy prophets from ancient times—Salvation from our enemies, And from the hand of all who hate us; To show mercy to our fathers, And to remember His holy covenant, The oath which He swore to our father Abraham, To grant us that we, being rescued from the hand of our enemies, Would serve Him without fear, In holiness and righteousness before Him all our days. And you, child, also will be called the Prophet of the Most High; For you will go on before the Lord to prepare His ways; To give His people the knowledge of salvation By the forgiveness of their sins, Because of the tender mercy of our God, With which the Sunrise from on high will visit us, To shine on those who sit in darkness and the shadow of death, To guide our feet into the way of peace." (NASB).*

We also have the Branch being referenced in Isaiah 11:1 to indicate that the Branch will come from the stem of Jesse. Zechariah 3:8 refers to the Branch, where Yahweh God tells Joshua that He will bring forth His servant, the "Branch." Jeremiah 23:5-6 confirms that the Branch is the Messiah. Jeremiah 23:5-6 says,

"Behold, the days are coming," declares the LORD, "When I will raise up for David a righteous Branch; And He will reign as king and act wisely, And do justice and righteousness in the land. In His days Judah will be saved, And this is His name by which He will be called, The LORD Our Righteousness.'" (NASB).

The Branch will be for us both a Priest and a King. He will intercede for humanity before the Father and be our King and rule over humanity. This occurs during the Millennial Kingdom. Some have come through the tribulation, and those born during this time will still need that intercession.

In verse 14, we are told that the crown will be placed in the Temple as a reminder to four men: Helem, Tobijah, Jedaiah, and Hen. These are not all the same names of the men who returned from exile and provided the silver and gold to make the crown. Two of the four are the same: Tobijah and Jedaiah. But Helem and Hen are not the same names as Heldai and Josiah. Perhaps they are the same men and have nicknames or less formal names. Josiah in verse 10 and Hen in verse 14 are said to be the son of Zephaniah, indicating that it is the same man called by a different name. This crown was to be kept in the Temple as a reminder. To me, that would be something to remember and speak of in other places, but to my knowledge, this crown is never spoken of again. It makes sense that if this were literal, there would be a literal crown as a memorial. If it were literal, I would expect to hear of it again. I would expect some mention of it from Jesus.

Finally, verse 15 tells us that people from far away will come to contribute to rebuilding the Temple. This will occur after the tribulation, at the beginning of the Millennial Kingdom. I anticipate that both Jews and Christians (in their immortal bodies), as well as those who recognize Jesus Christ as the King, will all want to contribute to the building effort. This will be the greatest church-building campaign ever. We will empty our pockets to give our all for this building. The next part of the verse is in quotes, and it appears that Jesus is speaking here: "Then you will know that the LORD of armies has sent me to you." He is telling them that on that day, there will be no doubt that Jesus is the Messiah when they see the Temple rebuilt. Finally, Jesus tells them it will occur "if you completely obey the LORD your God." The Jews have yet to obey the voice of the LORD completely. One day, though, when enemies surround them, and their only salvation is God, they will see Jesus whom they have pierced and mourn for Him. Then, they will completely obey.

Zechariah 7
Don't Fast for the Wrong Reason

Now we will see a couple of things about the reign of Darius. When Darius became king of the Medes and the Persians, the Jews were able to resume rebuilding their Temple. Prior to his reign, the work had been hindered and abandoned. It was also in the first year of the reign of Darius that Daniel received the prophecy of the 70 weeks. Daniel was in Babylon, and Zechariah was in Israel. We are now in Darius's 4th year, and this is the last we hear of Darius in the Old Testament.

This is a hard chapter for anyone to read. It is easier for us to seek a formula to please God than to dispense true justice and practice kindness and compassion to one another.

Zechariah 7:1-6 (NASB) In the fourth year of King Darius, the word of the LORD came to Zechariah on the fourth day of the ninth month, which is Chislev. 2 Now the town of Bethel had sent Sharezer and Regemmelech and their men to seek the favor of the LORD, 3 speaking to the priests who belong to the house of the LORD of armies, and to the prophets, saying, "Shall I weep in the fifth month and fast, as I have done these many years?" 4 Then the word of the LORD of armies came to me, saying, 5 "Say to all the people of the land and to the priests, 'When you fasted and mourned in the fifth and seventh months these seventy years, was it actually for Me that you fasted? 6

'And when you eat and drink, do you not eat for yourselves and drink for yourselves?

Chapter 7 begins by providing a timestamp, marking the start of a new section of the book. It begins by stating that the town of Bethel sent men to seek the favor of the LORD, and they spoke to the priests who belonged to the house of the LORD of hosts and the prophets. They came to Jerusalem to seek the counsel of the priests and prophets on whether they should fast and weep in the fifth month as they had been doing while in captivity. The passage informs us that they are currently in the ninth month and inquiring whether they should fast and mourn in the fifth month, indicating that they are planning eight months in advance.

Why are they fasting and mourning in the fifth month? According to Jeremiah 52, it was the month when Babylon came and destroyed the Temple and Jerusalem in 586 BC. Therefore, the Jews in exile adopted this practice of fasting and mourning in the fifth month to remember the destruction of the Temple and the Holy City. They were also remembering their sin that led to the destruction of their land and the Temple. I'm sure this practice began as genuine sorrow, but it has evolved into a duty or obligation. Now, with the Temple and Jerusalem in the process of being rebuilt, the question is whether they should continue fasting and mourning in the fifth month. At this point, the Temple is approximately 2 years away from completion.

God has four responses to the question, and these four responses start in chapter 7 and continue through the end of chapter 8. Each response to the question begins with, "Then the Word of the LORD of armies came to me."

In the first response, God returns a strong word for them. God says, "When you fasted and mourned in the fifth and the seventh months these seventy years, was it actually for Me that you fasted?" Is that question not a wake-up call? They were mourning and fasting because they had been defeated and carried away to a foreign land. They felt sorry for themselves. They wanted to be home in Jerusalem, living a comfortable life. They did not want to be in Babylon, living in a faraway land under the rule of a gentile king. Did they miss the presence of the LORD? They fasted and mourned out of duty. They fasted and mourned as a ritual without genuine sorrow for the sin that led them to Babylon. The presence of the LORD is like an oasis in the desert, and yet we find it so hard to stay in His presence. We are able to stay for a while, but then life gets in the way, and we slack off from spending time with Him. We become comfortable living in the world and adapting to its ways. The Jews eventually reached a point where they became comfortable in Babylon, and many of them chose to stay there rather than return to Judah and Jerusalem. Babylon is a picture of the world, and Jerusalem is a picture of God's presence. We must make a sincere effort to live in God's presence. Further, we must remember that sin will drive us out of His presence.

God wants us to desire His presence. He wanted the people to fast and to mourn because they missed Him. David knew how to seek God's presence. In Psalm 27:4, David says,

"One thing I have asked from the LORD, that I shall seek: That I may dwell in the house of the LORD all the days of my life, To behold the beauty of the LORD And to meditate in His Temple." (NASB).

David was a man after God's own heart because he sought God's presence and beauty! Most of the time, we seek the favor of God to have an easier time, happiness, or stuff. We miss the true treasure of being in His presence. He is the treasure, yet we seek the things He provides, not His presence.

This passage reminds me of the Church of Ephesus in the book of Revelation. The Church of Ephesus had left its first love. They were going through the motions out of duty. God is speaking these same words to Zechariah. The Jews had been going through the motions out of duty, but their hearts were not in the spirit of the Law. God is a jealous God. He deserves and wants our love. He is the source of all good things in life and gives us good things because He loves us. Life gets hard, not because God made it hard, but because sin entered the world. He offers us redemption, a way to fix all the problems sin caused in this world. When this life is over, we will have a life with God at its center, and all the blessings God intended for us in this life will be realized in the life to come. Being the source of all good things, God wants our love and devotion. It is not enough that we do things out of duty to Him. He wants our love and worship. Who is satisfied if their spouse does things for them out of duty? We might accept this for a time if we are struggling and working to strengthen our marriage, but we want our spouse to love us and do things for us out of genuine affection, not out of a sense of duty. My wife's love language is me just spending time with her. God desires the same from us, to be in His presence.

God also refers to fasting in the 7th month. Basically, there was a civil war among the Jews who were left in the land, and this happened in the 7th month. Jeremiah 41 discusses this issue. It was a big mess, but the people also fasted during the 7th month because of this rebellion and civil war.

Zechariah also mentions that when they were eating, they were doing so out of selfishness. Is there another way to eat and drink? Yes, we often do not think about it, but God loves for us to celebrate in our acknowledgment of Him and His greatness. There were seven feasts that the Jews were to celebrate in their lives. Apparently, they were not celebrating the feasts in the spirit of the Law. They were just going through the motions. God wants us to make a big deal by celebrating and remembering special occasions and observances. They had been sent to Jerusalem for a purpose, and that purpose was to rebuild Jerusalem and the Temple. Haggai states that they had fixed up their own houses, but did not care for the house of God. They became discouraged, and the work on the Temple had gone undone for 16 years. They had become comfortable in life, eating and drinking, even fasting, but had not fulfilled the purpose that God had for them. They were just going through the motions of their religious duties. In New Testament terminology, "they were not seeking first the kingdom of God and His righteousness."

Zechariah 7:7 (NASB) 'Are these not the words which the LORD proclaimed by the former prophets, when Jerusalem was inhabited and carefree along with its cities around it, and the Negev and the foothills were inhabited?'

In verse 7, Zechariah reminds the people that what God says here is not new. He has been saying this to His people throughout the years through His prophets. The message is not new. God has always desired the love and worship of His people. He has continually called His people back to Himself, that they may be in His presence.

Zechariah 7:8-14 (NASB) Then the word of the LORD came to Zechariah, saying, 9 "This is what the LORD of armies has said: 'Dispense true justice and practice kindness and compassion each to his brother; 10 and do not oppress the widow or the orphan, the stranger or the poor; and do not devise evil in your hearts against one another.' 11 "But they refused to pay attention, and turned a stubborn shoulder and plugged their ears from hearing. 12 "They also made their hearts as hard as a diamond so that they could not hear the Law and the words which the LORD of armies had sent by His Spirit through the former prophets; therefore great wrath came from the LORD of armies. 13 "And just as He called and they would not listen, so they called and I would not listen," says the LORD of armies; 14 "but I scattered them with a storm wind among all the nations whom they did not know. So the land was desolated behind them so that no one went back and forth, since they made the pleasant land desolate."

In verses 8 through 14, God gives us a second response to the question. He asks, "Why are you in this condition? Because you refuse to listen to my prophets, you have not understood what it is that I am seeking from you.

As I mentioned in verses 1 through 7, the first thing God wants is for us to be in His presence. However, in this response, God is more specific. He wants us to be His hands and feet or, at the very least, do no harm. Verses 9 and 10 give us the message: "This is what the LORD of armies has said: 'Dispense true justice and practice kindness and compassion each to his brother; and do not oppress the widow or the orphan, the stranger or the poor; and do not devise evil in your hearts against one another.'" (NASB). God was looking for them to show His love to the world and be a witness of His grace and mercy. There was not much grace and mercy before the coming of Jesus Christ. The nation of Israel was to be a witness to the greatness of God. Today, we Christians are to be witnesses to the greatness of God. By greatness, I mean the entirety of His character. Not just His power, not just His justice, not just His love, not just His mercy, but the entirety of His character wrapped together. An all-powerful God who has a standard and will send you to hell for violating that standard, and a God who loved you so much He sent His only Son to pay the price of your sins. To accept that payment for your sin, you must follow Him. He is a God who loves justice for the poor, the orphan, the widow, and the stranger.

What God asks of us is simple: show kindness and compassion to one another. Stop trying to scheme so that you get ahead of the guy next to you at his expense or the expense of the poor and widows. Trust that God will take care of you, and He asks that you help care for those who are less fortunate.

To see how badly they missed it, read Ezekiel 22. This is why God scattered them among the nations. God, in His goodness, did not discipline them without first trying to get their attention to turn from their sin. Verse 12 tells us that He sent His prophets to warn and call them back to Himself and His ways, but they would not listen. Verses 11 and 12 are a stern rebuke. In verses 11 and 12, He says, "But they refused to pay attention, and turned a stubborn shoulder and plugged their ears from hearing. They also made their hearts as hard as a diamond so that they could not hear the Law and the words which the LORD of armies had sent by His Spirit through the former prophets". (NASB). This wasn't just ignorance; this was willful disobedience. A heart without Jesus Christ can be as hard as a diamond.

He invites them to stop mourning and fasting and celebrate life with Him. To take His compassion, grace, and mercy to the less fortunate. Fasting was a means of repenting, but instead of constantly needing to repent, why not obey His laws? I've said many times we are not different than Israel. It is easier for us to go through religious rituals than it is for us to hear the voice of His Spirit and obey. We can go through religious rituals and still have a corrupt heart, but you cannot enter God's presence without His Spirit working on you to change your heart. It takes a change of heart even to desire to be in His presence.

What was the consequence of their not hearing and not obeying the law of the LORD? Because they would not listen to Him when He called them, He would not listen to them when they called Him. Instead, God says He scattered them with a whirlwind among all the nations they did not know. This was a hard lesson for the people of Israel, but it was not without warning. God warned them at the very beginning, when He brought them out of Egypt what would happen if they turned from Him and disobeyed His laws. Therefore, God scattered them among the nations, and now He has brought them back to the land. He is trying to tell them, as Samuel told Saul in 1 Samuel 15:22-23, "Does the LORD have as much delight in burnt offerings and sacrifices as in obeying the voice of the LORD? Behold to obey is better than a sacrifice, and to pay attention is better than the fat of rams. For rebellion is as reprehensible as the sin of divination, and insubordination is as reprehensible as false religion and idolatry." (NASB). God prefers obedience over mourning and fasting. Further, they were mourning and fasting over the loss of a land that God had returned to them.

As you read the Scripture, you begin to understand that God loves the land. The land is a gift to the people because it helps them sustain life. God does not care that the scattering of the people made the land desolate, even though

He loves this land and chose it for His people. The land is a gift to the people; therefore, the obedience of the people is more important than a vibrant land. Understand that He can make the land vibrant once more whenever He chooses. By His blessings, the land is fertile and vibrant, and He can decide to make it fertile and vibrant at His will.

Returning to the question, "Should the people weep and fast in the fifth month?" The answer is to obey the laws of the LORD, to dispense true justice, and to practice kindness and compassion to one another. God does not want them to oppress the widow, the orphan, the stranger, or the poor, and He doesn't want them to devise evil in their hearts against one another. As a Christian, God is calling us to the same standard. We should act in the same way to be a witness to people for Jesus Christ.

Fasting is a spiritual discipline that Christians are encouraged to practice. We should not fast out of obligation or religious ritual, but rather seek the LORD, His presence, and His favor to intercede on behalf of those who need Him. We should fast to break spiritual strongholds. The discipline of fasting is necessary in the Church in America today.

Kenneth Giesman

Zechariah 8
Jerusalem, the Beautiful

Notice that Zechariah continues to address God as the LORD of armies or, in some translations, as the LORD of hosts. This gives us a mental image of God's power. While Assyria, Babylon, and Medo-Persia are all thought to have these strong and powerful armies, God reminds us that He is the LORD of armies. God's army is the most powerful, and all other armies bow to His will. His army is a host of angelic warriors. According to 2 Kings 19:35, the angel of the LORD killed 185,000 Assyrian soldiers. This is an angel of the LORD. An angel is not the pre-incarnate Jesus Christ. One angel was able to kill 185,000 soldiers, and the LORD has a host of angelic warriors. "LORD of the Armies" is a military term that suggests God is a Warrior God. He is fighting for Israel and the redemption of mankind. To gain an understanding of the meaning of this term, read Psalm 46. God is over all nations and will be exalted on the earth! There is no one and no nation that can stand against Him. It is a Psalm that speaks to His second coming and His Millennial Kingdom. Psalm 46:8-11 reveals that God is truly the LORD of armies.

> *Come, behold the works of the LORD, Who has inflicted horrific events on the earth. He makes wars to cease to the end of the earth; He breaks the bow and cuts the spear in two; He burns the chariots with fire. "Stop striving and know that I am God; I will be exalted among the nations, I will be exalted on the earth." The*

106

LORD of armies is with us; The God of Jacob is our stronghold. Selah (NASB).

Thus far in the Book of Zechariah, we see this phrase, "The LORD of armies," used in Chapters 3, 7, and 8. When used, it is a reminder that the God of Israel is the most powerful. Whether He is confronting Satan or a nation, God will not be defeated. Chapters 7 and 8 are reminders that all that has happened and will happen to Israel is from the hand of God. He uses nations as His tools of chastisement, and nations will not be victorious against God's chosen ones unless God uses them as tools. Zechariah 8 offers hope that God will once again reside in Jerusalem and bring peace to the city. The term "The LORD of armies" is significant. It says, "Do not fear. Your God is omnipotent. You can trust in what He says."

Father, help me to understand this truth fully. Too often, I beg for crumbs while You have prepared a feast for me.

Zechariah 8:1-8 (NASB) Then the word of the LORD of armies came, saying, 2 "The LORD of armies says this: 'I am exceedingly jealous for Zion, yes, with great wrath I am jealous for her.' 3 "The LORD says this: 'I will return to Zion and dwell in the midst of Jerusalem. Then Jerusalem will be called the City of Truth, and the mountain of the LORD of armies will be called the Holy Mountain.' 4 "The LORD of armies says this: 'Old men and old women will again sit in the public squares of Jerusalem, each person with his staff in his hand because of age. 5 'And the public squares of the city

will be filled with boys and girls playing in its squares.'
6 "The LORD of armies says this: 'If it is too difficult in
the sight of the remnant of this people in those days,
will it also be too difficult in My sight?' declares the
LORD of armies. 7 "The LORD of armies says this:
'Behold, I am going to save My people from the land of
the east and from the land of the west; 8 and I will bring
them back and they will live in the midst of Jerusalem;
and they shall be My people, and I will be their God in
truth and righteousness.'

Verses 1 through 8 are a strong encouragement to the people. While they are struggling to rebuild their city and to overcome those around them who are rooting for and actively working toward failure for the returning Jews, God is telling them that Jerusalem will again be a great city. He loves Jerusalem, the land of Israel, and the people of Israel, and they are not forgotten. As I read this, I see He is encouraging the Jews in Zechariah's day. However, the message is to give hope for that day when Jerusalem will be the capital of the world, and Jesus will reign from Jerusalem, bringing peace.

The first thing God says is, "I am exceedingly jealous for Zion, yes, with great wrath I am jealous for her." God is like a jealous husband in two regards. The first regard is that Israel is His bride, and His bride is stepping out on Him with other gods. God sent them into exile in order to bring them back to Him. The second regard is that He will not let someone disrespect or abuse His bride. They are His people, and He will be their protector. He loves His bride with fierce love, and He reminds His people of this fact in this passage.

Thoughts On Zechariah

Zechariah 8:3 tells them God is returning to Zion and will dwell in Jerusalem. God loves His people, and He loves His city. When He dwells in Jerusalem, it will be called the City of Truth, and the surrounding mountains will be known as the Holy Mountains. We cannot pinpoint a specific time in history when this might have occurred, so I believe this section of Zechariah 8 refers to the Millennial Kingdom, when Jesus will rule from Jerusalem for 1,000 years. At the end of the Great Tribulation, Jesus will come back to fight for Israel, and He will destroy the enemies of Israel. He will march through the desert, freeing the captives and destroying His enemies. As He fights His way to victory, He will stand on the Mount of Olives, and the Mount of Olives will split in two, with one-half of the mountain moving northward and one-half of the mountain moving southward (Zechariah 14:4).

As I read prophecies about the Millennial Kingdom, it is apparent that the Jews will live in Israel and Jerusalem. The Gentiles will continue to live in their lands (Zechariah 8:7-8 and 10:10). Gentiles will make pilgrimages to Jerusalem to observe the Feast of Tabernacles (Zechariah 14:16) and for other purposes. Additionally, I recently heard Joel Richardson confirm my thoughts and say that the Jews will inherit Israel, and the Gentiles will inherit the world. At this point, I am jealous that I am not a Jew because I would like to live in Jerusalem, where Jesus will have His throne.

I am glad that I am a Christian and that I will be there to see it, whereas if I were a Jew, there is a strong possibility that I would not know Jesus as the Messiah and my Savior.

There are Jews who are coming to Jesus today, and there will be a remnant of Jews who survive the Tribulation and get saved at the end of the Tribulation, but that will be a tough road to travel. Zechariah 13:8-9 tells us that 2/3rds of the people in the land will be cut off and perish, but only a remnant, 1/3rd, will survive. The 1/3rd that remains will call on the name of the LORD, and He will answer them, and He will say to them, "They are My people," and they will say, "The LORD is my God." (NASB). Those who say, "The LORD is my God," will need to confess Jesus as their savior, and they will. Zechariah 12:10 tells us, "They will look at Me whom they have pierced; and they will mourn for Him, like one mourning for an only son, and they will weep bitterly over Him like the bitter weeping over a firstborn." (NASB).

Verse 3 reminds us of God's special connection with the City of Jerusalem. He will dwell in Jerusalem, which will be called the City of Truth. The City will take on the Character of God. It will be known as the City of Truth. God loves truth. We see in this chapter and the last chapter that He wants us to be truthful with one another. Ever since Satan lied to Eve about the Tree of the Knowledge of Good and Evil, lies have been a part of this world. Jesus said, "I am the Way, the Truth, and the Life." There is no deception or untruth in the character of God. When Jesus rules from Jerusalem, only truth shall emanate from His government. Imagine if only the truth came from our governments today.

The mountain upon which Jerusalem will sit will also take on the character of God. The mountain will be called the

Holy Mountain. The Holiness of God refers to His absolute moral perfection. All moral law and perfection have their eternal and unchangeable basis in His nature. The angels around the throne constantly sing, "Holy, Holy, Holy, is the LORD God Almighty." His holiness is perfection. Everything He does and says is right and good. My words fail to capture the essence of His holiness. Jesus living and ruling from Jerusalem will serve as an example of God's holy nature. Even the mountains of Jerusalem will take on the character of Jesus.

The more I read the Bible, the more I am struck by God's love for the land of Israel and the City of Jerusalem. This is why I want to live in Jerusalem during the Millennial Kingdom and when there is a new heaven and a new earth. God has a love for Jerusalem, and if it is that special to God, it must be the place to live.

Verses 4 and 5 tell us that Jerusalem will be a place of peace and safety. Think of the most idyllic setting, the picture of Americana. The town square features a gazebo at its center, where older people are seated on the park benches and children play on the grass. There will be peace, safety, and no fear of criminals, people with bad intentions, or war. Jesus will reign, and the land will be at peace. This starkly contrasts what the Jews in Zechariah's day were experiencing. The land remains sparsely populated and littered with rubble from the city's destruction. Jesus is telling them to hold onto hope that their God loves them and will return them to the land and be their God. When Jesus rules from Jerusalem, all their troubles will be no more.

In verse 6, God asks them, "Is this too difficult for the people of Zechariah's day to believe?" Then He asks them, "Is this too difficult for God to accomplish?" I love the places in the Bible where God says, "Is the LORD's arm too short?" Can you imagine God asking us if His arm is too short to save? The answer is a resounding No! However, He understands their reluctance to believe. The living conditions in Jerusalem at this time are vastly different from those described in the text. God wants them to know that nothing is too difficult for Him. If they would only trust and obey Him, they would see great and marvelous miracles. God wants them to have faith in Him. God wants us all to have faith in Him.

Regardless of their faith, this will happen because God has decreed it here in Zechariah. People are generally realists or even pessimists. They see with their eyes and only believe what they see before them. God is asking them to believe in Him, to put their faith in Him. For me, the difficult part is that I am an impatient person. I want everything to happen now. I am sure that the Jews were also impatient and wanted this to happen now. However, for the most part, God is not a God of instant gratification. His promises unfold over time. The prophecy we are reading is still being fulfilled nearly 2,500 years later. This is easy stuff for God to do, but it will happen on His schedule, not ours. Remember, at the beginning of this study, I mentioned that the names of the author, his father, and his grandfather conveyed a message to the reader. Twice in the first chapter, we read "Zechariah, the son of Berechiah, son of Iddo." While we are being told who authored the book,

God also provides us with a message about Himself and His love for His people and land. Zechariah means "The LORD remembers," Berechiah means "The LORD blesses," and Iddo means "The appointed time." When we put this phrase together, it means the LORD remembers and blesses in His appointed time.

God declares that He will bring His people back to the land to populate it. As of the writing of Zechariah, the land is still sparsely populated, and after the death of Christ, the Jews are scattered again. When Mark Twain visited Israel, he told the world it was a desolate and unlovely place, a blistering, naked, treeless land. But what have we seen in recent history? Since the beginning of the 1900s, you have witnessed Jews coming back to their land. This return has been hastened since the end of World War II. First, the Jews from Europe came back after the war, declaring never again. Then, they helped other Jews come back to the land from communist countries and other lands of oppression. I recently watched a show on TV that was all about the return of Jews to the land and how the State of Israel has done everything it can to bring Jews back to the land. When Russia opened to allow Jews to leave, Israel sent flight after flight to get as many as they could while the door was open because they knew it would close again. They did the same thing when the door opened in Ethiopia.

Verse 8 is the beautiful part of this promise. Jesus Christ will dwell in the midst of Jerusalem, and they will be His people. He shall be their God in truth and righteousness. This will happen in the Millennial Kingdom. We read later in

Zechariah that it will take up to the end of the Tribulation for the people to believe in Jesus Christ, and many will not survive the Tribulation. But when they see Him coming in the clouds, they will look on Him whom they have pierced and mourn for Him. That will be a glorious day, but between now and then, there will be heartache.

> Zechariah 8:9-10 (NASB) "The LORD of armies says this: 'Let your hands be strong, you who are listening in these days to these words from the mouth of the prophets, those who spoke in the day that the foundation of the house of the LORD of armies was laid, so that the temple might be built. 10 'For before those days there was no wage for man nor any wage for animal; and for him who went out or came in there was no peace because of his enemies, and I sent all the people against one another.

I've begun to love it when the prophet says, "The LORD of armies says." What a great God we have. He reminds us that He has a vast army that is the most mighty in all creation. Serving "The LORD of armies" should fill you with great confidence. It was also supposed to fill the people of Zechariah's day with great confidence. They seemed small and insignificant; they had to rely on a foreign king to allow them to return to Jerusalem and rebuild the walls and the Temple. They had enemies all around them trying to discourage them as they tried to rebuild the walls and the Temple. Remember, the people laid the foundation, and then the work was halted for 16 years as the people gave in to discouragement.

God reminds them of His power, that He is their God, and they are His people. All they could see with their physical eyes were enemies all around them, trying to stop the work and slow the progress of a hard, difficult task. God wanted them to see that they were the people of "The LORD of armies." They had reason to hope and believe. Kings and enemies follow the plan of "The LORD of armies." Most of the time, they don't know they are following His plan, but they are following His will (Psalm 46). We must also remember that we serve a great God, and His plan will come to pass. If it comes out of the mouth of God, it is as good as done.

What does the LORD of armies say? He tells them to let their hands be strong so that the Temple may be built. He lets them know to whom He was speaking. He says to those "who are listening in these days to these words from the mouth of the prophets, those who spoke in the day that the foundation of the house of the LORD of armies was laid." (NASB). The enemy doesn't want us to build the Temple of the LORD. The enemy doesn't want us to have a place to worship the LORD. We can get busy with so many things in our daily lives that seem so important that we forget the most important thing: building the Temple of the LORD. For Israel, this was literal. For us today, I am speaking figuratively. The enemy will try everything he can to get us to neglect spending time with the LORD to metaphorically build our Temple daily by spending time with Him! Let your hands be strong! Spend that time with the LORD so that your hands can be strong.

A key point to remember is that this entire discourse was initiated by men from the town of Bethel, who came to ask if they should continue fasting. They were fasting for a Temple and a city that the Babylonians destroyed. The most important job now is for them to put their hands to work and finish the job. There is a time for fasting, but there is also a time for putting your hands to work and completing the task. Now was the time to complete the job. I must also say that fasting is a weapon seldom used by the Church today. If you fast in the right way for the right reasons, fasting can be a part of putting your hands to work.

Haggai chapter 1 gives us insight into what God was thinking. He is not pleased with the people because they have allowed themselves to get discouraged and distracted from rebuilding the Temple. He tells them that they have all paid attention to their own houses and built their own homes while His house lies in ruins. Because of that, He says in Haggai 1:7-11, "The LORD of armies says this: "Consider your ways! Go up to the mountains, bring wood, and rebuild the Temple, that I may be pleased with it and be honored," says the LORD. "You start an ambitious project, but behold, it comes to little; when you bring it home, I blow it away. Why?" declares the LORD of armies. "It is because of My house which remains desolate, while each of you runs to his own house. Therefore, because of you the sky has withheld its dew, and the earth has withheld its produce. And I called for a drought on the land, on the mountains, on the grain, on the new wine, on the oil, on what the ground produces, on mankind, on cattle, and on all the products of the labor of your hands." (NASB).

Zechariah 8:10 says the same thing. Before the foundation of the Temple was started, the LORD made the economy even worse than it was, and there was no peace in the land. At this point, they have already begun rebuilding the Temple, and they are nearing completion. God reminds the people of the blessings that come with obedience and the consequences of disobedience. He says, "For before those days there was no wage for man nor any wage for animal; and for him who went out or came in there was no peace because of his enemies, and I sent all the people against one another." (NASB). God is sovereign. I don't understand it all. When does He cause things to happen, and when does He allow things to happen? Here is what I know. Romans 8:28 says, "And we know that God causes all things to work together for good to those who love God, to those who are called according to His purpose." (NASB). He is at work in all things and uses all things for His purposes. In this case, He used the economy and the trouble caused by the enemy for His purpose. If you do not listen to Him when He speaks to you, He will bring trouble or trials into your life to get your attention. Praise God. These are to help you get back in line with His will. His will is best for you! That is what He is doing here. He wants to get Israel to build His house so that they have a place to worship Him and enjoy His favor.

> Zechariah 8:11-13 (NASB) 'But now I will not treat the remnant of this people as in the former days,' declares the LORD of armies. 12 'For there will be the seed of peace: the vine will yield its fruit, the land will yield its produce, and the heavens will provide their dew; and I

will give to the remnant of this people all these things as an inheritance. 13 'And it will come about that just as you were a curse among the nations, house of Judah and house of Israel, so I will save you that you may become a blessing. Do not fear; let your hands be strong.'

Verses 11 through 13 are a transition. The LORD is talking about this generation of Jews living in the land. Still, He is also talking about when Christ will be a sacrifice for all nations, and He appears to be discussing the future in the Millennial Kingdom. For this generation of Jews in Zechariah's day, the LORD will bless them for completing the work of the Temple. That blessing will be with the produce of the land and also with peace from their enemies. Then, it transforms into a prediction of the coming Christ, who will be a blessing to all nations. The coming Christ shall come from the nation of Israel.

Furthermore, Israel shall be transformed from a curse among the nations to a blessing among the nations, and they shall be recognized as a blessing. In fact, today, there is still great antisemitism in the world. After this was written, the Romans destroyed Jerusalem and the Temple. The Jews were scattered all over the world. World War II occurred with the great persecution of the Jews. This Scripture addresses the Jews of that day, as evident in verses 14-17, but it also provides a comprehensive discussion of the future in verses 20-23. In verses 9-13, we see that the LORD is speaking to the generation of Jews in Zechariah's time, but He has an eye on the future when the nations of the world will recognize Israel as a blessing.

In verse 11, the LORD addresses the current generation of Jews living in the land. He will not treat them as He did when they made their homes more comfortable instead of building the Temple. As Haggai tells us, they were working to make their dwellings nice, but neglecting the Lord's Temple. He will not treat them as He did their fathers, who disobeyed and caused the people to go into exile. He will not treat them as He did in verse 10 when He caused the economy to be poor and when He caused their enemies to be a thorn in their sides. He says His blessing will be upon them for their obedience in building the Temple. In verse 12, He provides a description of what this blessing will entail. The seed will be prosperous, the vine will give its fruit, the ground shall give the increase, and the heavens shall give their dew, and He will cause the remnant of the people to possess all these things. This is a direct blessing to those living in the land at that time for their obedience in building the house of the LORD of armies.

Israel was always meant to be a blessing to the people of the world. Israel was to be a witness to the world of the One True God. Just as Christians are to be witnesses of Jesus Christ and His greatness, Israel was meant to be a witness of the greatness of God. However, for those neighbors directly around them, Israel was a curse as they occupied the land and worshipped a God different from their neighbors. They also became a curse because they became arrogant, thinking they were the people of God, rather than being a witness to the nations. Finally, they became a curse to the nations of the world by the will of God as a punishment for their disobedience. Deuteronomy 28 provides the blessings for obedience and the consequences for disobedience. One of the consequences of disobedience is that it would bring a curse upon the nations.

The second half of verse 13 marks a shift to the future, first in the coming of the Messiah through the line of Abraham and the nation of Israel. It doesn't specifically bring up the Messiah here, but that is the blessing that Abraham provides to the entire world. Genesis 12:2-3 says, "And I will make you into a great nation, and I will bless you, and make your name great; and you shall be a blessing; and I will bless those who bless you, and the one who curses you I will curse. And in you all of the families of the earth will be blessed." (NASB). Galatians 3:14 makes it clear that His blessing was fulfilled with the death of Christ for our sins, "so that in Christ Jesus the blessing of Abraham would come to the Gentiles. Then we would receive the promise of the Holy Spirit through faith." (NASB). The blessing of Israel was still five hundred years away, and Zechariah wrote that God would save His people, and they would become a blessing to the nations. I see this blessing in the birth, death, and resurrection of Jesus Christ. However, the salvation of Israel points us to the last days, and verses 20-23 direct us to the Millennial Kingdom. The tail end of verse 13 states, 'You are the beloved of God, and through you, the nations will be blessed.' So, pick up your heads, let your hands be strong, and finish the house of the LORD.

Zechariah 8:14-15 (NASB) "For this is what the LORD of armies says: 'Just as I determined to do harm to you when your fathers provoked Me to anger,' says the LORD of armies, 'and I have not relented, 15 so I have again determined in these days to do good to Jerusalem and to the house of Judah. Do not fear!

Verses 14 and 15 are a contrast. In verse 14, the prophet again refers to God as the "LORD of armies," which I have come to love. The contrast is that God reminds the Jews listening to and reading Zechariah that He punished their fathers for their disobedience, and God says, I am not sorry that I punished your fathers. Israel and Judah had both become wicked in their worship of idols. I think most Christians understand that idol worship is the worship of demons, but what we do not think about because we have grown up in Western civilization, civilized by the gospel of Jesus Christ, is that idol worship almost always includes sexual immorality, drugs, and drunkenness. These are the very things that are overtaking our country today.

If that were not bad enough, God refuses to share His accomplishments, life, and the fruit of life with created beings and inanimate objects. He causes the rain to fall to water the crops. He causes the sun to rise, providing the light and heat necessary for crops to grow. He allows us to take another breath and allows our hearts to continue beating. Israel was His chosen possession, and they were stepping out into a spiritual affair with another and giving His glory and His worship to evil entities made from material that He created.

He was not sorry. He needed to get their attention and bring His people back to Himself.

Verse 15 is just the opposite. God once again feels the love from His people as they rebuild the Temple, and He wants to show His favor to them. He says, "I have again determined in these days to do good to Jerusalem and to the house of Judah. Do not fear!" (NASB). Again, if we go back to Deuteronomy 28, God promises punishment for disobedience and blessings for obedience. They are now in the midst of those blessings. That doesn't mean that everything was rosy. Their enemies still surrounded them, and the city walls were not yet built. But the Father says, "Do not fear!" He gives them the confidence that the "LORD of armies" is with them.

> Zechariah 8:16-19 (NASB) 'These are the things which you shall do: speak the truth to one another; judge with truth and judgment for peace at your gates. 17 'Also let none of you devise evil in your heart against another, and do not love perjury; for all these things are what I hate,' declares the LORD." 18 Then the word of the LORD of armies came to me, saying, 19 "The LORD of armies says this: 'The fast of the fourth, the fast of the fifth, the fast of the seventh, and the fast of the tenth months will become joy, jubilation, and cheerful festivals for the house of Judah; so love truth and peace.'

He says now that we are walking together again, these are the things that I want you to follow: 1) Speak truth to one another; 2) Judge honestly and peacefully in your gates; 3) Don't devise evil plans against others; and 4) Do not swear falsely. Why does the LORD tell the people to follow these directives? Because all these things are what He hates: lying lips, a dishonest justice system, a heart that devises wicked schemes, and a false witness.

God loves people. He created people to spend eternity with Him. He loves all people. God doesn't judge us by our skin color, heritage, or looks. God judges us by our words and actions. He loves us all and wants us all to be kind to one another and love each other. God wants the people of Israel to take on His character. The enemy would love us to think that God is just an egomaniac who doesn't care what happens to us. Some believe He just wants to play with us as a child might play with toys. Nothing could be further from the truth. He loves us and has our best interests at heart. He created mankind, and He knows that since the fall, we are sinful. He gives us rules to follow for our good. He cares for all of us, especially those who are less fortunate. He wants us all to take on His character and love one another. God expects us to be His hands and feet.

Verse 18 tells us that the Jews fasted in four different months throughout the year. They fasted in the fourth, fifth, seventh, and tenth months. The fourth month, because that is the month that the Babylonians broke through the walls of Jerusalem (Jeremiah 39:2 and 52:6-7). The fifth month was the month in which the Babylonians burned the houses of the individuals and the house of the LORD and took the captives back to Babylon (Jeremiah 1:3 and 52:12-16). The seventh month was the month in which Ishmael, who was a royal heir, murdered the Babylonian-appointed governor of Israel at that time, Gedaliah (Jeremiah 41:1-3). Finally, the tenth month, because that is the month in which the Babylonians came and laid siege to Jerusalem (Jeremiah 39:1 and 52:3-4). The loss of their nation was a very traumatic event for the people, and they fasted for each major event that they saw as a part of this loss. Remember, this is still all a part of the answer to the question in Zechariah 7:3, "Shall I weep in the fifth month and fast, as I have done these many years?" God is saying that these fasts shall be turned into feasts and celebrations!

We have not seen the fasts turned into feasts and celebrations since this was written. This will only happen when Jesus rules and reigns from Jerusalem. One of the things that you begin to understand when you read the Old Testament Prophets is that there are several major events the prophecies point to: 1) the restoration of Israel, both after the captivity and at the second coming; 2) the first coming of the Messiah; and 3) the second coming of the Messiah. We read verses 18 and 19 and think this would surely happen soon after the prophet wrote these words. And yet, we are still waiting for the fasting and sorrow to be turned into celebration and feasts 2,500 years later.

> *Zechariah 8:20-23 (NASB) "The LORD of armies says this: 'It will yet turn out that peoples will come, that is, the inhabitants of many cities. 21 'The inhabitants of one city will go to another, saying, "Let's go at once to plead for the favor of the LORD, and to seek the LORD of armies; I also will go." 22 'So many peoples and mighty nations will come to seek the LORD of armies*

in Jerusalem, and to plead for the favor of the LORD.'
23 "The LORD of armies says this: 'In those days ten
people from all the nations will grasp the garment of a
Jew, saying, "Let us go with you, for we have heard that
God is with you."'"

Verses 20 through 23 provide a hint as to when all these things will occur. They will occur during the Millennial Kingdom. These verses refer to a time when the nations (Gentiles) will come to Jerusalem to seek the favor of the LORD. These verses go back to verse 13, where the LORD says, just as Israel was a curse to the nations (Gentiles), so the LORD will save Israel, and they will be a blessing to the nations. Even today, the Jewish people remain a hated people among the nations. Many of their neighbors would like to wipe them off the earth, and many of the nations would be happy to see this happen.

We have not yet seen the picture come to pass that we read here in verse 13 or verses 20 through 23. First, how many people from the nations are going to Jerusalem to plead for the favor of the LORD? Second, how many people are seeking friendship with the Jews because they have heard that God is with them? These are circumstances that are yet to happen and will happen after the second coming of the Messiah, when Israel recognizes their Messiah and Jesus Christ reigns in Jerusalem (Zechariah 12:10). Truly, as you read verses 20 through 23, this is different from what we see in the world today. To be a Jew on that coming day will be considered an honor. It will be a sign of blessing.

I've been going through Zechariah for a while now, and spending so much time in it makes me want to be Jewish and makes me want to live in Israel. You begin to understand how much God loves his people and how God loves the land of Israel. Don't ask me why, but God has made Jerusalem the center of the earth and very possibly the center of the universe. Jerusalem and Israel are that special to God.

Verse 23 says that ten Gentiles from all over the world will grasp the garment of a Jew and say, "Let us go with you, for we have heard that God is with you." (NASB). What a role reversal from today. This will all happen once they recognize the One whom they pierced, where Jesus will be their King, and they will be His people. Jesus will be the King of all on the earth during the Millennial Kingdom. The Old Testament saints, the Jews who survived the Tribulation, and the Church, will be the core of this Kingdom. There will also be those Gentiles who survived the Tribulation and put their faith in Him. But there will also be Gentiles who survive the Tribulation and never put their faith in Him, but they obey grudgingly because He will rule with a rod of iron (Revelation 19:15).

Zechariah 9
Settling Accounts

The work of Joel Richardson helped me tremendously to understand the book of Zechariah from this point forward. Joel's interpretation of Scripture has led me to think differently, and his understanding of the return of Christ makes the most sense and is the most biblically sound. Understanding how the Scripture reveals the return of Christ has helped me when reading Zechariah. Joel's knowledge of the Old Testament, the major prophets, and the minor prophets helps reveal how these Scriptures build upon each other. I don't agree with Joel's interpretation of events because he is the first one I've heard. I agree with his interpretation of the Scripture because I am well aware of the other views, and they left me with too many questions. Even before I read "Sinai to Zion," I was leaning toward a post-tribulation rapture because the argument for a pre-tribulation rapture is like trying to put a jigsaw puzzle together, and the pieces don't quite fit right.

Nowhere in Scripture does it directly tell us of a pre-tribulation rapture. You must piece it together, and you are still left with parts that don't fit together well. Joel's knowledge of the Scriptures and his interpretation of events left my spirit in agreement with him. As you look through the Scriptures, too many are saying the same thing to ignore the reality of Jesus' triumphant march through the desert, including those here in Zechariah. I highly recommend Joel's book, "From Sinai to Zion," for anyone seeking to understand the Second Coming of Jesus Christ.

> *Zechariah 9:1-8 (NASB) The pronouncement of the word of the LORD is against the land of Hadrach, with Damascus as its resting place (for the eyes of mankind, especially of all the tribes of Israel, are toward the LORD), 2 And Hamath also, which borders on it; Tyre and Sidon, though they are very wise. 3 For Tyre built herself a fortress, And piled up silver like dust, And gold like the mud of the streets. 4 Behold, the Lord will dispossess her And throw her wealth into the sea; And she will be consumed with fire. 5 Ashkelon will see it and be afraid. Gaza too will writhe in great pain; Also Ekron, because her hope has been ruined. Moreover, the king will perish from Gaza, And Ashkelon will not be inhabited. 6 And a people of mixed origins will live in Ashdod, And I will eliminate the pride of the Philistines. 7 And I will remove their blood from their mouth And their detestable things from between their teeth. Then they also will be a remnant for our God, And be like a clan in Judah, And Ekron will be like a Jebusite. 8 But I will camp around My house because of an army, Because of him who passes by and returns; And no oppressor will pass over them anymore, For now I have seen with My eyes.*

Many passages throughout the Old Testament Prophets seemingly have their fulfillment in two different events that are very much alike. It is as if God gives us his blueprint in the first event, and he follows that blueprint for the second event. It also seems that God wants to know if we will dig through His Word to find the truth or just settle for the event we already know happened and accept the easy truth without seeking the deeper meaning. Chapter 9 is one such place where we need to dig for the deeper meaning. The vast majority of commentaries point you to Alexander the Great and His march through places we, in our modern day, call Lebanon, Gaza, and Israel. It appears that Zechariah 9:1-6 is primarily referring to the conquest of Alexander the Great. However, as we read Joel 3, we see the LORD discussing these same cities and lands. However, it is apparent in Joel 3 that the Prophet Joel is talking about the last days. Joel 3:18 even mentions the fountain that we see in Zechariah 13:1.

> Joel 3:17 says, "Then you will know that I am the LORD your God, Dwelling on Zion, My holy mountain. So Jerusalem will be holy, And strangers will no longer pass through it." (NASB).

> And Joel 3:20-21 finishes with, "But Judah will be inhabited forever, And Jerusalem for all generations. And I will avenge their blood which I have not avenged, For the LORD dwells in Zion." (NASB).

Joel 3 speaks of the last days, as evidenced by its opening verses in Joel 3:1-3.

> "For behold, in those days and at that time, When I restore the fortunes of Judah and Jerusalem, I will gather all the nations And bring them down to the Valley of Jehoshaphat. Then I will enter into judgment with them there On behalf of My people and My inheritance, Israel, Whom they have scattered among the nations; And they have divided up My land. They

have also cast lots for My people, Traded a boy for a prostitute, And sold a girl for wine so that they may drink." (NASB).

Then Joel 3 turns to discuss Tyre, Sidon, and the regions of Philistia, just as Zechariah 9 does. The events of October 7th, 2023, are just a birth pain as foretold by Jesus, but when I read Joel 3:3-8, it very much reminds me of October 7th. On October 7th, 2023, approximately 1,400 Hamas fighters breached the border of Southern Israel from Gaza (Philistia), kidnapped over 250 people, and killed 1,139 people in attacks on Israeli Kibbutzim. Many of those killed were women who were sexually assaulted before they were killed. The stories are horrific. The women were assaulted to "make them dirty" and mutilated out of pure hatred. Experts say rape isn't about sex; it is about dominance and violence, and October 7th proved that point. Why do I bring this up? This is what comes to mind when I read Joel 3:2-3, which we just quoted above. In particular, verse 3.

"They have also cast lots for My people, Traded a boy for a prostitute, And sold a girl for wine so that they may drink." NASB).

Joel 3:4 tells us who will face judgment: Tyre, Sidon, and all the regions of Philistia. Where are Tyre, Sidon, and the regions of Philistia? They are Lebanon, where Hezbollah resides, and Gaza, where Hamas resides. Two enemies that are a constant threat to Israel, not enough to threaten their existence as a nation currently, but a constant threat of terror attacks. Today, Israel is determined to eliminate Hamas, and they currently are not stopping until they achieve that goal. However, Joel chapter 3 tells us that there will be future attacks from the area of Gaza and Lebanon. Thus, there will be a coming judgment on the location of Gaza, Philistia, Lebanon, Tyre, and Sidon. On that day, though, these will not be small terror attacks that Israel can defend against. These attacks will be part of the war of Gog and Magog, and Israel's existence will hang by a thread. October 7th showed us the treatment that the Jews can expect, being taken captive and being subjected to sexual violence. Joel 3 tells us that you can include human trafficking of both boys and girls.

Zechariah 9 includes cities in Syria, Lebanon, and Philistia. I see two countries that will be part of the Antichrist's alliance. Turkey and Syria. Both countries are to the north of Israel. I don't know if you can still count Lebanon as a country, as Hezbollah is basically ruling it, but they will also be part of this alliance, as will the Palestinians in Gaza. Think of the enormous amount of hatred currently being built up in the minds and hearts of the Palestinians. Presently, you have Iran funding terrorist organizations to fight against Israel, with Hamas being Sunni and Hezbollah being Shia. It does not currently matter to the Muslim world if they work with Sunni or Shia Muslims, provided they are working for the destruction of Israel. Turkey and Syria are both majority Sunni, while Iran is majority Shia. Whether Hamas or Hezbollah remains a strong force in the future, you can count on Gaza, Lebanon, and the West Bank as being areas from which attacks against Israel will come.

Unfortunately, most Bible scholars are from years ago, before Israel became a nation. Although the Scriptures tell of a restored Israel, most scholars could not see it. Also, we are more comfortable expounding on what someone else said than blazing our own trail. Therefore, many commentators continued down the same path as their predecessors. I tend to do that also to ensure that I do not stray from orthodox doctrine. I must admit that the teachings of Joel Richardson have opened my eyes to these Scriptures. Most commentators spoke of what they could see, and what they could see here in Zechariah 9 was the historical march of Alexander the Great through the areas of Lebanon, Gaza, and Israel, bringing judgment on those cities mentioned here in Zechariah 9. But what they could not see, and we have the ability to see because of the period in which we live, is the restored nation of Israel and the interactions between Israel and her neighbors. Where does Israel's trouble come from today? It is mainly from Lebanon and Gaza.

I also have the benefit of hindsight in writing these words, having passed the first anniversary of October 7th. The world can see the destruction that Hamas did to Israel in their attack coming out of the area of Gaza, or Philistia. Consequently, Israel is making itself a pariah on the world stage. Yes, she is only defending herself as most countries would, but the narrative is being twisted, and the world believes Israel's attempt to secure its borders goes too far, and it looks like Israel is committing genocide. Yes, the destruction is great, but what would most countries do if they were attacked like Israel was on October 7th?

From a historical perspective, the cities mentioned in Zechariah 9:1-7 trace the path of Alexander's march through the Promised Land in 332-331 BC. The march of Alexander the Great through Syria, down through Lebanon, and then through the Promised Land was an interim fulfillment of Zechariah 9:1-7. Also, it appears that the current fighting going on between Israel, Hamas, and Hezbollah is an interim fulfillment.

As you read through this chapter, you will see that it would be easy to interpret it as pertaining to Alexander the Great and his successors, and what happened in the past. However, like many prophecies, Zechariah 9 points to an interim fulfillment with an earlier event and a complete fulfillment with a later event. It is clear that the latter half of the chapter speaks of the end times and the Millennium, while you must pair the beginning of the Chapter with Joel 3 and Amos 1 to understand that this is a future judgment. This chapter is also related to Daniel 8, which provides more detailed information about the rise of the Greek empire and its significance for Israel. The rise of Greece and the subsequent events were events that the LORD wanted the Jews and us to know. Antiochus IV Epiphanes, a key successor to Alexander the Great, is the most prominent figure in the Bible who bears a resemblance to the Antichrist up to the point of the actual Antichrist.

The amazing thing here is that while Alexander the Great went through all these cities and destroyed them or put them under heavy bondage, he was very gentle with Israel and Jerusalem. Alexander the Great was tutored by Aristotle, who taught him that there was a creator. They called him "first cause." They believed that there was a god who created the world and then left it to its own devices to determine its path. When Alexander came to Jerusalem, the high priest, Simon the Just, feared what would happen to him. (It should be noted that Josephus attaches this story to Jaddua, although it appears that Jaddua was Simon's grandfather. The Talmud tells the story that Simon the Just was the High Priest.)

When the Jews could see that Alexander and his army were marching through their neighbors, destroying everything in their path, they were concerned about what would happen when they came through Israel and Jerusalem. Simon told the people that they should make sacrifices to God and seek God's favor for the nation. One night, after Simon had made a sacrifice, God directed him in a dream that the best course of action was to reach an accommodation with Alexander the Great. They were to take courage, adorn the city of Jerusalem, and open the gates. The people were to appear in white garments, while the priests wore their priestly attire. When Simon approached Alexander the Great, Alexander got off his horse and bowed to Simon. Alexander said that he saw Simon in a dream, in his proper priestly garments, and in this dream, he was encouraged to bring his army against the Persians because he would conquer them. That is why he bowed to or saluted Simon.

Additionally, Alexander the Great entered the Temple and offered a sacrifice to God. He was shown the book of Daniel, which prophesied that the Greeks would conquer the Persian Empire. Alexander the Great, believing that he was the one who would conquer the Persians, was even more favorably disposed to the people and the nation of Israel. Because of the dreams given to Alexander the Great and Simon the Just, and the prophecies in the Book of Daniel, the LORD's favor was with Jerusalem and its people. Alexander the Great asked what favors they would ask of him. They asked that he allow them to continue to enjoy the laws of their forefathers and not pay tribute in the seventh year. Alexander granted all the requests they asked of him. This was an enormous concession because Alexander was rarely that accommodating with anyone.

Verse 1 says that the LORD will bring judgment upon Hadrach and Damascus because the LORD has been watching mankind, especially the tribes of Israel. The thought is that the LORD is going to judge these cities and regions for their treatment of the Jews. The Pulpit Commentary, examining the original language, states that the literal interpretation is "for to Jehovah (is or will be) the eye of man and of all the tribes of Israel." The Pulpit Commentary further states, "This gives the reason why Hadrach and Damascus are united. Because Jehovah has his eye on men and on Israel." This goes along with verse 8 of chapter 9, which says, "For now I have seen with My eyes." (NASB). Although the NASB and the Tree of Life version, regarding verse 1, both say, "for the eyes of mankind, especially all the tribes of Israel are toward the LORD," the ESV translates it as "For the LORD has an eye on mankind and on all the tribes of Israel." Given the nature of the verse, the translation of the ESV appears to be the most logical. Additionally, several commentaries, including Benson's Commentary and the Pulpit Commentary, support this translation. Syria dealt harshly with Israel, especially the Northern Kingdom.

Notice here that Chapter 9 starts with "The burden of the word of the LORD" (NASB and Tree of Life) or "The oracle of the word of the LORD" (ESV). The next time we see this phrase used is at the beginning of Chapter 12. The phrase is used when the LORD tells us of the judgment of a people or land. That is how it is used here in Chapter 9; it informs us of the judgments imposed upon all the cities mentioned in the chapter.

The subject of Hadrach was a matter of controversy for a long time. The scholars were unsure until recently whether this was a person, an idol, or a place. The name Hadrach was discovered "in the catalog of Syrian cities tributary to Nineveh." Hadrach was a neighboring city to Damascus, located in Syria. Syria and Aram are different names for the same country. While David was King of Israel, he subjugated the Syrians (Arameans), but they broke free of that subjugation under Solomon and were a thorn in the side of Israel thereafter. The Syrians are the ones who fought with Ahab twice, and the second time they killed King Ahab.

What we see from this first verse is that the LORD will bring judgment upon Hadrach and Damascus. There is very little written about Hadrach, so little that scholars had difficulty determining that Hadrach was a city. Therefore, there is very little to understand why this judgment was made against Hadrach. I assume that it was part of the Syrian empire and joined in whatever Syria did to the people of Israel and Judah. In fact, we know that Syria allied with Israel against Judah (2 Kings 16).

Hamath, mentioned in verse 2, was the capital city of one of the kingdoms in upper Syria, located on the Orontes River in the valley of Lebanon. The land that God gave to Israel extended all the way to Hamath. Depending on the version of the Bible you read, it appears as Lebo-hamath or Hamath. The city is mentioned in Numbers 13:21, Numbers 34:8, Joshua 13:5, and Jeremiah 49:23. Hamath is included in this judgment of God upon Syria.

Many times, we see what appears to be the wicked prospering, and we wonder why God allows it. Our lifespan seems so long to us. A year is a long time, but the Bible says our life is but a vapor. To God, who is eternal, one day is as one thousand years and one thousand years as one day. If we use that as a guide to God, forty-one years is like an hour; that is, half of our lifetime. A person may think they get away with sin, but God is patient, and His timing is vastly different from ours. God will judge sin on His timetable, not ours. The LORD reminds His people that He sees all and He judges the wicked. However, He doesn't do it when we think He should. He gives people and nations time to repent. History is repeating itself. Again, we see Syria, Lebanon, and Gaza locked in battle with Israel.

In verse 2, we come upon the cities of Tyre and Sidon and, after them, the cities of Philistia. The Pulpit Commentary states, "These Syrian towns, as well as those below in Phoenicia and Philistia, shall be visited, because they were all once included in the territory promised to Israel (see Genesis 15:18; Exodus 23:3l; Numbers 34:2-12; Deuteronomy 11:25; and comp. 2 Samuel 8:6, etc.; 1 Kings 4:21; 1 Kings 8:65; 2 Kings 14:25)." From what I could tell from reading the scriptures, it appears that Hamath is on the border of Israel, but not given to Israel. The other cities would be included in the most expansive maps of the boundaries given to Israel.

Ezekiel speaks about the judgment of Tyre. She was the little sister of Sidon, but she had surpassed Sidon. Ezekiel 28:1-10 tells us that the ruler of Tyre was proud and thought he was a god in the heart of the sea. God tells the ruler of Tyre that he is only a human and not a god. Tyre was wise, so wise that she amassed much wealth. It is as if God is saying she was wise, but at the same time, she was not as wise as she thought she was. Her wisdom brought her arrogance, the kind of arrogance that draws the attention of God to humble you. It should also be noted that Tyre was known for exploiting its neighbors and was a city filled with unscrupulous merchants.

Thoughts On Zechariah

I find it interesting that Ezekiel 28:1-10 appears to be speaking of the human king of Tyre, while verses 11 through 19 seem to transcend the human king and begin to describe Satan. The pride and arrogance of Tyre were so great that they could only be eclipsed by Satan himself. So much so that Ezekiel could write about the human king of Tyre and then go right into a description of Satan's downfall.

During David's reign, he had a close relationship with King Hiram I of Tyre, who supplied David and Solomon with wood and craftsmen needed to build the Temple. Israel maintained close ties with Tyre during the reign of King Ahab. Ahab married the Phoenician princess, Jezebel, daughter of Ethbaal, King of Sidon, and their union led to a greater infiltration of pagan worship and idolatry in the Northern Kingdom (1 Kings 16:31). Ezekiel 28:24 compares Tyre and Sidon to a thorn bush or a briar that ensnares Israel. The passage tells us they despise Israel. Tyre was a snare to Israel and caused Israel to go after false gods and participate in their detestable practices. Gotquestions.org informs us that both Tyre and Sidon were notorious for their wickedness and idolatry, which resulted in numerous denunciations by Israel's prophets, who predicted the ultimate destruction of Tyre (Isaiah 23:1; Jeremiah 25:22; Ezekiel 26; Ezekiel 28:1-9; Joel 3:4; Amos 1:9-10; Zechariah 9:2-4). Tyre and Sidon were a land and a people that helped to lead Israel away from God and into idolatry and all the detestable practices that came with idolatry. After the restoration of Jerusalem in Nehemiah's time, the people of Tyre violated the Sabbath rest by selling their goods in the Jerusalem markets on the Sabbath

(Nehemiah 13:16). These actions are cited as reasons for the judgment of Tyre and Sidon.

In 332 BC, after a seven-month siege, Alexander the Great conquered Tyre, thereby ending Phoenician political control. But the city retained its economic power. In 1291, Tyre was utterly destroyed by the Saracens, eerily fulfilling Ezekiel's prophecy: "They will destroy the walls of Tyre and tear down her towers; and I will sweep her debris away from her and make her a bare rock. She will become a dry place for the spreading of nets in the midst of the sea, for I have spoken, declares the Lord God, and she will become plunder for the nations." (Ezekiel 26:4-5 NASB). The Island has remained desolate ever since. (GotQuestions.org)

Verse 3 continues the description of Tyre, detailing its strength and prosperity. Tyre was on the coast. Tyre was also located on an Island across from the coastal city, which was known as Coastal Tyre. The Babylonians laid siege to the island city for thirteen years to no avail, and the city was not conquered. As this verse states, Tyre was a fortress and also renowned for its wealth due to its location as a port city on a major trade route.

Verse 4, however, tells us that Tyre is not strong enough nor prosperous enough to avoid the judgment of the LORD. This verse tells us that the LORD will dispossess her and throw her wealth into the sea, and she will be consumed with fire. As stated previously, Alexander the Great destroyed the coastal city of Tyre and used the rubble from those buildings to build a land bridge to the island city of Tyre, captured the city, and took its wealth. Alexander the Great did in seven months what the Babylonians could not do in thirteen years.

The following verses inform us that the Philistine cities witnessed the destruction of Tyre and were filled with terror. The LORD pronounces judgment on these cities. Five major Philistine cities made up the nation of Philistia, which continued to wage war with Israel throughout its history.

However, if you read this passage, you will note that Gath is not mentioned among these cities for judgment. Gath was the home of Goliath, and later, David fought a series of battles against the Philistines, where four other giants were killed. They were also from Gath (2 Samuel 21:22). A race of giants is said to have lived in Gath after being driven out of their land (Joshua 11:22). Gath is noteworthy because, on multiple occasions, it served as a refuge for David as he sought to escape from Saul. Eventually, David and his men settled in Gath, and David asked the King of Gath to assign him to live in a small town rather than live in the royal city of Gath. Could it be that Gath was excluded from this judgment because it offered David refuge?

Four of the major cities of Philistia are mentioned in verses 5-7. Ashkelon is mentioned first. Although Judges 1 tells us that Judah took Ashkelon, they only held it temporarily. Judges 1:18 says, "And Judah took Gaza with its territory, Ashkelon with its territory, and Ekron with its territory" (NASB). Judges 3:1-7 says, "Now these are the nations that the LORD left, to test Israel by them (that is, all the Israelites who had not experienced any of the wars of Canaan; only in order that the generations of the sons of Israel might be taught war, those who had not experienced it previously). These nations comprise the five governors of the Philistines, all the Canaanites, the Sidonians, and the Hivites who lived on Mount Lebanon, from Mount Baal-Hermon to Lebo-Hamath. They were left to test Israel to see if they would obey the Lord's commandments, which He had given to their fathers through Moses. The sons of Israel lived among the Canaanites, the Hittites, the Amorites, the Perizzites, the Hivites, and the Jebusites. They took their daughters as wives, gave their own daughters to their sons, and served their gods. So the sons of Israel did what was evil in the sight of the LORD, and they forgot the LORD their God and served the Baals and the Asheroth" (NASB).

Nowhere does it mention that the Philistines took Ashkelon back, but if you read through the Old Testament, it is treated as a Philistine city (Judges 14:19; 1 Samuel 6:17; 2 Samuel 1:20). I assume that the tribe of Judah conquered the city, but they never completely drove out the inhabitants, and the Philistines took it back. Perhaps Judah did not occupy it, but the Philistines were left there to instruct Israel in fighting and defending themselves, and also to test their faithfulness to God. Throughout the Old Testament, God used various nations for His purposes, which He later judged for their actions. God does not make those nations commit cruelty against His people. He just uses their own desires and actions for His purposes, but He still holds them accountable for their actions. Romans 8:28 says, "And we know that God causes all things to work together for good to those who love God to those who are called according to His purpose" (NASB). God uses all things for His purpose. Also, Galatians 6:7-8 says, "Do not be deceived, God is not mocked; for whatever a person sows, this he will also reap. For the one who sows to his own flesh will reap destruction from the flesh, but the one who sows to the Spirit will reap eternal life from the Spirit" (NASB). Although God may use evil nations for His purposes, He also holds them responsible for their actions.

Amos chapter 1 also includes judgments against Damascus, Gaza, Ashdod, Ashkelon, and Tyre. The LORD is patient, but He does not forget those who war against or persecute His people. When I read Amos 1:6, I think of the captivity in Edom that we will see in the war of Gog and Magog.

> Amos 1:6 says, "This is what the LORD says: "For three offenses of Gaza, and for four, I will not revoke its punishment, Because they led into exile an entire population To turn them over to Edom. (NASB).

There are two possible meanings to the first half of Zechariah 9:7. The first is that the LORD will turn the "Philistines" away from idol worship and offering sacrifices to idols. The reference is to drinking the blood of sacrifices as an act of worship. The second meaning is similar to the first. The Philistines would eat the victims of their conquests, including the blood. Eating the blood of either a sacrificed animal or a human was forbidden by God for the Israelites. Abominations were typically referred to as partaking in worship, which included blood sacrificed to the idols. The first half of verse 7 indicates that the "Philistines" will turn away from these evil practices. The second half of the verse states that there will be a remnant of Philistines that belong to the LORD. This will happen at the end of the war of Gog and Magog and the beginning of the Millennium Kingdom.

The second half of verse seven seems to be clear in that a remnant of Philistia shall be a remnant for God. Today, approximately 21% of Israel, or 1.9 million citizens of Israel, identify as Palestinian. The last part of the verse indicates that they will be like the Jebusites in that they will be incorporated as a part of the people of Israel. The majority of these citizens are Muslim. However, the remnant will be a remnant of God. That will mean more than being a citizen of Israel. It will mean recognizing and worshipping Jesus as the Christ. The timing of this is not exact, but I would think that this would happen at the same time as the Jews come to see Jesus as their Messiah. When the forces of the Antichrist come against Israel, and Jesus comes back as King and Ruler of this world to save the Jews, the Jews will recognize the One that they have pierced, and apparently so shall a remnant of the Palestinians. The second half of verse 7 serves as a transition, shifting our focus away from the historical interpretation of Zechariah 9:1-7 and toward the future, when Jesus will establish His reign on earth.

Many commentators believe that verse 8 has already occurred when Alexander the Great marched through the Middle East and treated Israel more favorably than he did the surrounding nations. However, we cannot say that we see a time in history when Israel was protected to such an extent that no oppressor has been able to overrun them. After Alexander the Great, the nation was subjugated by the Romans, and eventually, the people were dispersed from the land by them. When I read verse 8, I see a larger meaning here. I see this occurring when Jesus returns to be the King and Ruler of the world. Never again will Israel be trampled; never again will foreign nations rule over the land or the people of Israel. Jesus Himself will make Jerusalem His home, and He will watch over them. As I get into verse 9 and continue through the end of the chapter, it is perfectly clear that the end of verse 7 and the entirety of verse 8 are pointing us squarely to Zechariah prophesying that the Messiah shall protect the nation of Israel and rule the entire world in peace.

Zechariah 9:9-10 (NASB) Rejoice greatly, daughter of Zion! Shout in triumph, daughter of Jerusalem! Behold, your king is coming to you; He is righteous and endowed with salvation, Humble, and mounted on a donkey, Even on a colt, the foal of a donkey. 10 And I will eliminate the chariot from Ephraim And the horse from Jerusalem; And the bow of war will be eliminated. And He will speak peace to the nations; And His dominion will be from sea to sea, And from the Euphrates River to the ends of the earth.

In verse 9, what we have is a verse that can point us to both the first and the second coming of Christ. We see the first coming of Jesus in that the verse points us to Jesus as being the Christ. I sat thinking about why verse 9, which points to the first coming when He comes as a suffering servant, is sandwiched between two verses that speak to His ruling of the world in peace. Verse 9 is put there so that all of us, particularly the Jewish people, can identify that Jesus is the Christ. Jesus literally fulfilled this prophecy on Palm Sunday. Most Christians are aware of this occurrence in the week prior to His death. Matthew 21:4 even tells us this happened to fulfill what is said here in Zechariah 9:9.

However, we can also look at verse 9 regarding His second coming. The coming of Jesus on a donkey, even on a colt—the foal of a donkey—is a sign of a king during peacetime. In the Old Testament, horses were often associated with war and power. Kings rode horses when they went out to make war. But when they were among their people and wanted to signify peace, they rode a donkey through the streets. When David wanted Solomon to be proclaimed as king, David had him put on his own donkey (1 Kings 1:33). There is an important distinction here: Jesus came to bring peace and reconciliation between God and man. The Jews were looking for a king who would come and throw off the rulership of whatever nation happened to be oppressing them. In this case, they wanted the Messiah to overthrow Roman rule. However, Jesus' first coming was not to establish an earthly kingdom but a spiritual kingdom and to bring peace between God and mankind. When we see Jesus in the second coming, it will also be to rule in peace. However, it will be after He has conquered and judged the nations. This is a picture of Jesus as the Christ after He establishes His rule, and the earth is at peace. Jesus will be the unchallenged ruler of the earth.

Verse 9 also reveals some of Jesus' characteristics. He is righteous, or it could be translated as "just" or "legitimate." If we look at Revelation, we find that He is the only one worthy to open the scroll. Therefore, He is the only one worthy of ruling on this earth. He is the only one worthy because He went to the cross and paid the price for our sins, bringing salvation to all people who are willing to accept His rule. He is also the only human who lived a sinless life on this earth. He is victorious over sin and Satan. He comes the first time, meek and lowly. The only one who is worthy of ruling this world, or for that matter, all of creation, and He comes not with an army but with 12 disciples preaching the good news of salvation to mankind. God, who became man, was born in a stable to parents of noble lineage, yet lived a common Jewish life. Contrast that with the King who is coming in Revelation 1:13-16 or Revelation 19:11-16.

In both passages, we have the picture of a King who will be victorious and will rule with a rod of iron. I love this picture of Jesus because it shows a strong and all-powerful Jesus. Even as He is ruling with a rod of iron, He will also be a kind, compassionate, and approachable king. During the Marriage Supper of the Lamb, King Jesus will serve us, Luke 12:37. Luke 12:37 says, "Blessed are those slaves whom the master will find on the alert when he comes; truly I say to you, that he will prepare himself to serve, and have them recline at the table, and he will come up and serve them" (NASB).

Translations commonly refer to the master's return from the wedding feast, but the word for return used in Luke 12:36 can be translated as "departure." The only other place it is used in the Bible is in Philippians 1:23, where it is translated as "departure." Strong's Concordance defines this word as "to unloose for departure." The servants are waiting for their master to return to the earth, or to depart heaven for earth, for the Marriage Supper of the Lamb, and at that feast, He serves His bride. This is a picture of a true leader. I'm thankful for Jesus as the Lamb of God, but I love the picture of Jesus as the conquering King. The world would tell us that the humble servant is a weak Jesus, but only a strong man could have redeemed mankind by enduring the pain of the cross. Only the toughest of men could willingly allow himself to be put to this kind of death to save humanity. But I love to see Jesus as a conquering King during the Millennial Kingdom. He puts sin and evil under His feet. No longer will women and children be used and trafficked by evil men who don't care about anyone but themselves. There will no longer be war because of evil men who don't care that they are ordering the death of many.

In verse 9, we encounter Jesus, who came as the Lamb of God or as the suffering servant. However, the phrase also depicts a king who rules during times of peace. Verse 9 marks a transition, where we begin to see our King, who has subdued the nations. Verse 10 tells us that his rule is established, and there is no opposition to it; however, there shall be peace for Israel and the entire world. In verse 10, we see that the weapons of warfare are no longer needed. He will eliminate the chariot from Ephraim and the war horse from Jerusalem. Both Ephraim and Jerusalem are mentioned here to encompass the entire nation of Israel. Ephraim represents the ten tribes of the northern kingdom (Ezekiel 37:15-28), and Jerusalem represents the two tribes of the southern Kingdom, Judah and Benjamin. Notice how Israel is at the center of this kingdom. Yes, the Church is His bride, and He has made a blood covenant with the Church, but His original blood covenant is with Israel. He made a blood covenant with Abraham when Abraham passed through the heifer, the female goat, and the ram, which were all cut in half (Genesis 15). He also made a blood covenant with Israel at the foot of Mt Sinai (Exodus 24:4-8). Israel is the true bride, but we, the Church, are grafted in and join Israel as the bride, being the spiritual children of Abraham, Romans 11:11-32.

The LORD Jesus will reign from sea to sea. This geographically represents the nation of Israel, from the Dead Sea on the East to the Mediterranean Sea on the West. Verse 10 also tells us He will rule from the River to the ends of the earth. The river spoken of here is the Euphrates River. The NASB includes the word "Euphrates," whereas most other versions simply refer to it as "River." The passage says, "from the Euphrates River to the ends of the earth" (NASB). This represents not only His rule over Israel but also over the entire world. Yes, Israel is the apple of His eye, and He has made a blood covenant with them, but "For God so loved the world, that He gave His only Son." Christ also made a blood covenant with anyone who would believe in Him. He loves the entire world and is not willing for any to perish. He has invited the nations to be His people and to be grafted into Israel. The believer is a spiritual child of Abraham with faith like Abraham. Jesus will rule the entire world in peace, the nation of Israel, and the rest of the nations.

> *Zechariah 9:11-12 (NASB) As for you also, because of the blood of My covenant with you, I have set your prisoners free from the waterless pit. 12 Return to the stronghold, you prisoners who have the hope; This very day I am declaring that I will restore double to you.*

Verse 11, I believe, speaks to both the blood covenant made with Abraham and Israel (Genesis 15 and Exodus 24), as well as the blood covenant created by the shedding of Jesus Christ's blood for the cleansing of sin. Today, most Jews are deceived, blinded, and in bondage to sin. The Bible tells us in Romans 11:25-27, "that a partial hardening has happened to Israel until the fullness of the Gentiles has come in; and so all Israel will be saved; just as it is written: "The Deliverer will come from Zion, He will remove ungodliness from Jacob." "This is My covenant with them, When I take away their sins" (NASB).

When Zechariah 9:11 says, "As for you also, because of the blood of My Covenant with you," Zechariah is saying that the covenant made to all mankind at the cross is also for the Jew. No longer will the Jew be partially hardened to this covenant of blood, but it is for him also. Although they have rejected Christ in the past, no longer will they reject Jesus Christ. They will see Him and mourn for the One whom they have pierced. He will set them free from their bondage to sin.

I believe this refers to the waterless pit. When we are not in Jesus Christ, we are captives of the enemy and slaves to sin. Only by accepting Jesus Christ are we freed from our captivity. There will also be a literal fulfillment of Jesus releasing the prisoners from the waterless pit. When Jesus returns, Israel will be in a life-and-death struggle with the forces of the Antichrist, and they will be on the verge of annihilation. Many Jews will be killed, and many will be taken prisoner. Verse 11 tells us that Jesus will free the prisoners and return them to the land. This will be the beginning of the final return to the land, with the Jews coming back to the land of Israel that God has given them. I also believe that at this time, during the Millennium, the nation of Israel will extend to its full boundaries, as given to the people of Israel.

Verse 12 says, "Return to the stronghold, you prisoners, who have the hope." Edward Pusey, Regius Professor of Hebrew at the University of Oxford, stated that based on the grammar in the text, the "hope" here meant "the Hope of Israel" of which Paul spoke in Acts 26:6-7 and Acts 28:20. That Hope is Jesus Christ, the deliverer that they were promised and for whom they have been looking and waiting.

Verse 12 reinforces the call of all Jews back to the land. The land of Israel shall be a stronghold under the protection of the conquering King. Zechariah 2:5 states, "But I," declares the LORD, "will be a wall of fire to her on all sides, and I will be the glory in her midst" (NASB). Never has Israel occupied the entirety of the land that God gave them. But they will occupy the entire land given to them during the Millennial Kingdom. The Word says that God will restore double to them. They shall occupy the land all the way from the Euphrates River to the Mediterranean Sea.

Isaiah 61 is particularly enlightening when we consider the double portion that the LORD will give to Israel. As I read Isaiah 61, I am compelled to believe that this passage was intended for Israel, yet also encompasses the Church, the spiritual descendants of Abraham. It is a fascinating chapter. It is the chapter that Jesus quoted and the reason the people attempted to stone Him. Jesus was letting them know that Isaiah 61 was meant to describe Him. Isaiah 61:1-3 speaks more directly to Jesus' first coming to earth, and verses 4-11 refer to Jesus' time ruling on earth during the Millennium. I recall Pastor Mark McGaughey teaching the men on early Saturday mornings that after the Battle of Armageddon, the world would be in a state of disrepair due to the plagues and battles that occurred during the Tribulation. Our first job would be to rebuild the world, and then we would inherit the goods and wealth of those who had rejected Christ and who would no longer be on this earth. This is exactly what Isaiah 61:4-11 is saying.

> *"Then they will rebuild the ancient ruins, They will raise up the former devastations; And they will repair the ruined cities, The desolations of many generations.*

Strangers will stand and pasture your flocks, And foreigners will be your farmers and your vinedressers. But you will be called the priests of the Lord; You will be spoken of as ministers of our God. You will eat the wealth of nations, And you will boast in their riches. Instead of your shame you will have a double portion, And instead of humiliation they will shout for joy over their portion. Therefore they will possess a double portion in their land, Everlasting joy will be theirs. For I, the LORD, love justice, I hate robbery in the burnt offering; And I will faithfully give them their reward, And make an everlasting covenant with them. Then their offspring will be known among the nations, And their descendants in the midst of the peoples. All who see them will recognize them Because they are the offspring whom the LORD has blessed. I will rejoice greatly in the LORD, My soul will be joyful in my God; For He has clothed me with garments of salvation, He has wrapped me with a robe of righteousness, As a groom puts on a turban, And as a bride adorns herself with her jewels. For as the earth produces its sprouts, And as a garden causes the things sown in it to spring up, So the Lord God will cause righteousness and praise to spring up before all the nations. (NASB).

Zechariah 9:13 (NASB) For I will bend Judah as My bow, I will fill the bow with Ephraim. And I will stir up your sons, Zion, against your sons, Greece; And I will make you like a warrior's sword.

Verse 13 takes us back a little before the peace of the Millennial Kingdom to the Second Coming of Christ, when Jesus conquers the forces of the Antichrist and saves Israel. We have already spoken of how the LORD will bring peace once the battle of Gog and Magog is over. But here we are speaking of making Judah and Ephraim his instruments of war. As we said earlier, Ephraim is representative of the northern tribes of Israel. Verse 13 takes us back to the battle of Gog and Magog, discussing how the nation of Israel will fight against her neighbors. As we read through the prophecies of Zechariah, we see that his writing is not always chronological. Many times, he discusses an event, then returns to it and speaks of it again, providing us with more detail. That is what we have here in verse 13. We are going back to the battle with Gog and Magog. One of the reasons this passage is difficult to understand is due to the English translations. The second half of the verse says,

"And I will stir up your sons, Zion, against your sons, Greece; And I will make you like a warrior's sword" (NASB).

The Hebrew word translated as "Greece" is Ya-van or Ya-wan, according to the Strong's and the NASB Lexicon. Ya-van / Ya-wan is used to indicate the area of Ionia or the descendants of Japheth. Per Joel Richardson, the Jews have typically interpreted Ja-van / Ja-wan as the lands of Turkey, Syria, and Northern Iraq. When the passage refers to the sons of Zion being stirred up against the sons of Greece, Greece represents the forces of the Antichrist. The base of the Antichrist's coalition comes from Turkey, Syria, Northern Iraq, and Iran. We see Ya-van used in Daniel 8:21 to describe the goat in Daniel 8:5-14. Daniel 8:5-14 starts out talking about Alexander the Great and the way in which his kingdom was split into four kingdoms, but it ends talking about a little horn that grows up out of the goat, particularly out of the four horns. This little horn is the Antichrist, as you see when you read Daniel 8:18-26.

The greatest type or foreshadowing of the Antichrist that we have to date is Antiochus IV Epiphanes. Even his name suggests that he is a type of the Antichrist. He took upon himself the title "Epiphanes," which means "illustrious one" or "god manifest." Antiochus IV Epiphanes ordered what many consider to be a precursor to the "abomination of desolation" spoken of in Daniel 9:27. We know that the Antichrist will be the one who commits the "abomination of desolation." Still, Antiochus IV Epiphanes had committed a similar act as early as 167 BC. Antiochus raided the Temple in Jerusalem, stealing its treasures, setting up an altar to Zeus, and sacrificing a pig on the altar. When the Jews protested, he slaughtered a significant number of Jews and sold others into slavery. He decreed that the rite of circumcision would be punishable by death and ordered the Jews to sacrifice to pagan gods and eat the flesh of pigs. Antiochus is the greatest picture we have of the Antichrist that is to come. He came out of the Greek empire, which would be the area of Ya-van. The areas he ruled were the modern-day countries of Turkey, Syria, and Northern Iraq. Daniel 8:9 tells us he extended his dominion toward the South, toward the East, and toward the beautiful land. His base was Turkey, Syria, Northern Iraq, and he was extending his dominion over lands toward the South and East, including Israel.

Zechariah and Daniel are revealing events that were going to happen in their near future but would be repeated during the end times. A ruler from the Northern Kingdom would wage war with the Southern Kingdom, ultimately conquering the Southern Kingdom. The Southern Kingdom is then added to Northern Kingdom through force and Israel is caught in the middle. At the end of days, Israel is not just caught in the middle but is nearly annihilated.

In Daniel 11, we see the King of the North emerging to wage war against the King of the South. This Scripture refers to the division of Alexander the Great's kingdom into four kingdoms, which eventually evolved into two large kingdoms. The Northern Kingdom was the Seleucid Kingdom, which was basically comprised of modern-day Turkey, Syria, Iraq, and Iran. The Southern Kingdom was the Ptolemaic Kingdom, which consisted of modern-day Egypt, Sudan, and Libya. The King of the North is the Antichrist, who battles against the King of the South and ultimately defeats him, as described in the Book of Daniel Chapter 11. He then turns his attention to Israel and fights against it in the book of Daniel, Chapter 12. The interesting part is that the nations that oppose Israel today are the nations that line up with the King of the North, and the nations that are friendly with Israel today and who have signed the Abraham Accords are the nations that line up with the King of the South. Before he goes against Israel, the Antichrist will defeat the nations of the King of the South. They will then join his coalition.

Ya-van is basically a son of Japheth. Google stated that "Almost all the Ottoman historians of the 15th century claimed that the Ottoman dynasty stemmed from Japheth, the son of Noah. Japheth was generally regarded as the ancestor of the Turks in Muslim historiography." It should be noted that Google states that the people of Syria and the people of Iraq are descendants of Shem. The Jews have historically referred to this northern region comprised of Turkey, Syrian, and Iraq as Ya-van.

The technical definition of Ya-van is Ionia, which is represented by Western Turkey and Ancient Greece. When we read this passage, "against your sons, O Greece," we are really referring to the area of Turkey, Syria, and Northern Iraq, which comprised a large part of Alexander the Great's kingdom. The conclusion is that Zechariah 9:13 is referring to the war of Gog and Magog, also known as the war between Israel and the forces of the Antichrist. The most specific definition of Ya-van is western Turkey, specifically the area of Ionia. I believe the usage of the word Ya-van is telling us that Turkey will be aligned with Syria, and Iraq, and will most likely lead the coalition.

> *Zechariah 9:14-16 (NASB) Then the LORD will appear over them, And His arrow will go forth like lightning; And the Lord GOD will blow the trumpet, And march in the storm winds of the south. 15 The LORD of armies will protect them. And they will devour and trample on the slingstones; And they will drink and be boisterous as with wine; And they will be filled like a sacrificial basin, Drenched like the corners of the altar. 16 And the LORD their God will save them on that day As the flock of His people; For they are like the precious stones of a crown, Sparkling on His land.*

Many commentators believe that verse 13 refers to the Maccabees' fight against Antiochus IV Epiphanes. If this is true, it is only partially true because this does not seem to fit the description we read in verses 14 through 16. While it can be said that the Maccabees did well and won back a measure of independence from the Greeks, restoring proper worship to the Temple, I do not see the description of total victory that we read about in Zechariah 9:14-16. Many commentators come from the 1800s or earlier and could not even fathom the current-day nation of Israel. Interpreting "Ya-van" as "Greece" really sends the reader down the wrong path in attempting to translate this verse. If we translate Ya-van as Greece without understanding the subtle geographical differences, we would be inclined to believe that this verse refers to Alexander the Great's conquest. However, it really refers to Antiochus IV Epiphanes as a foreshadowing of the little horn that is to come.

The remaining verses here expound upon the victory that Jesus wins for Israel. Verses 14 through 16 expound on how it will be the Lord God who saves Israel. Verse 14 says His arrow flashes like lightning, and He will blow the trumpet to gather the army together. It will be the trumpet (shofar) that calls us to Jesus as the Christ at the end of the tribulation. Verse 14 is very similar to Habakkuk 3 and reminds us that the LORD will come in the storm clouds, and lightning will flash from His hands. He is riding the storm clouds with strong storm winds as He makes his way through the desert, rescuing those who have been captured. This will be a storm that causes men's hearts to faint and knees to buckle. Habakkuk 3:3-15 says,

> "God comes from Teman, And the Holy One from Mount Paran. Selah His splendor covers the heavens, And the earth is full of His praise. His radiance is like the sunlight; He has rays flashing from His hand, And the hiding of His might is there. Before Him goes plague, And plague comes forth after Him. He stood and caused the earth to shudder; He looked and caused the nations to jump. Yes, the everlasting mountains were shattered, The ancient hills collapsed. His paths are everlasting. I saw the tents of Cushan under distress, The tent curtains of the land of Midian were trembling. Did the LORD rage against the rivers, Or was Your anger against the rivers, Or was Your rage against the sea, That You rode on Your horses, On Your chariots of salvation? You removed Your bow from its holder, The arrows of Your word were sworn. Selah You divided the earth with rivers. The mountains saw You and quaked; The downpour of waters swept by. The deep raised its voice, It lifted high its hands. Sun and moon stood in their lofty places; They went away at the light of Your arrows, At the radiance of Your flashing spear. In indignation You marched through the earth; In anger You trampled the nations. You went forth for the salvation of Your people, For the salvation of Your anointed. You smashed the head of the house of evil To uncover him from foot to neck. Selah You pierced with his own arrows The head of his leaders. They stormed in to scatter us; Their arrogance was like those Who devour the oppressed in secret. You trampled on the sea with Your horses, On the foam of many waters. (NASB).

In Habakkuk 3:16-19, Habakkuk goes on to say that this picture left him trembling and in distress, the state of your body when you are afraid and resigned to calamity coming against you. Yes, Habakkuk sees the great victory, but he also knows the terrible circumstances that occurred before the victory. He is waiting quietly for the day of distress for the people to arise who will attack Israel. He knows the terrible circumstances that this will create, yet he will triumph in the LORD and rejoice in the God of salvation. Habakkuk expounds upon Zechariah 9:14 with an entire chapter. The picture Habakkuk paints is of total war on the land and the destruction that comes from total war. He paints a picture of Israel being defeated until Jesus shows up to save the nation and the people. Habakkuk 3:16-19 says,

> *"I heard, and my inner parts trembled; At the sound, my lips quivered. Decay enters my bones, And in my place I tremble; Because I must wait quietly for the day of distress, For the people to arise who will attack us. Even if the fig tree does not blossom, And there is no fruit on the vines, If the yield of the olive fails, And the fields produce no food, Even if the flock disappears from the fold, And there are no cattle in the stalls, Yet I will triumph in the LORD, I will rejoice in the God of my salvation. The Lord God is my strength, And He has made my feet like deer's feet, And has me walk on my high places. (NASB).*

Zechariah 9:15 states that the LORD of armies will protect them, and under His leadership, they will conquer the enemy. It is as if the LORD covers them with a shield over their heads. The Jewish people will devour the enemy and trample them down as if they were common stones. This compares to verse 16, where the Jewish people are called precious stones. The people will be drunk on the blood of their enemies and boisterous in their victory. Revelation 14:20 says, "And the wine press was trampled outside the city, and blood came out from the wine press, up to the horses' bridles, for a distance of 1,600 stadia" (NASB). One thousand six hundred stadia is approximately 184 miles or 296 kilometers. The Jewish people will be drunk with victory on the blood of their enemies. Zechariah describes the blood as filling the sacrificial basin and drenching the altar. Verse 15 describes the victory with the LORD leading them. There will be joy and rejoicing overflowing.

Verse 16 tells us that the LORD shall save them because they are His flock. They are like jewels in a crown, shining for His glory in the land. This verse reminds us of God's love for the people of Israel. Right now, they are like a wayward spouse, and it is hard for Him to show His love to them. However, then, they will be a faithful spouse, and He will shower them with love. They are His prized possession, the apple of His eye, as they were always meant to be.

Zechariah 9:17 (NASB) For how great will their loveliness and beauty be! Grain will make the young men flourish, and new wine, the virgins.

Verse 17 concludes by stating that His love and provision for the people of Israel will cause them to flourish and be beautiful. Verse 17 presents a beautiful picture of reconciliation in the relationship as if none of the unfaithfulness and chastisement had occurred. God provides the nurture and care that will allow the Jewish people to be lovely and beautiful.

Zechariah 10
A Call to Return

The promises of chapter 10 will ultimately be completed when Jesus returns. Still, even now, we have partial fulfillment of this prophecy with the bringing of the Jews back to Israel beginning after World War II. Even now, it is such a tiny country that it seems as if there is no more room for the Jews to return to the land, and still, they go back to the land.

As you read chapter 10 in total, you get the feeling that it is part remembrance and part prophecy of restoration. Zechariah begins by discussing how Israel has sinned against the LORD by relying on idols and false gods for their sustenance. Oh, how the LORD yearns that the people would have only asked Him to send the rain and increase the yield of the crops. God then turns His attention to the leaders of the people, who were supposed to lead them toward God and righteousness, but they have not. As I've said 100 times by now, God cannot forget His love for His people. It is like a father with the prodigal son, you understand that the son is being rebellious, but you love him and want him to turn to you in love. Fortunately, God has more power than we earthly fathers and has ways of helping wayward children understand their errant ways. Israel will return to God and to Jesus. When they do return, God will gather them up and make them great. The relationship between Israel and God shall be restored. However, as we shall see later in Zechariah, it will take the Great Tribulation, also known as The Time of Jacob's Trouble, to get the nation of Israel to recognize that Jesus is indeed the Christ, their Messiah.

Zechariah 10:1-2 (NASB) Ask for rain from the LORD at the time of the spring rain— The LORD who makes the storm winds; And He will give them showers of rain, vegetation in the field to each person. 2 For the household idols speak deception, And the diviners see an illusion And tell deceitful dreams; They comfort in vain. Therefore the people wander like sheep, They are wretched because there is no shepherd.

In verse 1, you can almost hear the pain in the voice of the LORD as He tries to get the people to trust in Him for their provision, for the rain that is so necessary for the growth of their crops. He is the true God and wants them to ask Him for the rain, but instead, they turn to idols and ask them for rain. The same could be said about us today. In ancient times, they wandered off to follow false gods of fertility, believing that they would bring rain and provide prosperity. The LORD says, "Ask of me and I will bring the rain!" God wants us to put our faith in Him! We want to trust in what we can see, but He wants us to trust in Him! In our society today, we believe that we are self-sufficient, and we do not need God, but that is the furthest thing from the truth. The verse ends with "And He will give them showers of rain, vegetation in the field to each person" (NASB). God wants to provide an abundance for everyone!

The Prophet begins by discussing the recurring issues that often plague Israel. Bad leadership frequently leads people astray into idol worship. Idol worship is false hope and leaves people empty. For a time, these false idols may fill that part of us that was meant to be filled with the true God, but in time, they just leave us empty. The passage describes people as wandering like sheep without a shepherd. But God says that He will provide the ultimate leader for the people (see verse 4). Lately, I keep going back to Isaiah 61, and I get the picture of the ultimate Shepherd. Jesus quotes Isaiah 61 in Luke 4:18-19 and says,

> *"THE SPIRIT OF THE LORD IS UPON ME, BECAUSE HE ANOINTED ME TO BRING GOOD NEWS TO THE POOR. HE HAS SENT ME TO PROCLAIM RELEASE TO CAPTIVES, AND RECOVERY OF SIGHT TO THE BLIND, TO SET FREE THOSE WHO ARE OPPRESSED, TO PROCLAIM THE FAVORABLE YEAR OF THE LORD." (NASB)*

What a difference between idols who utter deceit, lies, and false dreams compared to the Messiah who proclaims good news to the poor and freedom to the captives. Notice in Luke 4, Jesus stops after "to proclaim the favorable year of the LORD" and does not quote "and the day of vengeance of our God." The day of vengeance comes at the end of the tribulation; it was not to come with the first coming of Jesus Christ.

> *Zechariah 10:3 (NASB) "My anger is kindled against the shepherds, And I will punish the male goats; For the LORD of armies has visited His flock, the house of*

Judah, And will make them like His majestic horse in battle.

Verse 3 starts with His anger against the shepherds and the leaders whom He will punish. Why? Because He cares for His flock, and He knows we are like sheep who need a shepherd to follow. The leaders of the nation of Israel were to be their shepherds and were to lead them in the way of the LORD. Instead, most leaders lead them astray, guiding them in the way of the world to worship false idols. The LORD talks about how much He cares for His people and how He will make them like His royal steed, His war horse. They shall be like mighty men who defeat the enemy in battle. Is this happening even now? What have we seen from Israel since its rebirth as a nation? They have won all the wars against their neighbors who have tried to wipe them out. We are only seeing a foretaste of what this passage means today. During the Millennial Kingdom, I believe that we shall see Israel and Judah strong and mighty, no longer the whipping boy of the world and the devil. They will be like a royal war horse, but there will be no battles for them to fight, because Jesus will rule the entire world. Isaiah 2 tells us that there will be no war during the Millennial Kingdom, that people will convert their weapons into commercial productive uses.

Zechariah 10:4 (NASB) "From them will come the cornerstone, From them the tent peg, From them the bow of battle, From them every tyrant, all of them together.

Verse 4 tells us this very thing, that Jesus is coming to rule, but after he wins the victory over Satan and the Antichrist. Out of Judah shall come the cornerstone, the tent peg, and the battle bow. This Ruler that is to come out of Judah will unite the people of Israel and shall set the foundation of the nation, and nations, to hold all things together. He will be the Fierce One who will lead His people in battle when necessary. There are only two battles that the Messiah shall have to fight. The battle at the end of the tribulation, where He destroys the armies of the nations of the world with just the breath of his mouth, and at the end of the Millennium, when Satan is released from his prison and deceives the nations to lead them to war against the Messiah. As I think about the battle that shall come at the end of the tribulation, I thought for a long time that He will say it, and it will happen. However, as I read the remainder of this chapter, I am thinking that, as He speaks it, they will do it. It is just as we read prophecy in the Bible, the LORD says it, and others do it. His Words cannot return void; all that He says comes to pass. Every Word that comes from the mouth of Jesus Christ is prophecy, or, more accurately, a command that both nature and humanity must obey.

His reign shall be mostly a reign of peace. He will be a leader of leaders, and all of the leaders of Israel shall report to Him. This verse shows Jesus as the foundation of the building, as well as the one who secures our dwelling. It also shows Jesus as the military and political leader of His people and of the world. Jesus fulfills every one of these descriptions in verse 4. Verse 4 begins with, "From them." The word "them" refers to "The house of Judah." From the House of Judah will come:

1. The cornerstone
2. The tent peg
3. The bow of battle; and
4. A strong leader who will unite the people and rule over their enemies.

All four of these descriptions point to the Messiah, to Jesus Christ. Jesus Christ is referred to as the cornerstone in Ephesians 2:20, and the Messiah is called the cornerstone in Isaiah 28:16. Jesus also refers to himself as the chief cornerstone in Luke 20:17.

Jesus is also the tent peg that will crush the head of Satan. There is much symbolism with the use of the term "tent peg" in verse 4. Joel Richardson covered the significance of the "tent peg" in one of his videos (I think it was the "Fulfilled" series). It starts all the way back in Genesis 3:15 when God said to the serpent,

> *"He shall bruise you on the head, And you shall bruise Him on the heel." (NASB)*

According to Strong's Lexicon, the word used there can be interpreted as either "bruise" or "crush." I believe that "crush" is the better interpretation based on the ultimate fulfillment of this prophecy. Christ is the "tent peg" that shall crush the Devil's head. This idea is illustrated by the story of

Deborah and Barak in Judges 4 and 5. The Israelites were being punished because they did evil in the sight of the LORD, so they cried out to the LORD and he sent a deliverer to them in the persons of Deborah and Barak. He provided the opportunity to Barak, but he was afraid to go without Deborah, so she got the glory.

The commander of the Canaanite army was Sisera. The LORD drew Sisera and his army into a trap to rout them. Sisera fled on foot and came to the tent of Jael, the wife of Heber the Kenite. Jael drew Sisera into her tent with kind words. She gave him a place to sleep and some milk and stood watch for any danger to him. Once he fell asleep, she took a tent peg and a hammer and drove the tent peg into his temple and killed him. Verse 4 tells us that from Judah will come the "cornerstone" and the "tent peg," both of which are names for Jesus the Messiah. He is the Chief Cornerstone of Israel, and He is the Tent Peg that will crush the head of the serpent. Ultimately, Jesus Christ will defeat the Antichrist and Satan, and the Antichrist will be killed, and Satan will be thrown into the lake of fire forever. (Habakkuk 3:13 and Revelation 20:7-10) Habakkuk 3:13 says,

> *You went out for the salvation of your people, for the salvation of your anointed. You crushed the head of the house of the wicked, laying him bare from thigh to neck. Selah (ESV)*

I used the ESV for this passage because it is more descriptive. Jesus will cut the Antichrist open all the way from his thigh to his neck.

The term "bow of battle" refers to an instrument of war, a conquer. When the Antichrist and his army are very close to annihilating the nation of Israel, the people shall need the Messiah to be an instrument of war, a conqueror. That is precisely what He will be for them, a deliverer. We read in Zechariah 9:10 that once we are in the Millennial Kingdom, the bow of war will be eliminated, as there will be no need for the Messiah as an instrument of war; instead, He will be a ruler who maintains peace.

The last description is a little more difficult because none of the translations provides an accurate translation to convey the meaning of what the Prophet intended to say. The NASB translates the phrase as "From them every tyrant, all of them together." The ESV translates that phrase as "from him every ruler, all of them together." The Tree of Life Version translates that phrase as "from him every leader together". When I examine the Strong's Hebrew Lexicon and analyze the passage word for word, it translates it as "from him comes every ruler together."

When I look at the meaning of the words, particularly "every," "ruler," and "together," it conveys to me the idea of a strong leader who will unite the people, and together they shall rule over their enemies. The word "every" is a versatile term used to denote totality or completeness, often represented by the Hebrew word "kol." Strong's states, "In the Hebrew Bible, "kol" is used to express the entirety of a group, the completeness of an action, or the totality of an object or concept. It can refer to all people, all things, or the whole of something, emphasizing the inclusiveness or comprehensiveness of what is being described." The Hebrew word used for ruler is "nagas" and is defined as "to oppress, to drive, to exact, to press, to urge". Strong's states the context usage of nagas "primarily conveys the idea of exerting pressure or force upon someone, often in the context of oppression or demanding labor. It is used to describe the actions of taskmasters or oppressors who impose burdens or exact tribute."

The Hebrew word translated as "together" is "Yachad," which means "unity, together, or union." Yachad's historical usage primarily denotes the concept of unity or togetherness. It is used to describe a state of being joined or united, often in a communal or collective sense." Thus, I see this phrase as referring to a strong leader who will unite his people and subject their enemies to his will.

The descriptions in verse 4 point to a leader who will lead his people to victory over their enemies. Verse 5 brings us directly into war. I don't think it is a coincidence that verse 5 starts with, "They will be like mighty men in battle, trampling the foe in the mud of the streets." I believe that the battle of Gog and Magog will last for 42 months, and it will be the battle that Christ ends when he returns to this earth.

Zechariah 10:5 (NASB) "And they will be like warriors, Trampling down the enemy in the mud of the streets in battle; And they will fight, because the LORD will be with them; And the riders on horses will be put to shame.

I think it is significant that verse 5 talks about the warriors trampling the foe in the mud of the streets because when you read Ezekiel 38:22 we find, "With plague and with blood I will enter into judgment with him; and I will rain on him and on his troops, and on the many peoples who are with him, a torrential rain, hailstones, fire, and brimstone. "(NASB). I see that the battle of Gog and Magog lasts the entire length of the Great Tribulation, also known as "The Time of Jacob's Trouble," which is 42 months. The battle will go so badly for Israel that two-thirds of the Jewish people will die, Zechariah 13:8-9. But when Jesus returns, He shall give His people victory over the invaders, and they will trample the foe in the mud due to the torrential rains that Jesus will send. The more I study Old Testament prophecy, the more amazed I am at how it all fits together.

The second half of verse 5 says,

"And they will fight, because the LORD will be with them; And the riders on horses will be put to shame." (NASB)

Israel will fight before the LORD returns, but they will be fighting a retreating and losing action, giving ground grudgingly and trying to hold the line. But when Jesus returns, they shall become victorious, and their small army, lacking adequate equipment at that time, will defeat the army of the Antichrist and all his mechanized troops. We are not given details here; this chapter serves as a summary of God calling His people to Himself, ultimately uniting Israel with their Messiah, Jesus.

I believe that during the battle of Gog and Magog, the forces of the Antichrist will capture Jerusalem, and half the population will have been killed or removed from Jerusalem. That is when Jesus returns. Many of the Jews will either be captured and placed in prison camps, or they will be refugees who have scattered to the wilderness of Jordan or Egypt.

> *Zechariah 10:6 (NASB) "And I will strengthen the house of Judah, And I will save the house of Joseph, And I will bring them back, Because I have had compassion on them; And they will be as though I had not rejected them, For I am the LORD their God and I will answer them.*

Based on the scenario presented, it is easy to understand what is happening here. The war, which has been ongoing for three and a half years, will have taken a toll on Israel, and for all intents and purposes, they are defeated. The people of Israel will be scattered and will be prisoners and refugees all over the Middle East when Jesus returns to this earth to lead His people. He will call the prisoners and the refugees back to the land. We also see this in Chapters 12 through 14.

The use of "Judah and Joseph" here refers to the entire house of Israel, encompassing both the Northern Kingdom and the Southern Kingdom. It could also be said that He has been calling his people back to the land since 1946. The land is special and is an inheritance. In Numbers 34, the LORD gives instructions on portioning the land to the Israelites by lot, all the way from the tribe down to clans and families, to the individual head of households. In Leviticus 25:23, the LORD tells them that they are just strangers and sojourners with Him. They were not to sell the land in perpetuity; instead, the land was to be returned to the family that had inherited it from the original distribution of the land. Today, the Jews and Palestinians are fighting over the land and their right to the land, but God declares that He owns the land. This is special land owned by God and given to the Children of Israel (Deuteronomy 4:40). The LORD loves both the land of Israel and the people of Israel. He declares here in Zechariah that He will bring the Jews back to the land that He has given them, and He will have compassion on them. Amos 9:14-15 states,

> "I will also restore the fortunes of My people Israel, And they will rebuild the desolated cities and live in them; They will also plant vineyards and drink their wine, And make gardens and eat their fruit. I will also plant them on their land, And they will not be uprooted again from their land Which I have given them," Says the LORD your God." (NASB)

Amos 9 fits very nicely alongside Zechariah 10:6. These two passages are companion passages that speak to the same events, the same deliverance, and the same reunification of the people with the land and with their God.

Based on the picture of what is happening at this time, right before the LORD makes his second appearance, the people of Israel will be in dire straits. The entire world, or so it seems, is coming down on them to wipe them off the face of the earth, and what allies they did have are destroyed or powerless to stop the onslaught. There will be only one place for the Jews to turn, and that is the LORD their God. The second part of verse 6 says,

"And I will bring them back, Because I have had compassion on them; And they will be as though I had not rejected them, For I am the LORD their God and I will answer them." (NASB).

The LORD will have compassion on His people, and He will see the dire situation they are in and move to save them. Unfortunately, for all of us hardheaded, stiff-necked people, God often must put us in dire situations before we reach the point where we call out to Him for help and repent of our sins. That is the situation that we have here: the people are calling out to God for help, and He answers them. The LORD spurned the people because they spurned Him, and they have not been found to be faithful.

At Mount Sinai, they choose to be the bride of God, the apple of His eye. He proposed to them, and they accepted His proposal. But they turned away from him many times. The entire Book of Hosea is a picture of God's love for the people of Israel and the fact that Israel chose to be unfaithful instead of being a faithful wife. Israel continues to reject the God who loved her and wanted to care for her. The nation continued to sell herself to others for a night at a time.

In Matthew 23:37-39, Jesus laments that the people were not willing to gather to their God at that time. Jesus said, "Jerusalem, Jerusalem, who kills the prophets and stones those who have been sent to her! How often I wanted to gather your children together, the way a hen gathers her chicks under her wings, and you were unwilling. Behold, your house is being left to you desolate! For I say to you, from now on you will not see Me until you say, 'Blessed is the One who comes in the name of the LORD!'" (NASB) Jesus is telling his people, unfortunately, it will take the Time of Jacob's Trouble for them to recognize Jesus as their Messiah, after they have called out to God.

He will answer them in a mighty way. Verse 6 says,

"And I will strengthen the house of Judah, And I will save the house of Joseph." (NASB)

Verse 7 says,

Zechariah 10:7 (NASB) "Ephraim will be like a warrior, And their heart will be joyful as if from wine; Indeed, their children will see it and be joyful, Their heart will rejoice in the LORD.

Picture the scene, the people of Israel are desperate, 2/3rds of them have perished in this war against the Antichrist, and 1/3rd are fighting, have fled as refugees, or are prisoners in prison camps. Their allies are in the same situation and have either collapsed or are on the verge of collapse. At a time when the situation seems lost, Jesus returns with a vast army of warrior angels and saints that are gathered to Him. The people shall rejoice and be glad, the warriors and mighty men are strengthened. As Jesus is crowned and set on the throne of David, all of Israel is strengthened.

At this point, many of the people will be scattered as they flee from the armies of the Antichrist. We know that many will flee into the wilderness of Petra / Basra, into Egypt, and any place they could take refuge. Also, many will be taken prisoner. In verses 8 through 10, Jesus discusses how He will gather them back to the land and to Himself, and how He will restore them. In verses 8 through 10, Jesus says,

> Zechariah 10:8-10 (NASB) "I will whistle for them and gather them together, For I have redeemed them; And they will be as numerous as they were before. 9 "When I scatter them among the peoples, They will remember Me in distant countries, And they with their children will live and come back. 10 "I will bring them back from the land of Egypt And gather them from Assyria; And I will bring them into the land of Gilead and Lebanon Until no room can be found for them.

I see the regathering of the people of Israel as something that started after World War II and something that is still ongoing today. God has been bringing His people back to the land for 70 years now, since 1946. Though they will be scattered again during the tribulation, and they flee the land to any place safe because of the war. After the tribulation and after the war, God will regather them again. He will bring them from all the areas where they flee for safety. I like verse 10, which says, He will bring them back, Until no room can be found for them." (NASB) Many will return, and they will also inhabit Lebanon, north of Israel, and Gilead, east of Israel. Satan's hatred for Israel is so fierce that even as the attack is happening in Israel to remove the Jews from the land, Jews all over the world are persecuted. Even today, after Hamas attacked Israel, Jews in Germany had their property defaced and their lives threatened, and a Jewish woman in Detroit was stabbed to death for being Jewish.

In his book, "Sinai to Zion: The Untold Story of the Triumphant Return of Jesus", Joel Richardson states that Jesus will come back to earth and touch down in Egypt. He will start a march, much like the Israelites took with Moses out of Egypt, to gather his people and to rescue them from the hiding and captivity that occurred during the tribulation.

> *Zechariah 10:11-12 (NASB) "And they will pass through the sea of distress And He will strike the waves in the sea, So that all the depths of the Nile will dry up; And the pride of Assyria will be brought down, And the scepter of Egypt will depart. 12 "And I will strengthen them in the LORD, And in His name they will walk," declares the LORD.*

What we see here in verses 11 and 12 is a reference to the exodus from Egypt that Israel experienced when God called them to be His people for the first time at Mount Sinai.

Here, in verses 11 and 12, we see part of the reason that Joel Richardson believes Jesus will march from Egypt through the desert to Jerusalem. These verses do reference the crossing of the Red Sea and the exodus from Egypt, but Zechariah states this as a future event. Verse 11 begins with "He will cross," "He shall pass," or "And they shall pass," indicating a future event. Verse 11 is an imitation of the first time they crossed the Red Sea, the Tree of Life version says,

> *"He will cross the turbulent sea and calm its raging waves. All the depths of the Nile will dry up, the pride of Assyria brought down, the scepter of Egypt removed." (TLV)*

This is the picture of a future coming out of Egypt. Jesus begins in Egypt and makes His way through the desert, freeing prisoners and taking in refugees as He marches toward Jerusalem. Not only will He cross the Red Sea, but Assyria and Egypt will also be brought low.

Verse 12 indicates that this pilgrimage will also have the effect of strengthening the people of Israel through the LORD. The name used here is Jehovah, which was often used in the Septuagint to indicate the Lordship and authority of God. It contains the concept of dominion, rulership, and ownership. They will follow their Messiah, their King, their Ruler, and He will strengthen them; they will follow Him. This is the beginning of an approximately 30-day march from Egypt to Jerusalem, building up the people of Israel and putting their enemies under their feet and under the feet of their King, Jesus. As Jesus proceeds along this march route,

He frees captives, and people emerge from hiding to follow Him. When they reach Jerusalem and destroy the armies of the Antichrist, they will install Jesus as their King on the throne of David in Jerusalem. Verse 12 finishes by saying, "declares the LORD". That phrase conveys the finality of this prophecy. God has spoken it; it will come to pass.

Zechariah 11
The Flock Destined for Slaughter

In verses 1-3, we have a continuation of Chapter 10, verse 10, where the LORD says that so many Jews will come back to the land that there will not be enough room in the land. Verses 1-3 serve as a clearing of the land to prepare it for the people who are returning and will need the space to live. The LORD causes the prophet to use poetic language to speak of the room that will be made in Lebanon, Gilead, and Bashan (adjacent to Gilead to the north). Verse 1-3 says,

> *Zechariah 11:1-3 (NASB) Open your doors, Lebanon, So that a fire may feed on your cedars. 2 Wail, juniper, because the cedar has fallen, For the magnificent trees have been destroyed; Wail, oaks of Bashan, Because the impenetrable forest has come down. 3 There is a sound of the shepherds' wail, For their splendor is ruined; There is a sound of the young lions' roar, For the pride of the Jordan is ruined.*

This refers to a land devastated by war. Fire will devour the cedars and everything else. The fire of bombs and rockets and the explosions that wreak destruction during war. Since October 7th, northern Israel has been attacked by rockets from Hezbollah, and Israel has struck back. Southern Lebanon and Beirut have suffered significant damage. Israel has fought many times in southern Lebanon since their formation in 1948. Lebanon has been turned into a staging ground for terrorists and continues to be destroyed by Israel to secure its northern border. Lebanon and Syria will be the front lines in the War of Gog and Magog, as the land that will be fought over for three and a half years during the Great Tribulation.

Many commentators see these first three verses as describing the destruction of Jerusalem after the rejection of Jesus Christ by the nation of Israel. That is an easy conclusion when you read the remainder of Chapter 11. Joseph Benson, in his Commentary, states, "proceeds now to foretell the ruin which should come on the body of the Jewish nation for rejecting him, with the destruction of their temple and capital city. To this only can the first three verses of this chapter relate, for no calamities happened to that people, from the time of Zechariah till that event, of which the expressions here used can with propriety be understood."

We must understand that many commentators like Benson lived and died before Israel had again become a nation, and many commentators failed to see or believe that Israel would again become a nation. Many of the commentators spiritualize the discussion about the nation of Israel and say that the Church has replaced Israel and the people of Israel. To be fair to Benson, he does not hold this view, but many commentators from the 1800s did not believe that Israel would again rise to become a nation. Therefore, it is quite natural for them to look for fulfillment of these passages in history. As I have said many times, you can find an interim fulfillment of passages within one time period, with the ultimate fulfillment to occur in another or a future time period. Additionally, we must remember that the prophet did not separate the book into chapters; that was done later. Although I would imagine those who decided where chapters started and ended had a good reason for separating the chapters where they did.

These first three verses serve as a bridge between a passage that speaks about the second coming of Jesus Christ and the first coming of Jesus Christ. After the first coming of Jesus Christ, the Roman armies came and destroyed Jerusalem and the temple, and the nation of Israel was scattered. This was a result of their rejection of Jesus as the Christ, the Son of God. The second coming of Jesus Christ results in bringing the nation back into the land and unifying the people under Christ's rule. Chapter 10 of Zechariah details the second coming of Jesus Christ, while chapter 11 prophesies about the rejection of Jesus Christ during the 1st coming.

In Deuteronomy 28, the Israelites are told of blessings if they are faithful to the LORD and chastisement if they disobey the LORD. It is hard for me to read that passage without feeling sympathy for the people of Israel. We all question, how could a people who had just come through the Red Sea make a golden calf? How could they be afraid to take the land that the LORD had promised to give to them? Yet we would be just like them. When I was reading Deuteronomy, I could see the Holocaust in several of those verses.

Deuteronomy 4:25-27 says, "When you father children and have grandchildren, and you grow old in the land, and you act corruptly, and make an idol in the form of anything, and do what is evil in the sight of the LORD your God to provoke Him to anger, I call heaven and earth as witnesses against you today, that you will certainly perish quickly from the land where you are going over the Jordan to take possession of it. You will not live long on it, but will be utterly destroyed. The LORD will scatter you among the peoples, and you will be left few in number among the nations where the LORD drives you." (NASB)

But just a few verses away is a promise of redemption in the latter days.

Deuteronomy 4:30-31 says, "When you are in distress and all these things happen to you, in the latter days you will return to the LORD your God and listen to His voice. For the LORD your God is a compassionate God; He will not abandon you nor destroy you, nor forget the covenant with your fathers which He swore to them." (NASB)

The purpose of the severity of the punishment is to restore the relationship, to drive Israel back into the arms of their God. As horrible as the Holocaust was, would the Jews have returned to the land without it? They have returned to the land, and yet they have not recognized their Messiah.

Unfortunately, in Zechariah 11, we are still caught in this cycle of rejection and chastisement, and we see that through the rejection of their Messiah, the people of Israel will undergo further chastisement and scattering. Verse 3 tells us that the shepherds are wailing, the leaders of the people of wailing for their glory has been destroyed, and the young lions are roaring, the warriors are roaring, for Jordan's thickets are ruined. Why, because the land and the people have been devastated. Look at what verse 4 says, "Shepherd the flock marked for slaughter!" Unfortunately, before the flock recognizes their Messiah, they must suffer much to show them the truth, so that they will see their Messiah.

> *Zechariah 11:4 (NASB) This is what the LORD my God says: "Pasture the flock doomed to slaughter.*

Verse 4 is part history lesson and part prophecy. It tells of the history of bad shepherds that people have endured, but the chapter also tells of the Good Shepherd that they reject (verse 7). Their rejection of the Good Shepherd speaks of their rejection by God. This is a hard declaration. I think of the history of the hardships of the Jewish people, and I have compassion for them. I believe surely their sin is not so great that they must suffer all these things. The Jews were to be a witness to the rest of the world, and not only did they fail to remain faithful to God, but they also failed to be a witness to the world.

Therefore, Romans 11 tells us that the Jews were branches that were broken off due to unbelief, and the Gentiles were grafted into the tree due to their faith. But Romans 11:25 tells us that the partial hardening of the Jews is only until the fullness of the Gentiles has come in, then, "and so all Israel will be saved, just as it is written: "The Deliverer will come from Zion, He will remove ungodliness from Jacob." "This will be My covenant with them, when I take away their sins." (NASB) All that has happened, and all that will happen, was meant and is meant to restore the nation to its God. He has never ceased being their God and has never stopped loving them. What we see in the following chapters is intended to restore the Jewish people to God and lead them to recognize Jesus as their Messiah.

As I sit here thinking about this, we in the Church today think about a God of grace and mercy because of the sacrifice of the Lamb. We don't like to think about a God of judgment. Romans 11:22 says, "See then the kindness and severity of God: to those who fell, severity, but to you, God's kindness,". (NASB) God is patient and He is merciful, but that patience and mercy will not last forever. I am trying to reconcile the God I have been taught as full of mercy and grace with the God I see here in Zechariah and in Revelation. He does not want to be a God of judgment and vengeance, but a third of the angels rebel and mankind rebels, and He must ultimately reward the righteous and judge the unrighteous. God is God, and He is in control of all creation,

He has a plan that He is in the process of carrying out. Romans 11:22 tells us that the consequences for being in rebellion against Him are severe; they are not light. It feels like we have so emphasized the love of God that we have forgotten to preach His judgments. We love to think about the Savior who is meek and lowly, but we forget about the Son of Man.

"His head and His hair were white like white wool, like snow; and His eyes were like a flame of fire. His feet were like burnished bronze when it has been heated to a glow in a furnace, and His voice was like the sound of many waters. In His right hand He held seven stars, and out of His mouth came a sharp two-edged sword; and His face was like the sun shining in its strength. When I saw Him, I fell at His feet like a dead man. And He placed His right hand on me, saying, "Do not be afraid; I am the first and the last, and the living One; and I was dead, and behold, I am alive forevermore, and I have the keys of death and of Hades." (Revelation 1:14-18 NASB)

As I read this chapter and engaged in a lot of listening and thinking about the coming end times, I asked God to show me His love. What came to mind was the cross. When you think about the cross, you can see the severity of sin, the seriousness of the punishment for sin, and the great love that the Father has for us that He would send His Son to take the punishment for us. His Son was punished in a brutal way that was severe, which demonstrates the severity of sin. His judgments are severe. Revelation 6:8 tells us that a quarter of the earth will be killed by sword, famine, plague, and the wild beast of the earth. Revelation 9:18 tells us that another third of the world will be killed by three plagues released in the verses immediately preceding verse 18. Hell, in and of itself, is severe.

We need to understand the severity of God's judgment so that we can appreciate the urgency of sharing the redemption offered through Jesus Christ with the world. We need to understand the severity of God's judgments so that we grasp the seriousness of our own sin, to the point where our sin repulses us.

You are either on God's side or you are not. You are either living in obedience to God or you are living in rebellion to God. God made a covenant with Israel, and He will not forget His covenant; however, He also warned Israel (Deuteronomy 4 and 28) of the consequences that would follow if they disobeyed His commands. In chapter 11, here we see the severity of God's judgment upon Israel. That is not to say that God is the cause of everything that has happened or happens to the Jews; part of the chastisement is just the removal of His hand of protection. When you are the favored of God and the Messiah is promised to come through your people, the enemy is going to try to destroy you. He tried to destroy Jesus (Revelation 12:4-6), and all He did was further the plan of God. Since He can't destroy Jesus, He will try to destroy the people with whom God has made a covenant.

In verse 4, Yahweh says, "Shepherd the flock marked for slaughter!" (TLV) To whom does He say this? I believe that He is asking Zechariah to play out this part in a vision; He does not actually shepherd an actual flock, but he plays a part. He plays several parts in this chapter. He plays the part of Jesus Christ shepherding the flock, he plays the part of Judas throwing the money in the Temple, and finally, he plays the part of the foolish shepherd that we see in the end times. In a sense, a prophet is a shepherd to the flock to whom he prophesies; however, there are many parallels between this role and that of Jesus Christ.

Verse 10 says, "And I took my staff Favor and cut it in pieces, to break my covenant which I had made with all the peoples." (NASAB) Who can make a covenant with all people? Certainly not Zechariah, but the LORD makes a covenant with all the peoples. Verses 12 and 13 refer to the 30 pieces of silver for which Judas betrayed Jesus Christ. Thus, Zechariah is playing a part within the vision. In verses 4 through 12, he plays the part of Jesus Christ.

Notice the term, "marked for slaughter." (TLV) The NASB and ESV say "doomed for slaughter." This reminds me of Romans 11, in which we are told that the Jewish people were partially hardened "until the fullness of the Gentiles has come in". (NASB) Romans 11:28 says, "As regards the gospel, they are enemies for your sake. But as regards election, they are beloved for the sake of their forefathers." (ESV) They have been marked for slaughter because they rejected Jesus Christ. Because of their unbelief, they have been blinded to the truth of Jesus as their Messiah so that we, the Gentiles, would have the opportunity to receive the gospel. It reminds me of Romans chapter 1, where those who sin are given over to their sin, allowing them to believe a lie, since they refuse to acknowledge the truth that is evident before them. The more we sin and become addicted to that sin, I believe God allows us to get to the point where we can't even recognize that activity as sin any longer. We become blind to the truth.

What we are seeing here is the fruit of the rebellion of the flock and the removal of the Father's hand of protection. When God's hand of protection is removed, unless God limits what the enemy can do, like He did with Job, the enemy is free to commit more violence and more slaughter than is appropriate. When you go back to Zechariah 1:15, we see the LORD seeming to say this very thing. Zechariah 1:15 says, "But I am very angry with the nations who are carefree; for while I was only a little angry, they furthered the disaster." (NASB) While God took his hand of protection off the nation of Israel so that they would be carried off into captivity, so that they would be chastised for their sin and come back to Him, the nations He used to carry out this judgment took it too far. Their violence and their treatment of the LORD's people and the LORD's land were greater than was appropriate for the sin.

> *Zechariah 11:5 (NASB) "Those who buy them slaughter them and go unpunished, and each of those who sell them says, 'Blessed be the LORD, for I have become rich!' And their own shepherds have no compassion for them.*

Thus, when we come to Zechariah 11:5, the LORD says, "Those who buy them slaughter them and go unpunished". It reminds me of Zechariah 1:15, where the LORD appears to be angry with the nations He uses as His instrument of chastisement. In a class that I was in at Church, we spoke of this very thing when it came to prodigals who are running from the LORD. Unfortunately, it often takes challenging and difficult circumstances to get the individual to turn back to

God, and that is what we find here. To get a nation to turn back to God, the circumstances must be as harsh as necessary to achieve the desired result, which is the restoration of the nation to God and for the nation of Israel to recognize Jesus as their Messiah.

In verse 5, we see not just those nations that slaughter the flock, but also the leaders of the nation of Israel, who have sold the flock. The second half of verse 5 says, "and each of those who sell them say, "Blessed be the LORD, for I have become rich, and their own shepherds have no compassion on them." (NASB) The leaders of the people were corrupt in their leadership and more concerned with accumulating wealth and prosperity through their positions of power than with guiding the flock of God into righteousness and holiness. They are deceived into thinking that the LORD is blessing them, and they fail to see the need to feed and water the flock with the truth of the Word of God.

It reminds me of King Josiah in II Kings 22. When a scroll of the law was found as they were restoring the temple, they read the scroll to the King. He immediately tore his clothes, realizing that they had not been keeping their covenant with the LORD. Before the reign of Josiah, a succession of poor kings ruled who did not follow the LORD, alongside a scattering of good kings who did follow the LORD. The nation had gotten so far from the LORD that, for many years before finding the scroll, there had been no reading of the law. When the law was finally read, the King and the priests recognized their sin and realized that they had not been keeping the covenant with God.

This is what a good shepherd does, but all too often, the shepherds of Israel did not care for the sheep properly; they only cared for their own interests. This is where we find ourselves in Zechariah 11, where we encounter both a recounting of the nation's history of sin and a prediction of the future rejection of the Messiah, the Son of God. It is up to the leaders to lead, to tear down the Asherah poles in the land and any other form of idol worship, and lead the people to follow the LORD who brought them out of Egypt. Unfortunately, the kings, priests, and prophets were more concerned with their own station in life; they forgot that their primary responsibility was to lead the people in the ways of the LORD and to worship the LORD only. These are the shepherds who sold the flock, concerned only for their own wealth.

> *Zechariah 11:6 (NASB) "For I will no longer have compassion for the inhabitants of the land," declares the LORD; "but behold, I will let the people fall, each into another's power and into the power of his king; and they will crush the land, and I will not rescue them from their power."*

What we see in verse 6 is a realization of the judgment that would fall on the nation for their disobedience to the covenant they made with God. Verse 6 bears a strong resemblance to Deuteronomy 4:25-27.

"When you father children and have grandchildren, and you grow old in the land, and you act corruptly, and make an idol in the form of anything, and do what is evil in the sight of the LORD your God to provoke Him to anger, I call heaven and earth as witnesses against you today, that you will certainly perish quickly from the land where you are going over the Jordan to take possession of it. You will not live long on it, but will be utterly destroyed. The LORD will scatter you among the peoples, and you will be left few in number among the nations where the LORD drives you." (NASB)

We also see this happening in the time of Josiah. When Josiah heard the words of the law, he tore his clothes, and he then inquired of the LORD, and the LORD gave him a reply.

II Kings 22:18-20 says. "This is what the LORD, the God of Israel says: 'Regarding the words which you have heard, since your heart was tender and you humbled yourself before the LORD when you heard what I spoke against this place and against its inhabitants, that they would become an object of horror and a curse, and you have torn your clothes and wept before Me, I have indeed heard you,' declares the LORD." Therefore, behold, I am going to gather you to your fathers, and you will be gathered to your grave in peace, and your eyes will not look at all the devastation that I am going to bring on this place.'" So they brought back word to the king." (NASB)

It is a terrible thing to fall under the judgment of God. The second half of Zechariah 11:6 says, "behold, I will let the people fall, each into another's power and into the power of his king; and they will crush the land, and I will not rescue them from their power." (NASB) Lest we think that God is just love, yes, He is love, but there is also a solemn nature to God. Israel is His bride, and she played the prostitute, and He was jealous for His bride. But this passage looks toward the day when they will despise the Good Shepard that the Father provides for them. You must look at verse 8, where the text says, "and their soul also detested me." (TLV)

We don't see this abandonment until after the death of Jesus Christ, when the people rejected Him and crucified Him. It was the leaders of the people who led the people in this rebellion against their Shepherd. Throughout history, the Jews suffered various persecutions and death, but I can't help but think of the Holocaust, since it was in the recent past. How tragic, how horrible it was for the Jewish people. I can't imagine being taken from my home, losing all my possessions, and being put in a prison camp where I was treated as something to be used up and thrown away. When you look at verse 6 and you think of it in the context of history, something as horrible as the Holocaust, you see how severe this judgment is. However, the Holocaust served another purpose: to bring the people back to the land.

> *Zechariah 11:7 (NASB) So I pastured the flock doomed to slaughter, therefore also the afflicted of the flock. And I took for myself two staffs: the one I called Favor, and the other I called Union; so I pastured the flock.*

Verse 7 tells us Christ did indeed feed the flock. In Mark 4:18-19, Jesus quotes from Isaiah 61:1-2 saying,

"THE SPIRIT OF THE LORD IS UPON ME, BECAUSE HE HAS APPOINTED ME TO BRING GOOD NEWS TO THE POOR. HE HAS SENT ME TO PROCLAIM RELEASE TO CAPTIVES, AND RECOVERY OF SIGHT TO THE BLIND, TO SEE FREE THOSE WHO ARE OPPRESSED, TO PROCLAIM THE FAVORABLE YEAR OF THE LORD" (NASB)

Notice that everyone mentioned in Isaiah could be considered the afflicted of the flock that is mentioned in Zechariah 11:7. He was here to feed the flock, and particularly the afflicted of the flock. The first two verses of Isaiah 61 refer both to the first coming and the second coming of Christ, while the remainder of Isaiah 61 refers exclusively to the second coming. But as you can see in Zechariah 11:7-11, He does not shepherd the flock long. He comes to shepherd the flock, but the leaders reject Him, and they do their best to keep the people from following the Shepherd.

Joseph Benson, in his Commentary, says that a shepherd has two staffs. Benson's Commentary says, ""The shepherds of old time," says Lowth, "had two rods, or staves, one turned round at the top, that it might not hurt the sheep: this was for counting them, and separating the sound from the diseased, Leviticus 27:32; the other had an iron hook at the end of it, to pull in and hold the straying sheep." Zechariah says the Shepherd has two staffs. One is named Beauty or Favor and really denotes a graciousness to the flock. The other is called Union, and the Hebrew word means those that bind. The idea is to make one flock of the sheep. This union is a reunion between Israel and Judah, the reuniting of the

Northern and Southern kingdoms. Verse 14 tells us that is what the union means.

> *Zechariah 11:8 (NASB) Then I did away with the three shepherds in one month, for my soul was impatient with them, and their soul also was tired of me.*

Verse 8 says, In one month I destroyed the three shepherds (ESV). I look at this one month as being either in the same month or as a short period of time. As I see the person to whom God is asking to shepherd the flock as Jesus Christ, then it only makes sense that upon His death and resurrection, He put an end to the offices of king, priest, and prophet and took all those offices upon Himself forever. And thus, the three shepherds that were destroyed in that month were the offices of king, priest, and prophet, as these have historically been the leaders of the nation, the shepherds of the people. These also would have been the shepherds who sell the flock and say, "Blessed be the LORD, because I have become rich". Verse 5 says, "their own shepherds have no pity on them," or, I like the way the TLV says it, "Their own shepherds do not spare them." And with whom did the shepherd become impatient? In the original language, it begins a new paragraph; therefore, the Pulpit Commentary suggests that this refers back to the sheep, the flock.

> *Zechariah 11:9 (NASB) Then I said, "I will not pasture you. What is to die, let it die, and what is to perish, let it perish; and let those who are left eat one another's flesh."*

Verse 9 also makes the point that the Shepherd's impatience is with the flock, because the Shepherd addresses the flock and says, "I will not be your shepherd". He would not say that to the other shepherds, but He would say that to the flock.

The phrase "my soul became impatient with them" means the opposite of longsuffering, thus the translation of "impatient." Some of the translations stated this as "my soul was grieved at them." The Shepherd tires of the obstinacy of the flock, and the flock despises the Shepherd. Others have translated the flock's attitude toward the Shepherd as "Their soul also abhorred me", or their souls howled, bellowed, roared, or raised a horrible outcry against me." He was not the Shepherd they wanted. This Shepard asked them to repent, to love, and to forgive. They wanted a Shepherd who was going to overthrow the Romans. They were ready for the physical rule and reign of the Messiah, not the Messiah who was going to die for the sins of the world.

They rejected their Shepherd, and now, in verse 9, their Shepherd rejects them for a time. The passage does not say for a time, the passage says, "Then I said, "I will not pasture you. What is to die, let it die, and what is to perish, let it perish; and let those who are left eat one another's flesh." (NASB) However, as we read the remaining chapters of Zechariah, we see that the sheep will one day recognize and reconcile with the Shepherd (Zechariah 12:10-14). But in the intervening period, Jews around the world are persecuted.

The Jewish Encyclopedia refers to the persecution of the nation by the Roman Empire as the paganization of Jerusalem. This led many Jews to migrate to Europe, where they suffered persecution by a Europe that the Church heavily influenced. From 1096 to 1600, there were significant persecutions of the Jewish people in Europe. However, the greatest persecution in all of history was the Holocaust, where an estimated 6,000,000 Jews were killed just for being Jews. This is what it is like when the sheep have no Shepherd. God's hand of protection was removed from Israel, and the sheep were scattered and devoured as foretold in Deuteronomy, Zechariah, and by many of the other Old Testament prophets. This is a difficult thing to write and think about, but the words in Zechariah 11:9 are real; they are not just words on paper, but a story that holds meaning. These words are a prophecy that foretold the persecution and death of real people. The more that I read Zechariah, the more I see the truth of these words in history, the more I know the truth of the prophets and what is yet to come. The deeper I dig into the Word of God, the more impressed I am with its truthfulness and the more faith it builds in my life.

> *Zechariah 11:10 (NASB) And I took my staff Favor and cut it in pieces, to break my covenant which I had made with all the peoples.*

Verse 10 gave me much to ponder. It is saying that the Shepherd, which I believe to be the Prophet Zechariah representing the LORD Jesus, broke His covenant with Israel. However, this is not consistent with other verses, such as Leviticus 26:44, Judges 2:1, and Jeremiah 33:20-21, which state that the LORD would never break His covenant with Israel. What we are seeing here is the annulment of the conditional Mosaic Covenant, and it is being replaced with an unconditional covenant, the New Covenant. The New Covenant is an expansion of the Abrahamic Covenant and the fulfillment of the Davidic Covenant. The covenant being annulled is the one that the Jewish people have not fulfilled their part of the agreement. God is replacing it with a covenant where Jesus Christ has done all the work, and all they must do is believe in Him.

With the death of Christ, God broke the covenant of the law with Israel, and now, all men must come to God through Christ. With the rejection of Christ, that hand of protection was taken off Israel, and thus, many calamities have befallen the nation of Israel since the death of Christ. It is not just that the hand of protection has been removed; it is chastisement, chastisement to bring them back to God, to see their Messiah. Although the Mosaic (or Sinaitic) covenant was broken, God is not finished with Israel. The way in which Israel relates to God is broken forever, but they are still His bride. Romans 11:11 says, "I say then, they did not stumble so as to fall, did they? Far from it! But by their wrongdoing salvation has come to the Gentiles, to make them jealous.". (NASB) Israel is provoked to jealousy, so that they may see what they have lost and want it back. It will take much pain and suffering for them to recognize their Messiah.

The key to understanding Zechariah 11:10 lies in Jeremiah 31, Hebrews 8, and Romans 11. God abolished worship in the Temple and all the traditions associated with Temple worship. The Temple was to be a foreshadowing of Jesus' sacrifice, and now we have Jesus as the Christ. Because of their rebellion, God broke the Mosaic covenant with Israel, but He tells us in Jeremiah 31 that He will make a New Covenant with Israel and He will write His law on their hearts. Perhaps the term "broke His covenant" is not quite right. The Mosaic covenant was conditional; if Israel did not keep their part of the covenant, they would be chastised by God, and they have been chastised. This chastisement has led to what Paul calls the fullness of the Gentiles in Romans 11:25. Romans 11:23 and 24 say,

> "And they also, if they do not continue in their unbelief, will be grafted in; for God is able to graft them in again. For if you were cut off from what is by nature a wild olive tree, and contrary to nature were grafted into a cultivated olive tree, how much more will these who are the natural branches be grafted into their own olive tree?" (NASB)

With the rejection of their Messiah, God has rejected his natural bride, Israel, and has included the Gentiles to be a part of His bride. But God cannot forget His love for Israel, nor can he forget his promises. Jeremiah 31:1-4 says,

> "At that time," declares the LORD, "I will be the God of all the families of Israel, and they shall be My people." This is what the LORD says: "The people who survived the sword Found grace in the wilderness— Israel, when it went to find its rest." The LORD appeared to him long ago, saying, "I have loved you with an

everlasting love; Therefore I have drawn you out with kindness. I will build you again and you will be rebuilt, Virgin of Israel! You will take up your tambourines again, And go out to the dances of the revelers. (NASB)

He breaks His covenant, but He doesn't break His covenant. He replaces the conditional Mosaic Covenant, which Israel could not keep, with the unconditional New Covenant, which God will uphold by placing His Spirit within them. Jeremiah tells us that God will put a new covenant in their hearts.

Jeremiah 31:31-33 says, "Behold, days are coming," declares the LORD, "when I will make a new covenant with the house of Israel and the house of Judah, not like the covenant which I made with their fathers on the day I took them by the hand to bring them out of the land of Egypt, My covenant which they broke, although I was a husband to them," declares the LORD. "For this is the covenant which I will make with the house of Israel after those days," declares the LORD: "I will put My law within them and write it on their heart; and I will be their God, and they shall be My people". (NASB)

The curses of Deuteronomy 4 and 28 are in effect and for a prolonged period; God has rejected Israel, but only for a time, so that the fullness of the Gentiles may come in. What Zechariah is telling the people is that they will experience the rejection and chastisement of the LORD that will make them desire the favor of the LORD once again. Notice that the first staff broken with the rejection of Jesus Christ is Favor, they lose the favor of the LORD. It is as if they are wandering in the wilderness during this period, and the LORD is not leading them to the promised land until all the older generation has passed away. But He will not forget them. He can't forget them because of His promise to Abraham under the Abrahamic covenant, and His promise to David under the Davidic Covenant. Although the nation did not fulfill its part of the Mosaic covenant, God made an unconditional covenant with Abraham. Abraham was promised that he would become a great nation, that he would possess the land, and that all the world would be blessed through him. God made an everlasting covenant with Abraham in Genesis 17:7. He has a plan to restore Abraham's descendants, but after He has allowed the nations and opportunity to know Him and His grace.

Suppose I can compare this to the marriage relationship. God has every right to cancel; the Hebrew word used here is 'annul,' referring to the marriage contract. And if we are reading this passage correctly, He has annulled the marriage contract. But He can't forget that he found this bride as an infant and has cared for her. He later finds her as a young woman, still no one has cared for her, so He cares for her. He nurtured her, bestowed beauty upon her, gave her jewelry and fine clothes, and married her. Even with her unfaithfulness, He cannot forget this one that He cared for and upon whom He bestowed beauty, Ezekiel 16. After all that Israel has done, God still loves her and will forgive her. Although they are separated, they shall be reunited; however, Israel will have to come to the Father through their Messiah, Jesus Christ. There will be a reunification, but it will be under

God's terms, and He will cleanse the land of idols and sin (Zechariah 13).

> *Zechariah 11:11-12 (NASB) So it was broken on that day, and so the afflicted of the flock who were watching me realized that it was the word of the LORD. 12 And I said to them, "If it is good in your sight, give me my wages; but if not, never mind!" So they weighed out thirty shekels of silver as my wages.*

If you are following along and understanding what is occurring, verse 11 is a natural progression. Verse 11 tells us that the covenant was broken on that day, on what day? Verse 12 tells us the day on which the Shepherd was paid his 30 pieces of silver. The day that Jesus was betrayed and crucified.

The ESV does a poor job of translating the second half of verse 11 from the original language. The ESV says, "So it was annulled on that day, and the sheep traders, who were watching me, knew that it was the word of the LORD." My first thought was, who are the sheep traders? However, when you read the Tree of Life version, you gain a better understanding that makes more sense. The TLV says, "It was broken on that day. The afflicted of the flock that were watching me knew that this was the word of ADONAI."

The NASB also agrees with this reading as it states, "So it was broken on that day, and so the afflicted of the flock who were watching me realized that it was the word of the LORD." The Pulpit Commentary, which provides Commentary on the original language, translates verse 11 as, "It was broken. And so the poor of the flock that waited upon me (that gave heed to me) know". Verse 11 is telling us that a portion of the flock, who were the poor or afflicted portion of the flock, followed the Shepherd, and they listened to his voice. This portion of the flock knew that the covenant was being broken on that day because the Shepherd told them what was occurring. That the portion of the flock who knew these things were the poor and afflicted of the flock. This follows the way in which God operates.

> I Corinthians 1:26-31 says, For consider your calling, brothers and sisters, that there were not many wise according to the flesh, not many mighty, not many noble; but God has chosen the foolish things of the world to shame the wise, and God has chosen the weak things of the world to shame the things which are strong, and the insignificant things of the world and the despised God has chosen, the things that are not, so that He may nullify the things that are, so that no human may boast before God. But it is due to Him that you are in Christ Jesus, who became to us wisdom from God, and righteousness and sanctification, and redemption, so that, just as it is written: "Let the one who boasts, boast in the LORD." (NASB)

There was a small portion of the flock that followed Jesus, and they knew what was happening because Jesus had told them, and the Holy Spirit had also informed them. They were not the wise or learned; they were fishermen, tax collectors, and ordinary people, the poor and afflicted.

Deuteronomy 4:25-31 foretells the breaking of the covenant, and Romans 11 and Hebrews 8 provide a much better understanding of what is occurring. Romans chapter 8 is particularly enlightening in understanding the annulment of this covenant. Hebrews 8:7-13 says, For if that first covenant had been free of fault, no circumstances would have been sought for a second. For in finding fault with the people, He says,

> "BEHOLD DAYS ARE COMING, SAYS THE LORD, WHEN I WILL BRING ABOUT A NEW COVENANT WITH THE HOUSE OF ISRAEL AND THE HOUSE FO JUDAH NOT LIKE THE COVENANT WHICH I MADE WITH THEIR FATHERS ON THE DAY I TOOK THEM BY THE HAND TO BRING THEM OUT OF THE LAND OF EGYPT; FOR THEY DID NOT CONTINUE IN MY COVENANT, AND I DID NOT CARE ABOUT THEM, SAYS THE LORD. FOR THIS IS THE COVENANT WHICH I WILL MAKE WITH THE HOUSE OF ISRAEL AFTER THOSE DAYS, DECLARES THE LORD: I WILL PUT MY LAWS INTO THEIR MINDS, AND WRITE THEM ON THEIR HEARTS. AND I WILL BE THEIR GOD, AND THEY SHALL BE MY PEOPLE. AND THEY WILL NOT TEACH, EACH ONE HIS FELLOW CITIZEN, AND EACH ONE HIS BROTHER, SAYING, 'KNOW THE LORD,' FOR THEY WILL ALL KNOW ME, FROM THE LEAST TO THE GREATEST OF THEM. FOR I WILL BE MERCIFUL TOWARD THEIR WRONGDOINGS, AND THEIR SINS I WILL NO LONGER REMEMBER."

When He said, "A new covenant," He has made the first obsolete. But whatever is becoming obsolete and growing old is about to disappear." (NASB)

What did they know? They knew that this was the word of the LORD. They understood the Old Testament scriptures and saw Jesus Christ as their Messiah and Savior, as prophesied in the Old Testament. The writers of the New Testament were able to write what they did because they had a thorough understanding of the Old Testament. The Holy Spirit illuminated the Old Testament for them, helping them to understand how Jesus Christ fit into the Old Testament as the Messiah and the New Covenant He had made for all people. This is why the New Testament frequently quotes the Old Testament. This is why God miraculously chose Paul to be an apostle, due to his extensive knowledge of the Old Testament scriptures. Once God enlightened him on Jesus as the Messiah, the scriptures opened for Paul. It was this key that unlocked a treasure trove of information.

God is not finished with His people, Israel, but He has provided a New Covenant, and Israel must come to Him through this New Covenant. Zechariah chapters 12 through 14 and Jeremiah 31 make it plain that God is not finished with Israel, and the Church has not replaced Israel. Romans 11:23-36 makes clear that Israel will be saved, and Zechariah 12-14 tells us of the coming salvation of the remnant of Israel. Lest anyone think that we are saying God will save an entire nation without requiring any action on their part, they misunderstand. The final chapters of Zechariah reveal that the salvation of Israel comes at a significant cost to the nation. Two-thirds of the nation will perish in a war; many people will be scattered and become prisoners. The nation will be on the verge of extinction when Jesus appears, then they will be so overjoyed for their physical salvation, they will see their Messiah, and they will mourn for the one they have pierced.

Verse 12 is Jesus giving the leaders the opportunity to accept or reject Him. It is the voice of the Shepherd who has taken extraordinary care of the sheep, and He knows the value of what He provides for the sheep, but the sheep do not. He allows the sheep the opportunity to show gratitude for the care that the Shepherd has bestowed upon them. It has been this way since God created mankind; man has always had a choice to follow God or to live in rebellion. Dare I say to worship God? Paying the Shepherd His wages is very similar to giving God the worship that is due to Him. God has never forced humanity to follow Him; He has always given man a choice. Even in this passage, Jesus gave the nation of Israel a choice: they could follow Him or go their own way without the protection of the Shepherd.

> Zechariah 11:12-13 (NASB) And I said to them, "If it is good in your sight, give me my wages; but if not, never mind!" So they weighed out thirty shekels of silver as my wages. 13 Then the LORD said to me, "Throw it to the potter, that magnificent price at which I was valued by them." So I took the thirty shekels of silver and threw them to the potter in the house of the LORD.

Jesus doesn't need us; we need Him. He knows that there will be a group of people, the poor and afflicted, who will choose to follow Him. You can hear sarcasm or contempt in verses 12 and 13. He doesn't need our payment; the payment is more to show if the sheep appreciate all that the

Shepherd has done, is doing, and will do. Who is he talking to? Yes, it is to the sheep, so to speak, but the sheep are sheep. They don't have the responsibility to pay the shepherd. He is talking to the ones who have been put in charge of the flock, the three shepherds that were disposed of in verse 8, the kings, the priests, and the prophets. It was the rulers of the people who decided to pay 30 pieces of silver; it was the rulers of the people who rejected the Shepherd. So they paid him his wages, 30 pieces of silver!

Why 30 pieces of silver? This was not an extravagant amount. Exodus 21:32 tells us that 30 pieces of silver were the price that was due to the owner of an enslaved person if someone else were responsible for the death of his slave. Thirty pieces of silver were the value of an enslaved person. Jesus tells his disciples that anyone who wants to be great among them must be a servant to all, and those who want to be first among them must be their slave. Matthew 20:26-28 says,

> *"It is not this way among you, but whoever wants to become prominent among you shall be your servant, and whoever desires to be first among you shall be your slave; just as the Son of Man did not come to be served, but to serve, and to give His life as a ransom for many." (NASB)*

Jesus willingly humbled himself to be a ransom for us. The leaders of the people considered Him to be worth no more than the value of a slave. The Shepherd sarcastically calls this an extravagant sum. It is hardly an extravagant sum;

it was meant to be an insult. The Shepherd says, "If it seems good to you, pay me my wages, but if not, don't bother!". The Shepherd doesn't need the money, but He is testing the hearts of those who oversee the sheep. Those in charge of the sheep, the sheep traders, were more concerned with lining their own pockets than they were paying a good shepherd adequate wages to ensure that they had the right person to take care of the sheep (verse 5).

Verse 13 becomes even more specific when discussing this passage as a prophetic one about Jesus Christ. Verse 13 says, "Then the LORD said to me, "Throw it to the potter, that magnificent price at which I was valued by them." So I took the thirty shekels of silver and threw them to the potter in the house of the LORD." (NASB) When you get to the latter verses in Zechariah 11, this may be why many scholars believe that Zechariah is playing the part of the shepherd. We know that Jesus did not throw the silver into the temple, but Judas threw the 30 pieces of silver into the temple, and the priests, in turn, took the funds from the treasury and used them to buy a potter's field. They did this because they claimed it was blood money, and they could not deposit it into the Temple treasury.

Therefore, in verse 13, when the writer says, "The LORD told me", He is speaking to Zechariah, who in this part of the vision is playing the part of Judas, throwing the money on the temple floor. When the word "LORD" is capitalized, it represents the name "YHWH," which is the self-existent or eternal, the Jewish name of God. But YHWH is the personal name for God, the God of the covenant. When I read this passage, I understood this verse to mean that it was the will of the LORD that this should be done, and thus it was completed in this manner.

Matthew 27 is where we read that Judas took 30 pieces of silver to betray Jesus, and after they put Jesus to death, Judas regretted his decision to betray Jesus, and when they would not take the money back, he threw the pieces of silver down in the Temple. Matthew 27:9-10 attributes the prophecy of the 30 pieces of silver to Jeremiah saying, "Then that which was spoken through Jeremiah the prophet was fulfilled: "And they took the thirty pieces of silver, the price of the One whose price had been set by the sons of Israel; and they gave them for the Potter's Field, just as the LORD directed me." (NASB)

However, you do not find this specific prophecy in Jeremiah. Jeremiah 18:2 talks about the potter's house, and Jeremiah 32 talks about the purchase of land for 17 pieces of silver. However, neither of these passages really discusses the betrayal of Judas like Zechariah 11:11-13 does. The best explanation for why Zechariah is not mentioned involves the ancient Jewish custom of dividing the Old Testament into three main sections: the Law, the Writings, and the Prophets. When writers would quote from any of these sections, they would often refer to the first book in that section to indicate from what section they were quoting. In rabbinical order, Jeremiah came first among the prophetic books. In effect, "spoken by Jeremiah the prophet" is the same as saying, "recorded in the Prophets".

A more expansive explanation can be found at https://thirdmill.org/answers/answer.asp/file/40445.

Zechariah 11:14 (NASB) Then I cut in pieces my second staff Union, to break the brotherhood between Judah and Israel.

We have already read where Jesus breaks the first staff called Favor, and He makes a New Covenant with all people. In verse 14, He breaks the second staff called Unity. With the destruction of the nation, the people are scattered, and it breaks the brotherhood of unity between Israel and Judah. This whole chapter is a sad chapter and reveals that with their rejection of Jesus as the Christ, God rejects the nation for a time, as we see in Romans 11, so that the Gentiles will have the opportunity to know God and His love. We know that with the destruction of the people, they were scattered all over the earth, and the bond between Israel and Judah was broken.

Zechariah 11:15 (NASB) And the LORD said to me, "Take again for yourself the equipment of a foolish shepherd.

In verse 15, we see the prophet playing the part of another character; he portrays another shepherd, a wicked shepherd. The LORD is telling him to take up the instruments of a foolish shepherd, and this time the shepherd will play the part of the Antichrist. He is speaking of another shepherd who will come and will not care for the sheep but will use them to his advantage. The term "foolish shepherd" denotes a shepherd who is wicked. Sin is often represented as folly in the Bible, as seen in Job 5:2-3, Psalm 14:1, Proverbs 1:7, and Proverbs 14:9.

> *Zechariah 11:16 (NASB) "For behold, I am going to raise up a shepherd in the land who will not care for the perishing, seek the scattered, heal the broken, or provide for the one who is exhausted, but will devour the flesh of the fat sheep and tear off their hoofs.*

Verse 16 clearly tells us that God will raise up an evil shepherd who will not properly care for the sheep but will use them to his advantage. God must raise up this shepherd to show the sheep that they have rejected the good Shepherd. This shepherd does not care for the sheep as a proper shepherd cares for his sheep. He does not care for the dying, nor does he seek out the young; he neither heals the injured nor nourishes the healthy. Instead, he eats the meat of the choice sheep, even tearing off their hoofs. To tear off their hoofs indicates that he takes them over rocky and rough land, not caring that the path he takes will damage the sheep's hoofs. He cares nothing for this flock, only what this flock can provide for his benefit. Moreover, since this shepherd is a portrait of the Antichrist, we know that he wants to harm the flock and destroy the flock.

As I said earlier, Zechariah 11:1-3 is a transition from the second coming to the first coming of Jesus Christ. When we reach the end of Zechariah 11:15-17, we transition back to the second coming of Christ, with the raising up of the

Antichrist. John 5:43 is appropriate here in this chapter, it says, "I have come in My Father's name, and you do not receive Me; if another comes in his own name, you will receive him." (NASB)

> *Zechariah 11:17 (NASB) "Woe to the worthless shepherd Who abandons the flock! A sword will be on his arm And on his right eye! His arm will be totally withered, And his right eye will be blind."*

Verse 17 tells us that God will judge the worthless shepherd for his treatment of the flock. Revelation 13:3 says, "I saw one of his heads as if it had been fatally wounded, and his fatal wound was healed. And the whole earth was amazed and followed after the beast". (NASB) I recently listened to Joel Richardson as he hypothesized that the fatal head wound of Revelation 13:3 may actually be that of a kingdom seemingly dying only to be restored. The thought seemed to make sense and still does, but as I sit here and read Zechariah 11:17, I can't help but wonder if this passage is describing an actual wound that the Antichrist may suffer. I can't help but wonder if this is an actual physical description of the Antichrist? Does this head wound cause his right eye to be blind and his arm to be withered?

God raises up this shepherd to contrast the Good Shepherd with the evil shepherd. God raises him up, and Jesus will bring him down. All of history in which we have seen the persecution of the Jews has been leading them to this point in time, when they will be in a situation so dire that they have no salvation other than the Good Shepherd. I recently watched the documentary "Annihilation: The Destruction of the European Jews." I saw people digging their own graves and lining up to be shot. I saw women paraded naked to the pit to be shot. I thought of this passage of scripture (verses 7 and 9) and the image of sheep being led to the slaughter. Most of them just lined up to be shot without resistance. To be sure, I am not saying that anyone deserved this treatment; it was horrific, but I am saying that God used it for a purpose. This persecution served a purpose: to bring the Jews back to the land that God had promised to them, and it was part of the curse of Deuteronomy 4. It was the beginning of the plan to bring them to the point where they would recognize their Messiah, the one who would bring them salvation. Sadly, God has to chastise us to get us to obey Him. The more we rebel, if we truly belong to Him, the more He must chastise us to get us to turn back to Him.

Zechariah 12
They Will Mourn for the One They Have Pierced

Zechariah 12:1 (NASB) The pronouncement of the word of the LORD concerning Israel: The LORD who stretches out the heavens, lays the foundation of the earth, and forms the spirit of a person within him, declares:

Chapter 12 starts with "The burden of the word of the LORD" or "The pronouncement of the word of the LORD." When we see this in Zechariah, it lets us know that we are about to read of the judgment of a people or land. In this case, it tells us that the LORD is going to bring judgment upon the neighbors of Israel. We saw the exact phrase in Zechariah 9:1, and the Word went on to tell us of the judgments that would be visited upon the various cities that were mentioned in Zechariah 9. Zechariah 9 mentions cities that are well known for their wars against the Jews or persecution of the Jews, and here in Zechariah 12, judgment is coming upon the surrounding peoples who have warred against or persecuted Israel.

Chapter 12 could be simply titled "The Salvation of the LORD." Israel has not seen this kind of salvation since the Old Testament times, when many would come against Israel, and God would give Israel the victory over greater numbers. This is the salvation that the Jews prayed for through the many persecutions that they suffered since they rejected Jesus

215

Christ, and they were scattered from the land. To a degree, you could say that the salvation of the LORD began when the people started coming back to the land after World War II. I say to a degree because when we see these prophecies fulfilled, we shall see all Jewish people return to the land, and we shall not just see a restoration to the land, but also a reconciliation to their Messiah.

What we have seen thus far is just a precursor to the main event, the return of Israel to the land, which sets the stage for the return of the Messiah. As their neighbors have continued to attack them since 1948, tiny Israel has held and not just held, but they have soundly defeated those who have come against them, and Israel gained ground in these wars. However, Chapter 12 foretells the last war that will come against Israel, and as we shall see over the following several chapters, although there is salvation, victory will not come without significant costs. Only when all appears to be lost does the LORD Jesus Christ come to their rescue. Deuteronomy 32:36-43 tells us that God will wait until Israel has no strength left, and Israel will see His salvation and will recognize that He is the only God. Deuteronomy 32:36-43 says,

> *"For the LORD will vindicate His people, And will have compassion on His servants, When He sees that their strength is gone, And there is none remaining, bond or free. And He will say, 'Where are their gods, The rock in which they took refuge? Those who ate the fat of their sacrifices, And drank the wine of their drink offering? Let them rise up and help you, Let them be*

your protection! See now that I, I am He, And there is no god besides Me; It is I who put to death and give life. I have wounded and it is I who heal, And there is no one who can save anyone from My hand. Indeed, I raise My hand to heaven, And say, as I live forever, If I have sharpened My flashing sword, And My hand has taken hold of justice, I will return vengeance on My adversaries, And I will repay those who hate Me. I will make My arrows drunk with blood, And My sword will devour flesh, With the blood of the slain and the captives, From the long-haired leaders of the enemy.' Rejoice, you nations, with His people; For He will avenge the blood of His servants, And will return vengeance on His adversaries, And will atone for His land and His people." (NASB)

Today, Israel revels in their own strength, although it must feel like they are alone against the world.

These first verses lay a foundation. What is needed here is a miracle. Tiny Israel will be on the verge of being wiped out, and only a miracle will save it. The first two verses of Zechariah 12 explain where the miracle will come from: "The LORD who stretches out the heavens, lays the foundation of the earth, and forms the spirit of a person within him, declares: "Behold, I am going to make Jerusalem a cup that causes staggering to all the peoples around." (NASB) They need a miracle, and they get a miracle from the only One who can supply miracles. The Word makes it clear that this salvation is being delivered from the One who formed the heavens and the earth. In Numbers 11:23 and Isaiah 59:1, the question is asked, "Is the LORD's arm too short to save?" I love this question because it is sarcastic, as it is not meant to be a genuine question, but rather a reminder that the resounding answer is no! It is our God puffing up His chest as if to say, "You doubt me?" He is the action hero you love because you know he will save those who are being bullied by evil. That is what we see here in the first two verses: the God who created the heavens and the earth reminding the people that He is the Almighty, that He is omnipotent; His arm is not too short to save.

We are told in Ezekiel 38 and 39, as well as Revelation 16:12-21, from where their salvation comes. In Ezekiel 38:18 - 19 God says, "It will come about on that day, when Gog comes against the land of Israel," declares the LORD God, "that My fury will mount up in My anger. In My zeal and in My blazing wrath I declare that on that day there will certainly be a great earthquake in the land of Israel." (NASB)

Ezekiel 38 and 39 describe the war with Gog of the land of Magog. This also ties into Revelation 16:12-21. Ezekiel 38:19-23 describes a great earthquake that will occur throughout Israel, accompanied by pestilence, torrential rain, and hailstones. Revelation 16:12-21 describes lightning, rumblings, peals of thunder, and a great earthquake such as there has never been since man was on the earth. Every Island fled away, and no mountains were to be found. Great hailstones, about one hundred pounds each, fall from heaven on people. Ezekiel 38:23 says, "So I will prove Myself great, show Myself holy, and make Myself known in the sight of many nations; and they will know that I am the LORD." (NASB)

Verse 2 tells us why they need a miracle.

Zechariah 12:2 (NASB) "Behold, I am going to make Jerusalem a cup that causes staggering to all the peoples around; and when the siege is against Jerusalem, it will also be against Judah.

You could interpret the words "Jerusalem will be a cup of drunkenness." The people surrounding Israel have this blinding desire to remove Israel from the land and to occupy Jerusalem. The enemy (Satan) has put it in their minds that Jerusalem is their historic holy place; it is like a drug addict seeking his next fix or an alcoholic seeking his next drink. Common sense goes out the window, and they will do anything to have the next fix or drink.

The surrounding peoples will do anything to remove Israel from the land and occupy Jerusalem. In Islam, there is a belief in Dar al-Islam, which translates to "House of Islam" or "House of Peace." What this also means is that once a piece of land comes under the rule of a legitimate Muslim authority, it forever becomes an inalienable part of the Dar al-Islam. Suppose even one acre of Dar al-Islam becomes conquered and ruled by a non-Muslim authority. In that case, Muslims have an obligation to restore the land to Muslim authority, no matter the cost. This partially explains the fanatical drive to wipe Israel off the map. But it goes even deeper than that. The land and the people of Israel are the apple of God's eye, and Satan will do anything to wipe out the people and establish his rule in the land in his attempt to usurp God. It is the war that started when Satan rebelled against God, and now Satan is against anything God establishes.

Chapter 12 tells us what is happening, but we must read chapter 14 to understand the pain it will inflict on the Jewish people. Chapter 14:1-2 tells us, "Behold, a day is coming for the LORD when the spoils taken from you will be divided among you. For I will gather all the nations against Jerusalem to battle, and the city will be taken, the houses plundered, the women raped, and half of the city exiled, but the rest of the people will not be eliminated from the city." (NASB) The pain is intended to turn the Jewish people to their Savior, to their Messiah when He comes marching into the situation to save them. Zechariah 14:3 provides the timing of this salvation, which comes after all these horrible things have happened. Zechariah 14:3 says, "Then the LORD will go forth and fight." (NASB) It will take the Jewish people being defeated and on the brink of annihilation, and Jesus coming to their rescue, before they turn to Jesus as their Messiah. All of this is chastisement meant to bring the people of Israel back to their God, the God to whom they committed back at Mount Sinai when the LORD God brought them out of Egypt.

> Zechariah 12:3 (NASB) "It will come about on that day that I will make Jerusalem a heavy stone for all the peoples; all who lift it will injure themselves severely. And all the nations of the earth will be gathered against it.

The first thing to note about verse 3 is that it begins with the phrase "On that day" (ESV) or "in that day" (TLV and

NASB). It refers to the second coming of Jesus Christ to the earth. When I read the term "on that day," it gives the impression that everything occurs on a single day, but when I read the term "in that day," it suggests that a period of time is involved during which everything is happening. I believe that there will be a period of approximately 30 days when Jesus wages a campaign of war to free the captives that have been placed in prison camps as He marches from Egypt to Jerusalem. As He frees these Jewish prisoners, they will continue with him on this march as he conquers the enemy on His way to Jerusalem. As we read through the end of the chapter, we see that this is indeed the return of Jesus Christ. With Jesus coming to save the Jewish people from this annihilation, they will finally recognize Him as their Messiah, the anointed one. ("Sinai to Zion" by Joel Richardson lays out the scriptural evidence for this March from Egypt to Jerusalem.)

There is also judgment occurring here in these verses, including verse 3. The LORD says, "I am going to make Jerusalem a cup that causes staggering to all the peoples around." (NASB) The ESV states "all of the surrounding people," making it clear that this refers to the neighbors of Israel, specifically the countries that formed the Northern and Southern Kingdoms after Alexander the Great's kingdom was divided into four kingdoms. It is the LORD God who is bringing this about. Not only is He using these circumstances to chastise Israel so that they will turn and recognize Jesus as their Messiah, but He is using these circumstances to judge the surrounding peoples.

Using the term surrounding peoples is a good term, because even today, as you look at the news, it is not just a nation that troubles Israel; there are terrorist groups made up of people who are not a nation. However, on that day, it will be both nations and people without a nation who come against Israel. They will think they are finally winning, but verse 3 tells us a different story. Verse 3 says, "It will come about on that day that I will make Jerusalem a heavy stone for all the peoples; all who lift it will injure themselves severely. And all the nations of the earth will be gathered against it." (NASB) The enemy used various people throughout history to persecute the Jewish people. On this occasion, God will gather Israel's neighbors against Israel, but even as the nations think they are winning, Jerusalem and Judah will be a heavy stone that will devastate the armies that are coming against them.

> Zechariah 12:4 (NASB) "On that day," declares the LORD, "I will strike every horse with confusion and its rider with insanity. But I will watch over the house of Judah, while I strike every horse of the peoples with blindness.

Although the nations think that they are fighting against the Israeli Defense Forces, they will be fighting against the LORD, a battle they cannot win. Verse 4 says, "On that day," declares the LORD, "I will strike every horse with confusion and its rider with insanity. But I will watch over the house of Judah, while I strike every horse of the peoples with blindness." (NASB) The LORD will create confusion and panic in the forces opposing Israel. He will do this with the most traumatic natural events that we have ever seen. Additionally, my guess is that they will have many friendly fire incidents where they drop bombs and artillery on their own forces.

There are multiple passages in the Old Testament where the forces opposing Israel ended up killing each other in panic and confusion. The battle led by Gideon comes to mind, as does the siege of Samaria by the Syrians (Arameans), where they heard the sound of chariots, horses, and a great number of troops, and they fled (Judges 7 & 8; II Chronicles 20; II Kings 6 & 7). When the LORD delivers His people, it is often by confusing the enemy's mind. Fear will also play a part in the destruction of the enemy. There are so many natural disasters happening during this time, as well as the Messiah marching from the south to Jerusalem, freeing captives as he goes along.

Great fear will strike the enemy, and they will panic because of the awesome visage of the LORD. Revelation 19:11-16 tells us what our Conquering King looks like, "And I saw heaven opened, and behold, a white horse, and He who sat on it is called Faithful and True, and in righteousness He judges and wages war. His eyes are a flame of fire, and on His head are many crowns; and He has a name written on Him which no one knows except Himself. He is clothed with a robe dipped in blood, and His name is called The Word of God. And the armies which are in heaven, clothed in fine linen, white and clean, were following Him on white horses. From

His mouth comes a sharp sword, so that with it He may strike down the nations, and He will rule them with a rod of iron; and He treads the wine press of the fierce wrath of God, the Almighty. And on His robe and on His thigh He has a name written: "KING OF KINGS, AND LORD OF LORDS." (NASB) Isaiah 63:1-6 provides the details of what is happening in this passage. It says,

> "Who is this who comes from Edom, With garments of glowing colors from Bozrah, This One who is majestic in His apparel, Marching in the greatness of His strength? "It is I, the One who speaks in righteousness, mighty to save." Why is Your apparel red, And Your garments like one who treads in the wine press? "I have trodden the wine trough alone, And from the peoples there was no one with Me. I also trod them in My anger And trampled them in My wrath; And their lifeblood is sprinkled on My garments, And I stained all My clothes. For the day of vengeance was in My heart, And My year of redemption has come. I looked, but there was no one to help, And I was astonished and there was no one to uphold; So My own arm brought salvation to Me, And My wrath upheld Me. I trampled down the peoples in My anger And made them drunk with My wrath, And I poured out their lifeblood on the earth."

Verse 5 tells us that the leaders of Israel and Jerusalem are finally starting to see that it is the LORD who gives them their strength.

> Zechariah 12:5 (NASB) "Then the clans of Judah will say in their hearts, 'The inhabitants of Jerusalem are a

strong support for us through the LORD of armies, their God.'

They are defeated, having lost Jerusalem, and on the brink of annihilation before Jesus returns to save them. Not much land remains for them to hold. Their own strength has failed them; now they must trust in Jesus as He leads them in battle. They will see all of the destruction through the natural calamities and supernatural events that the LORD will bring upon the enemy, so that the leaders of Israel will know that the LORD is fighting for them. The people have confidence that the LORD is fighting for them. It is that LORD who has allowed them to fight and survive this long.

Furthermore, based on the language of "in that day" or "on that day," the Messiah has arrived on the scene and begun His march from Sinai, freeing captives as He makes His way to Jerusalem. The leaders and the people are seeing this march, and it gives them hope. The description used in verse 5 is "the LORD of armies" or "the LORD of hosts"! This is the description used for God when He comes as a Warrior King leading His army of angels and saints.

> *Zechariah 12:6 (NASB) "On that day I will make the clans of Judah like a firepot among pieces of wood and a flaming torch among sheaves, so they will consume on the right and on the left all the surrounding peoples, while the inhabitants of Jerusalem again live on their own sites in Jerusalem.*

Verse 6 tells us that not only will they see the LORD confuse the thoughts of the enemy and calamity fall upon the enemy, but the IDF will be performing much better than they have a right to perform. They will be like a fire in the woodpile. Although it may start small, it will grow using the fuel of the wood. A small fire in a woodpile will spread to become a large fire. Verse 6 says, "so they will consume on the right and on the left all the surrounding peoples." (NASB) As verse 2 says, the LORD will use Jerusalem as a cup of staggering to all of the surrounding peoples. Small Israel will be left to fight all by herself, will be like a firepot in the wood pile, Israel will devour all on her right and on her left. Let's not forget, I started this out by saying that they have been defeated, having lost Jerusalem, and on the verge of annihilation. They have paid a great cost; now, with Jesus leading them, they shall be victorious. Think of what chapter 14 says: the houses are plundered, the women are raped, and half of the people are taken into exile. Think of where we are in this battle for the armies of the enemy to have come far enough to capture Jerusalem. Yes, they will see the hand of the LORD fighting for them, but they should have been wiped out by this time.

The final part of verse 6 describes the restoration of Jerusalem. It says, "while the inhabitants of Jerusalem again live on their own sites in Jerusalem." (NASB) Jerusalem will be the capital city of the Messiah. With all the damage that the enemy will have done to it, Jerusalem will once again be inhabited by the Jewish people. Ultimate victory will come to the Jewish people from their Messiah.

Thoughts On Zechariah

In 2023, I went on a 21-day fast in response to a vital prayer request that I had before the LORD. I have not had my prayer answered yet, but what that fast did for me was bring me closer to the LORD, and the LORD showed me more truth about the end times through the teachings of Joel Richardson and Frontier Alliance International. It was one of those instances where their teaching aligned with my existing perspective, and their scriptural evidence was overwhelming. Whereas, before I asked Him to show me the truth of whether the rapture would occur before or after the tribulation, now I see it clearly. The teachings of Joel Richardson have greatly helped my understanding of the end times. Joel writes in his book, "Sinai to Zion," that Jesus will return riding the clouds, accompanied by the pillar of fire by night and the cloud by day, and will march from Sinai to Jerusalem, freeing the Jewish captives as He goes.

> *Zechariah 12:7 (NASB) "The LORD also will save the tents of Judah first, so that the glory of the house of David and the glory of the inhabitants of Jerusalem will not be greater than Judah.*

Verse 7 aligns with the idea that Jesus will march from the south to the north and first give salvation to those in Judah, as He comes north and gives salvation to the inhabitants of Jerusalem last. It is the order of His march, from south to north, seen in Isaiah 63:1-6, Isaiah 34:1-7, and Psalm 68. He will defeat His enemies and will be crowned King of all the earth in Jerusalem. Before understanding this truth, I was sitting here wondering why the LORD is saving Judah first, and then Jerusalem; it is the order of His march. Also, "the tents of Judah" contrast here with the fortified city of "Jerusalem." I am sure that the leaders of Israel will put forth their maximum effort to keep Jerusalem from falling. They will have to leave the tents of Judah to fend for themselves. With the war and destruction going on, great numbers of people will have fled to Petra and will be taking refuge anywhere they can find refuge, most likely in temporary shelters and tents. The Messiah will save the tents of Judah first, to show that this was His salvation, and the salvation of Judah and Jerusalem was not brought by human hands, as Isaiah 2:11-17 states.

> *Zechariah 12:8-9 (NASB) "On that day the LORD will protect the inhabitants of Jerusalem, and the one who is feeble among them on that day will be like David, and the house of David will be like God, like the angel of the LORD before them. 9 "And on that day I will seek to destroy all the nations that come against Jerusalem.*

Verses 8 and 9 are a continuation and expansion of verse 7. The LORD has come back, and He is marching toward Jerusalem. He will retake Jerusalem, and He will enable even those who are feeble, the old, and the sick, to be strong like David. Most likely, the feeble will have the strength they need to make their way to Jesus and take refuge behind him as He leads the battle. The LORD shall lead the remnant of Israel, and He will enable them to defeat the enemies who have Israel and Jerusalem on the edge of annihilation. The LORD Jesus Christ will retake Jerusalem and will enable the inhabitants to rise up and be strong. But as we see in verse 9, the victory belongs to the LORD. He will destroy all the nations that have come against Jerusalem. As verse 2 says, He draws them to Jerusalem to destroy them, a cup that causes staggering. This will be the second coming of Jesus as the Messiah.

The second half of verse 8 has a curious phrase. It says, "and the house of David will be like God, like the angel of the LORD before them." (NASB) I believe that this is an inference that Jesus is the head of the house of David, and Jesus is the angel of the LORD. It will be the head of the house of David and the Angel of the LORD that goes before them and wins this victory.

> *Zechariah 12:10 (NASB) "And I will pour out on the house of David and on the inhabitants of Jerusalem the Spirit of grace and of pleading, so that they will look at Me whom they pierced; and they will mourn for Him, like one mourning for an only son, and they will weep bitterly over Him like the bitter weeping over a firstborn.*

Verses 10 -14 point to an occasion that Jesus has been waiting for a very long time. These verses are up there among the most important verses in the Bible. The people know that their annihilation is assured. They know that except for the coming of Jesus as the Messiah, they will be destroyed. Jesus waits until disaster is inevitable for the Jewish nation so that there will be no doubt that He is responsible for their salvation. The Jewish people finally realize that Jesus is their Messiah, and they turn to Him as one, pleading for mercy. Romans 11:26 tells us the result, "and so all Israel will be saved." (NASB) Zechariah 12:10 says God will "pour out on the house of David and on the inhabitants of Jerusalem the Spirit of grace and of pleading." (NASB) As the Jews have been partially blinded so that the time of the Gentiles could be fulfilled, now God lifts the scales from their eyes so that they can see the truth of Jesus as their Messiah. What verses 10-14 reveal to us is a national repentance, by house and clan, "so that they will look at Me whom they pierced; and they will mourn for Him, like one mourning for an only son, and they will weep bitterly over Him like the bitter weeping over a firstborn." (NASB) They will recognize that they rejected Jesus for so many years and that it was their forefathers who put Him to death, and they will weep bitterly. They will weep bitterly because they will also recognize how they themselves rejected the truth that Jesus was the Messiah.

Zechariah 12:11 (NASB) "On that day the mourning in Jerusalem will be great, like the mourning of Hadadrimmon in the plain of Megiddo.

Verse 11 says, "On that day the mourning in Jerusalem will be great, like the mourning of Hadadrimmon in the plain of Megiddo." (NASB) The reference to "mourning like Hadadrimmon in the valley of Megiddo" appears to be a reference to when the last righteous king of Judah, King Josiah, was killed in battle with the Egyptians, and the nation mourned for him, II Chronicles 35:20-27.

Zechariah 12:12 (NASB) "The land will mourn, every family by itself; the family of the house of David by itself and their wives by themselves; the family of the house of Nathan by itself and their wives by themselves;

Verse 12 tells that "the land" will mourn. This is the entirety of the land; the entire nation shall mourn because they rejected Jesus as the Christ. I have heard many people who believe that the Church has replaced the Israel state, that the entire nation will not be saved, that this is not how God saves, God saves each individual as each individual makes their own choice. See what is happening here: each individual will be drawn by the Spirit of God to repentance, and each individual will repent; it will be a collective act of repentance.

> *Zechariah 12:12-14 (NASB) "The land will mourn, every family by itself; the family of the house of David by itself and their wives by themselves; the family of the house of Nathan by itself and their wives by themselves; 13 the family of the house of Levi by itself and their wives by themselves; the family of the Shimeites by itself and their wives by themselves; 14 all the families that are left, every family by itself, and their wives by themselves.*

Verse 12 through 14 tell us, "The land will mourn, every family by itself; the family of the house of David by itself and their wives by themselves; the family of the house of Nathan by itself and their wives by themselves; the family of the house of Levi by itself and their wives by themselves; the family of the Shimeites by itself and their wives by themselves; all the families that are left, every family by itself, and their wives by themselves." (NASB) Each individual and each family shall come to see the truth of Jesus as the Christ and will mourn. That is why God must allow them to go through such a horrific time, because their salvation will be so dramatic that they will have no choice but to realize their rejection of Jesus as the Messiah is a mistake. Why are the men and the women mourning by themselves? Due to the solemn nature of the occasion. In Jewish custom, men and women often had their separate places for times of religious observance. They had separate areas in the synagogue, and Paul instructs husbands and wives to separate by mutual agreement for the purpose of prayer and fasting. It removes the temptation to think about one another and allows them to focus solely on the LORD. It also points to the fact that the mourning will be so personally intense that it will transcend the husband-wife relationship; it is personal and individual. Everyone will want to be alone with God in that hour.

The mourning encompasses the nation's leadership and its people. The leadership of the land must lead the way, so that the people can follow them. It starts with the house of David, the King. It then goes to the house of Nathan, the Prophet, then to the house of Levi, the Priest, then to the house of Shimei, ordinary Levites, and finally, to all the families that are left. It encompasses the offices of King, Prophet, and Priest, culminating in the role of the ordinary man. The entire nation shall repent, each man and woman for themselves.

As I was sitting and thinking about what I had just read and what I had just written, the thought hit me: How long will the Jewish people mourn and repent? It will be such an emotional realization that they have missed Jesus as their Messiah. It will not be finished in an hour or in a day. I believe it is highly probable that the Jews will recognize their Messiah on the day of the Feast of Trumpets, now also known as Rosh Hashanah, and will spend the next 10 days in repentance and consecration until the Day of Atonement. Today, these 10 days are known as the 10 Days of Awe, serving as a time for reflection, repentance, and fasting. These 10 days are considered the holiest days on the Jewish calendar and finish on Yom Kippur, the Day of Atonement. The Bible doesn't explicitly state that Jesus will be recognized by the Jewish people on the Feast of Trumpets, but the 10 days of repentance and consecration seem to be a fitting time for this realization. Furthermore, God often utilizes pre-established templates, places, and events on significant days.

There are scholars and Messianic Rabbis who believe that, as the Jewish year follows the Jewish appointed times for holy convocations, the end of the age follows a prophetic timeline that imitates the Jewish calendar. The Feast of Trumpets and the Day of Atonement are near the end of the Jewish calendar, followed only by the Feast of Tabernacles. The Feast of Trumpets will call the nation to repentance, and the Day of Atonement will see their cleansing and forgiveness. Just as these days occur toward the end of the calendar year, the repentance of the nation and the acceptance of Jesus as their Savior and Messiah/Christ will occur toward the end of the age. With these feasts, the Bible is giving a template for the second coming of Jesus and his recognition by the people of Israel as the Messiah. I've listened to several Messianic Rabbis who are convinced that Jesus is returning on the Feast of Trumpets.

Shortly after I concluded that the Feast of Trumpets was significant to the Second Coming of Jesus, I was driving to work and listening to "One For Israel" on YouTube. The episode discussed the Feast of Trumpets and how Jesus is believed to return on that same feast. They also said something interesting. Because the Jewish calendar follows the lunar cycle, Jews did not know on which day the Feast of Trumpets would fall until they observed the new moon that marks the beginning of the Hebrew month of Tishri. Thus, when a new moon was sighted to start the month of Tishri, they would blow trumpets throughout the land to let the nation know that they were to observe the Feast of Trumpets. They never knew exactly on which day it would fall until the new moon occurred. According to the Days of Noah (days-of-noah.com) and the International Christian Embassy Jerusalem (icejusa.org), the Feast of Trumpets is also known as "The Day and the Hour No Man knows" due to the difficulty in determining the exact day every year. Was Jesus telling us the day he would return when he told his disciples in Matthew 24:36, "But about that day and hour no one knows"? (NASB). I do believe that the Feast of Trumpets will be a significant day in the second coming of Jesus Christ.

The Feast of Trumpets is the only biblical feast for which God did not provide a detailed explanation of its actual meaning or significance. Is that because He did not want the meaning or importance revealed until the right time? The next marker I am looking for regarding the prophetic timeline is the peace agreement with the Antichrist, which will bring peace to Israel and likely include an arrangement that allows

Israel to rebuild the Temple. If I were a betting man, I would bet that this agreement will be signed at the end of September or the beginning of October, a timeframe that coincides with the Feast of Trumpets. I expect that seven years later, Jesus will return.

If you read Leviticus 23, you will see that the appointed times of Jewish holy convocations on the calendar begin with Passover on the 14th day of the first month and conclude with the Feast of Tabernacles on the 15th day of the seventh month. The calendar begins with Passover, commemorating the death of Jesus Christ as our perfect Passover Lamb, and concludes with the Feast of Tabernacles, a time to celebrate and acknowledge all of God's provision. Zechariah 14:16 tells us that the Feast of Tabernacles shall be celebrated annually in the Millennial Kingdom. During the Feast of Tabernacles, people also brought their tithes and offerings to the LORD to recognize His provision and deliverance. Just like Israel remembered what God did for them in bringing them out of Egypt and into a new land, they will remember this time of salvation and national reconciliation with Jesus as the Messiah. Israel and the world will celebrate God's provisions and deliverance each year. The whole world will come to Jerusalem annually with their tithes and offerings to honor God for His provision.

To be fair, even as I write down my thoughts on the second coming of Jesus and incorporate Joel Richardson's thoughts from "Sinai to Zion," I am having difficulty understanding the timeline and aligning it with the last trumpet. I have a timeline in my head, but if Joel is correct and Jesus starts his return in Egypt and makes a march through the desert freeing and collecting prisoners as he goes, you can't have the last trumpet when he returns to start His march and have the last trumpet on the Feast of Trumpets. I do believe He will begin in Egypt and free the prisoners as he marches to Jerusalem. He will then stand on the Mount of Olives and split the Mount of Olives and defeat the Antichrist. I believe that the march will take approximately 30 days. Based on my understanding, that would mean that you will not have the last trumpet on the Feast of Trumpets.

God is so good. I am not a theologian or a Bible scholar; however, I do consider myself a student of the Word. The Holy Spirit prompted me to ask these questions: "How long will this mourning go on?" and "Is there an official time for mourning on the Jewish calendar?" Just by asking those two questions, he led me to different resources that seemed to unlock more understanding. Nothing God does is random. The deeper I dig, the more gold I find, the more I fall in love with God, with Jesus, and with His Word. Journaling through Zechariah has been an amazing journey.

Zechariah 13
Refiner's Fire

Zechariah 13:1 (NASB) "On that day a fountain will be opened for the house of David and for the inhabitants of Jerusalem, for sin and for defilement.

Chapter 13 picks up on the theme at the end of chapter 12, that of national atonement. Again, we read, "On that day." On what day? The Day of the LORD, the time of His return! What is going to happen? "A fountain will be opened for the house of David and for the inhabitants of Jerusalem, for sin and for defilement." (NASB) What a wonderful day, a day of restoration of Israel to their God, of the nations to see the one true God. It aligns with Chapter Twelve, where the Jews will recognize Jesus on the Feast of Trumpets, mourn and repent for the 10 Days of Awe, and then, on the Day of Atonement, they will wash themselves clean in the spring or fountain that Jesus opens for their cleansing. Nowhere does the Bible tell us on what day this is going to happen; I am assuming based on the character of God. God loves to set His holy days and have everything revolve around them. I could be totally wrong about the timing for this to happen, but it seems as if the LORD has already set aside the day on which this will happen.

The question is, will this be a physical spring or fountain, or will this just be a metaphorical spring or fountain? I believe this will be a literal spring, and the Jews will wash in it as they have been required to complete their ceremonial cleansing since meeting the LORD at Mount Sinai. It will be much like baptism; it will be a symbol of their repentant hearts and their acceptance of the sacrifice that Jesus paid for all of humanity. It is more fitting to say baptism is a symbol of the ritual cleansing of a bride before they meet their groom. It will also signal their acceptance of Jesus as their Messiah, their Savior, their King. The Mikveh (also spelled Mikvah) is an ancient Jewish ritual practice of water immersion, traditionally used for cleansing, purification, and transformation.

Almost every Jewish community has at least one Mikveh; in larger Jewish communities, you will find several mikv'ot. To be saved, they must recognize Jesus as God and King, the Lamb that has taken away the sins of the world. This occurred in chapter 12, where they mourned for the one whom they pierced. After this recognition, there will be a call to cleanse themselves in water that emanates from the throne of Christ here on earth. In Exodus 19, there was a betrothal of Israel to God at Mount Sinai. In Exodus 19:14-15, we can see the people being told to perform the ritual cleansing required of a bride before they meet their groom. I believe that is what we are seeing again here in chapter 13. The ritual cleansing of a bride before they meet their groom. After this, the marriage supper of the Lamb will be held on Mt. Zion, where the bride and the groom will celebrate the marriage.

We see this new river of living water in several passages. Zechariah 14:8 tells us, "And on that day living waters will flow out of Jerusalem, half of them toward the eastern sea and the other half toward the western sea; it will be in summer as well as in winter." (NASB) Zechariah describes the river as "living waters will flow." Ezekiel 47 tells us of a river of water that flows eastward out of the Temple. We see this river described in several different passages, and it is a river that flows out from the Temple from beneath the very throne of God. It is not described as living water, but Ezekiel 47:9 says,

> "And it will come about that every living creature which swarms in every place where the river goes, will live. And there will be very many fish, for these waters go there and the others become fresh; so everything will live where the river goes."

After the destruction of the earth and the pollution of the waters, of which we read in Revelation, it will be necessary to have a river of living water flow from the throne of God. (NASB) Ezekiel 47:12 says, "And by the river on its bank, on one side and on the other, will grow all kinds of trees for food. Their leaves will not wither and their fruit will not fail. They will bear fruit every month because their water flows from the sanctuary, and their fruit will be for food and their leaves for healing." (NASB) This is indeed living water. Jesus has already spilled his blood. Now, He truly is the living water where anyone who drinks from the river or immerses themselves in it shall be healed and live. Most likely, the leaves will be exported worldwide for their healing properties.

In John 4:10, Jesus tells the woman at the well that if she knew who she was speaking to, she would ask Him for living water. John 4:10 says, "Jesus replied to her, "If you knew the gift of God, and who it is who is saying to you, 'Give Me a drink,' you would have asked Him, and He would have given you living water." (NASB) Jesus clarifies further in John 4:14, "but whoever drinks of the water that I will give him shall never be thirsty; but the water that I will give him will become in him a fountain of water springing up to eternal life." (NASB) Jesus speaks more about living water in John 7:37-39, "Now on the last day, the great day of the feast, Jesus stood and cried out, saying, "If anyone is thirsty, let him come to Me and drink. The one who believes in Me, as the Scripture said,' From his innermost being will flow rivers of living water.'" But this He said in reference to the Spirit, whom those who believed in Him were to receive; for the Spirit was not yet given, because Jesus was not yet glorified." (NASB) Living water comes from Jesus, and it leads to eternal life; it also flows from those who believe in Him. It is a sign that you believe in Him as the Christ. In His first coming, He gave spiritual living water; in His second coming, it will be physical living water.

We see a similar river in New Jerusalem in eternity. Revelation 22:1-5 tells us,

"And he showed me a river of the water of life, clear as crystal, coming from the throne of God and of the

Lamb, in the middle of its street. On either side of the river was the tree of life, bearing twelve kinds of fruit, yielding its fruit every month; and the leaves of the tree were for the healing of the nations. There will no longer be any curse; and the throne of God and of the Lamb will be in it, and His bond-servants will serve Him; they will see His face, and His name will be on their foreheads. And there will no longer be any night; and they will not have need of the light of a lamp nor the light of the sun, because the LORD God will illuminate them; and they will reign forever and ever." (NASB)

Zechariah 13:2 is a continuation of the cleansing of the people and the land.

Zechariah 13:2 (NASB) "And it will come about on that day," declares the LORD of armies, "that I will eliminate the names of the idols from the land, and they will no longer be remembered; and I will also remove the prophets and the unclean spirit from the land.

Ezekiel 39:21-29 tells us what is on the LORD's mind. He will no longer put up with rebellion. All will know that He is God and He alone is to be worshipped. He is to be obeyed. No longer will He put up with our rebellion; He will be recognized as God, supreme, all-powerful, all-knowing, Creator of the heavens and earth! The world will realize that there is no one like Him!

Verse 2 tells us He is going to erase the names of the idols from the land, and they will no longer be remembered. There are things in life, such as trials, tribulations, and events that happen within our family or to us, that we would like to erase and forget. If we follow the Prophet Hosea, he saw his wife become a prostitute and continually ran to other men. I think that is something we would like to erase and forget if we were Hosea. The LORD allowed this in Hosea's life as a picture that the nation of Israel was the unfaithful wife who kept running to other lovers. Not just other lovers, but strange men, whom she would pay. When we get to the return of Jesus, the Messiah, He will erase the names of the idols and remove that memory from the land. He will indeed make all things new.

When my children were young, one of my children drank a red colored Kool-Aid or fruit drink, and he got sick and threw up on the new carpet that we had just placed in our home. I thought we would never be able to get that stain out, but somehow my wife managed to remove it. Jesus will take the stain of idol worship out of the land and off the people. Erasing the name of the idols so that they are forgotten is essential because it is the name that gives the idol its power. A wooden figure is just a wooden figure until you call it Baal, or Ishtar, or any other demonic name. The names will no longer be remembered. They will be cleansed from the land and the memory of the people.

This passage deals with Israel and the Land. When I googled 'idol worship in Israel,' I found an interesting article in The Jerusalem Post about an event called the Lag Ba'omer feast, also known as the Mount Meron Jamboree. They commemorate Rabbi Shimon Bar Yochai, the alleged author of the Zohar, a foundational work of Kabbalah. Each year,

Kabbalists make a pilgrimage to Mount Meron, where the Rabbi is buried, and celebrate a feast.

The article is entitled "Idolatry: The Jewish Version." (https://www.jpost.com/israel-news/article-742130)

More than half a million Kabbalists flocked to the event annually until 2021, when 45 people died in a stampede. In 2022, only 130,000 people attended the event, partly due to government control of the crowd. Many Ultra-Orthodox Rabbis consider this to be a pagan celebration.

Another thing that I thought of is that in our modern society today, we worship idols, and we don't even realize that we are worshipping idols. There is a picture that has come out of Israel since October 7th, and that of the young people dancing under a large statue of Buddha before the massacre at the music festival. I've heard Joel Richardson talk about the Jewish people worshipping many other religions in Israel today. In his book, "Return of the Gods," Jonathan Cahn describes the history of pagan worship, most of which involved sexual immorality.

All you need to do is open Apple News, and you will find plenty of stories/pictures in the entertainment or fashion section of celebrity after celebrity pushing the boundaries of modesty by wearing as few clothes as they can get away with, or wearing see-through items that do not hide the more delicate parts of the body. I bring this up because it is as if these women are the modern-day equivalent of the temple prostitutes that Jonathan Cahn describes in antiquity. Perhaps the idols and false prophets in the land are described in a manner that reflects the prophets' understanding of them, but their application in our time has evolved. However, their ability to lead people away from God remains unchanged.

> *Zechariah 13:2-5 (NASB) "And it will come about on that day," declares the LORD of armies, "that I will eliminate the names of the idols from the land, and they will no longer be remembered; and I will also remove the prophets and the unclean spirit from the land. 3 "And if anyone still prophesies, then his father and mother who gave birth to him will say to him, 'You shall not live, because you have spoken falsely in the name of the LORD'; and his father and mother who gave birth to him shall pierce him through when he prophesies. 4 "Also it will come about on that day that the prophets will each be ashamed of his vision when he prophesies, and they will not put on a hairy robe in order to deceive; 5 but he will say, 'I am not a prophet; I am a cultivator of the ground, because a man sold me as a slave in my youth.'*

In verses 2 through 5, we see the elimination of the need for a prophet. Even further, those who pretend to be prophets will be killed because they will be false prophets. Verses 4 and 5 inform us that being a prophet will be out of favor, and thus anyone who believes themselves to be a prophet will hide and deny their prophetic status, knowing they will be killed. Today, in our world, we have people called influencers who may lead others away from the LORD. These will be people who point people away from the LORD while acting as if they speak for the LORD. When you read verse 2, it indicates that these are false prophets connected with idols and unclean spirits, but verse 3 says, "You shall not live, because you have spoken falsely in the name of the LORD." (NASB)

Does history not continually repeat itself? Men will always find something other than God in which to direct their affections. They may even find something that is associated with God to make it seem like they are worshipping God, but they are in fact worshipping an idol. Satan wants us to mix our affection for the LORD with something else to turn our worship into something other than true worship to the LORD. No longer will the LORD allow a man to prophesy in His name and lead others astray.

There will no longer be a need for prophets, because in the Messiah, the whole world will have the one true King, one true Prophet, and one true Priest. The One who holds all three offices is Jesus, the Christ. The people of Israel and the nations will have Jesus speak directly to them. Therefore, they will not require a prophet to speak on behalf of the LORD. As with any kingdom, there will be representatives, governors, and emissaries, but they will take their orders and direction directly from Jesus Himself, who rules from Jerusalem. They will be implementing orders given by Jesus in Jerusalem.

Ezekiel 46:4 indicates that there will be a "prince" in Jerusalem, who is the local official in charge of the city. Just as we have a president who governs the entire country, we also have a mayor who governs a local town or city. Therefore,

Jesus will govern the whole world, and He will appoint local officials to assist with the administration of His government. In his book "Heaven," Randy Alcorn states that we will all be able to converse with Jesus on a daily basis. There will no longer be a need for a prophet to tell us what God is saying; we will have His officials, and we will speak to Him ourselves. 1 Corinthians 13:12 tells us, "For now we see in a mirror dimly, but then face to face; now I know in part, but then I will know fully, just as I also have been fully known." (NASB) There will be no need for a prophet; we will have the King with us here on earth, and we shall speak to Him face to face.

The punishment outlined in Deuteronomy 13:6-11 for being a false prophet and leading others to worship false gods was severe. It was death, and like Zechariah 13:3, Deuteronomy 13:6-11 prescribes that it should be someone very close to the false Prophet who should carry out the punishment. Deuteronomy 13:6 says, "If your brother, your mother's son, or your son or daughter, or the wife you cherish, or your friend who is like your own soul, entices you secretly," and is followed by Deuteronomy 13:9, which says, "Instead, you shall most certainly kill him." (NASB) It was expected that those who knew the false Prophet best would be the ones to erase the evil from the land. Zechariah 13:3 tells us that anyone who prophesies, his own father and mother will pierce him through when he prophesies.

Zechariah 13:4-6 (NASB) "Also it will come about on that day that the prophets will each be ashamed of his vision when he prophesies, and they will not put on a hairy robe in order to deceive; 5 but he will say, 'I am not a prophet; I am a cultivator of the ground, because a man sold me as a slave in my youth.' 6 "And someone will say to him, 'What are these wounds between your arms?' Then he will say, 'Those with which I was wounded at the house of my friends.'

Verses 4 through 6 tell us that prophets will be ashamed of their vision and instead will tell lies about their occupation and lies about how they received the scars on their body. Prophets used to wear a hairy cloak to distinguish themselves as prophets, but when Jesus reigns, they will not want to be identified as prophets, so they will not wear the clothing of a prophet. The idea behind the wounds between his hands is that they have cut themselves in the worship of a false god, similar to what the prophets of Baal did when they cut themselves in an attempt to get Baal to light the sacrifice on fire. 1 Kings 18:28 says,

"So they cried out with a loud voice, and cut themselves according to their custom with swords and lances until blood gushed out on them." (NASB)

They will not want to be recognized as a prophet, for in the day of Jesus' rule, it will be a death sentence to be a prophet.

Smith's Bible Commentary (Chuck Smith) offers an interesting perspective to consider when examining verse 6. Does Zechariah 13:6 go with Zechariah 13:5, or does it go with Zechariah 13:7? Chuck Smith and other commentators believe that verse 6 belongs with verse 7, rather than verse 5.

Zechariah 13:6-7 (NASB) "And someone will say to him, 'What are these wounds between your arms?' Then he will say, 'Those with which I was wounded at the house of my friends.' 7 "Awake, sword, against My Shepherd, And against the Man, My Associate," Declares the LORD of armies. "Strike the Shepherd and the sheep will be scattered; And I will turn My hand against the little ones.

The subject would have moved away from false prophets and shifted to the Shepherd. You can see that the Shepard starts this chapter by speaking about the cleansing of the lands, and now someone asks him about his wounds. The subject now changes, and the Shepherd becomes the subject. Jesus Christ did indeed receive His wounds at the house of a friend, a nation that He was to lead, a nation that had covenanted to follow Him. This interpretation is very interesting, and I am split on which interpretation is the most likely. In the original language, the passage says, "wounds between thy hands". Verse 6 could very well be describing the wounds Jesus received when being crucified. Although the Romans enforced the punishment, it was the leaders of the Jewish people (friends) who forced the issue and saw to it that Jesus was crucified.

Zechariah 13:7-9 is hard to read. These Scriptures go along with Zechariah 12:2-3 and Zechariah 14:1-2, which describe the horrendous toll their sin and rejection of Jesus as the Messiah will take on the Jewish people.

Zechariah 13:7-8 (NASB) "Awake, sword, against My Shepherd, And against the Man, My Associate," Declares the LORD of armies. "Strike the Shepherd and the sheep will be scattered; And I will turn My hand against the little ones. 8 "And it will come about in all the land," Declares the LORD, "That two parts in it will be cut off and perish; But the third will be left in it.

Verses 7 and 8 very much remind me of Zechariah 11:4-17. In that passage, we see that the people of Israel are the flock marked for slaughter, and they detest the Shepherd, and the Shepherd was impatient with them. What we also see is that the Shepherd leaves the flock on their own and says, "I will not pasture you. What is to die, let it die, and what is to perish, let it perish; and let those who are left eat one another's flesh." (NASB) This very much reminds me of Zechariah 13:8 that says, "That two parts in it will be cut off and perish." (NASB) In Zechariah 11:10, the Shepherd further says, "And I took my staff Favor and cut it in pieces, to break my covenant which I had made with all the peoples." (NASB)

This occurred at the time of the rejection of the Shepherd and ushered in the period of what Paul calls the fullness of the Gentiles in Romans 11. Zechariah 13:7 is a depiction of the death of our Savior and the scattering of the Jewish nation as a result. Verses 8 and 9 then bring us to the last days, when the tribulation of those days will require the salvation of the nation by their Messiah and their recognition of Jesus as the Messiah.

Verse 7 foretells of Jesus' death, and not just of His death, but that His death was planned and arranged by the Father. The term used, "Awake, O sword," implies any type of weapon that inflicts death. It is against the Good Shepherd, the Scripture says, "My Shepherd". If we assume the speaker was the Father, then we know who My Shepherd is. To leave no doubt, the passage goes on to say, "And against the Man, My Associate, Declares the LORD of armies" (NASB) or "against the man who stands next to me, declares the LORD of hosts". (ESV) The passage is foretelling the death of Jesus, the Christ.

To leave no doubt as to who this is, Jesus quotes Zechariah 13:7 in Matthew 26:31 and Mark 14:27. In these passages, Jesus and the disciples have gone up to the Mount of Olives on the day that Jesus is betrayed. He is telling them that on this night, they will fall away because the Shepherd is going to be struck. Jesus directly correlates Zechariah 13:7, in which He is identified as the Shepherd who is struck, with the scattering of His disciples. I believe that the broader meaning also correlates to the scattering of the nation that occurred after the Romans put down the rebellion in 70 AD. The true reason for the scattering is not the rebellion against Rome, but the rejection of the Shepherd, as we see in Zechariah 11. Israel broke their covenant with the LORD, and now the time of the Gentiles has been ushered into the Kingdom.

It is not just that Israel rejected their Messiah, it is that for a couple of thousand years before Jesus came, Israel had turned from God and turned to false gods. Israel was to be a kingdom of priests and a holy nation (Exodus 19:5-6) that would point others to God, but instead, they joined others in worship of false gods. I believe that this is why we see in Romans 11:7-8 and Romans 11:25 that God set Israel aside so that the fullness of the Gentiles might be fulfilled. God is not done with Israel, but He is allowing the nations an opportunity to enter His Kingdom. Israel was to be a Kingdom of priests and a holy nation, and they were to be a witness to the whole world. Instead, they strayed from the LORD and did not serve as a witness to the world.

What does the last section of verse 7 mean, "I will turn My hand against the little ones"? Many commentators seem to think these points provide protection for the young Church that is in the process of being established. However, the three translations that I am reading (NASB, ESV, and TLV) use the following language: "I will turn my hand against the little ones." If I read it in context, it appears to align with verse 8, which describes the cutting off of two-thirds of the people. It seems to me that several words contain the key to what is being said here. The first phrase is "I will turn", which is derived from a word meaning to "turn back, return". It is used in various ways and can have either a positive or negative connotation.

I believe in this case, it carries a negative connotation, and the words that best fit here are "return, repent, and revoke." The original word, translated here as "against," is a preposition that governs and usually precedes a noun. An example would be "the man on the platform". The word translated "against" means upon, above, or over. What does He specifically mean by the little ones? Strong's Lexicon states that this is a masculine plural verb, indicating an action is involved. The translation of the original word used here, as "little ones," means "to be or grow insignificant." After reading much of Zacheriah and keeping this phrase as pertaining to the Jewish people, I believe that this means that God is taking his hand off the Jewish people and revoking the betrothal covenant he made with them at Sinai. They were insignificant when He found them and established them as a nation, and they will be insignificant again. I believe that He is returning His hand from being on them or above them, similar to a double negative. His hand was on them or above them, and he is returning it and taking it away.

Ezekiel 16 tells that Israel was insignificant when God found this little child and nurtured her, grew her up, adorned her, and married her. Ezekiel 16 describes a small baby who had been born and not cared for, just left in a field in her own blood. The passage goes on to explain how God washed and cared for her, and when she was of age, He made a marriage covenant with her and adorned her in the finest clothes and jewelry. Even with all of this, she ran to other lovers. Therefore, God chastens her.

This little child, who became a full-grown, beautiful woman, is Israel. As I read Ezekiel 16:39-42, I see the pictures of the holocaust that I have watched in documentaries and on film. Jews being stripped naked and led to the slaughter, their houses being taken away from them and sometimes burned, their synagogues were burned. Ezekiel 16:39-42 says,

> *"I will also hand you over to your lovers, and they will tear down your shrines, demolish your high places, strip you of your clothing, take away your jewels, and will leave you naked and bare. They will incite a crowd against you, and they will stone you and cut you to pieces with their swords. And they will burn your houses with fire and execute judgments against you in the sight of many women. Then I will put an end to your prostitution, and you will also no longer pay your lovers. So I will satisfy My fury against you and My jealousy will leave you, and I will be pacified and no longer be angry." (NASB)*

God did all of this to bring them back to Him, and in Ezekiel 16:60, God says, "Nevertheless, I will remember My covenant with you in the days of your youth, and I will establish an everlasting covenant with you." (NASB) This is what God did for Israel. She was insignificant, and He made her significant. Now she will become insignificant again, until the fullness of the Gentiles is complete. He took his hand of protection away to bring her back to Him. Even today, God is positioning Israel for a final time of trouble, the time of Jacob's trouble, when their own strength will fail, and the only one who can save them is Jesus.

We must understand that God is love, but that is only one part of his character. In Romans 11:22, Paul talks about the severity of God. This is a difficult topic to write about, and when we consider its impact on real people's lives, it becomes even more challenging. It brings me no pleasure to write these words; I am just writing what the Scripture says. What is coming at the end of the age is going to be very hard for Jews, Christians, and non-Christians. The Jew will be put through the fire to be brought back to their Messiah, the Christian will be put through the fire to purify their faith, and the non-Christian will be judged. I recently heard Joel Richardson discuss the return of Christ. It is similar to the birth of a baby. You are not looking forward to the pain that the mother must endure in order to give birth to the child, but you look forward to the arrival of the child.

Was His hand strong against the people of Israel, who had become insignificant to Him for this period that is known as the fullness of Gentiles? His consideration of the Jewish people being insignificant and His hand being against them would certainly explain the past two thousand years of persecution. Think not of His hand being against them, but His hand of protection being removed from the Jewish people. In Zechariah 1:14-15, we read of the LORD's judgment against those nations that He had used to chastise Israel. We read that He brought judgment upon those nations because their treatment of Israel was too harsh. While God wanted to chastise Israel and bring nations against them to carry out the chastisement, once His hand of protection is removed from Israel, the punishment inflicted by these nations may be more severe than necessary. I am very unsure of this aspect of God's chastisement of Israel. How much is directed by God and how much is inflicted by the removal of God's hand of protection?

Zechariah 13:8 (NASB) "And it will come about in all the land," Declares the LORD, "That two parts in it will be cut off and perish; But the third will be left in it.

This would tie into verse 8, which says, "In the whole land, declares the LORD, two-thirds shall be cut off and perish, and one third shall be left alive." (ESV) It is one thing to read this and think dispassionately about it; it is quite another to think about the reality of what the Word is saying. Two-thirds of the nation of Israel will be killed in the war of Gog and Magog, the battle with the Antichrist. These people will die horrible deaths; many will be children and older adults who are just trying to stay out of the way of the war. It will be horrendous. The whole purpose of this chastisement is to bring the nation of Israel to recognize and worship Jesus, their Messiah! Deuteronomy 4:30-31 says,

"When you are in distress and all these things happen to you, in the latter days you will return to the LORD your God and listen to His voice. For the LORD your God is a compassionate God; He will not abandon you nor destroy you, nor forget the covenant with your fathers which He swore to them." (NASB)

The question that I am left asking is in Zechariah 13:8, "When does He say this will happen?" The Tree of Life Version begins the verse with "then it will happen." The term "then it will happen" originates from a single Hebrew word, which is translated as "to fall out, come to pass, become, or be." That doesn't really answer our question, but most commentators believe that this verse refers to the last days during the tribulation, based on verse 9.

Zechariah 13:9 (NASB) "And I will bring the third part through the fire, Refine them as silver is refined, And test them as gold is tested. They will call on My name, And I will answer them; I will say, 'They are My people,' And they will say, 'The LORD is my God.'"

We must use verse 9 to give us the timing of verse 8. As we saw in Chapter 12, the tribulation shall be so great that only the return of Jesus the Messiah will save the nation. Verse 9 tells us that God takes them through the fire, and that fire is what we see in verse 8. Two-thirds of the nation will die, and one-third will remain. Throughout the Scriptures, when you read of a remnant, this is that remnant. This is a difficult way to return to your God and finally recognize your Messiah. Israel is His betrothed, and He is doing what is necessary to bring His betrothed back to Himself so that they realize their Messiah, the One whom they rejected.

Zechariah 13:9 is very similar to Zechariah 8:8, which says, "they shall be My people, and I will be their God in truth and righteousness.'" It fits with Romans 11:25-27 which says, "For I do not want you, brothers and sisters, to be uninformed of this mystery—so that you will not be wise in your own estimation—that a partial hardening has happened to Israel until the fullness of the Gentiles has come in; and so all Israel will be saved; just as it is written:

"The Deliverer will come from Zion, He will remove ungodliness from Jacob." "This is My covenant with them, When I take away their sins." (NASB)

This all happens when the Deliver comes, the second coming of Jesus Christ. Zechariah 13:8-9 occurs during the Time of Jacob's Trouble and at the time of Jesus' return. After he saves the nation, He says, they are His people, and they will say, The LORD is my God.

Even in the revocation of the betrothal contract with Israel (Zechariah 11:10), God reveals His character. He has every reason in the world to revoke the contract, but instead, He comes back and forgives Israel. They are His bride, His chosen people, and even after all their whoring with other gods, He cannot forget His love for them. The wording in Zechariah 13:7 and Zechariah 11:10 indicates that God breaks the Mosaic Covenant with Israel, but He establishes a New Covenant with them. The Mosaic Covenant was conditional, and Israel failed to fulfill its part of the agreement. God has every right to break the betrothal contract made with Israel at Mt. Sinai. He says He is breaking it, but He gives them a New Covenant, and He comes back and marries the remnant of Israel and the Church. The Church has been grafted into Israel. It demonstrates His great love, faithfulness, and forgiveness. God is doing all of this to receive His bride and to stop her unfaithfulness.

The entire Bible tells the same story of how God created mankind and loves mankind. It is the story of how He takes one group of people from all the tribes and nations of the earth to use them to redeem humanity. His chosen people are to tell the rest of the world of Him and His goodness and love. He brought His Son to the earth through His chosen people to save the world, but they rejected Him, their Messiah; therefore, He went to the rest of the world. However, God is not done with His beloved bride, Israel; He will restore them to Himself. Verse 9 states that He will refine them like silver and gold through the fire. This will bring them to the point where they will call on Jesus, and He will be their God, and they will be His people.

He has another reason for saving Israel and restoring them to Himself, so that their enemies could not deny that Yahweh was God. Deuteronomy 32:26-27 says,

> "I would have said, "I will wipe them out, I will remove the mention of their name from humanity," Had I not feared the provocation by the enemy, That their adversaries would misjudge, That they would say, "Our hand is triumphant, And the LORD has not performed all this."' (NASB)

Not only does the LORD love His people, but He will not allow His name to be profaned by the unrighteous.

Zechariah 14
Jesus, King Over All

Remember that Zechariah did not put the chapter and verse separations in the book. That was done well after he wrote the book. I say this because the end of Zechariah 13 and the beginning of Zechariah 14 are the same message. It is a declaration and description of the chastisement and pain that Israel will experience to find their God and their Messiah. Daniel 12 tells us the same thing that we see in Zechariah 13 and 14, that Israel shall experience a great time of trouble. Daniel 12:1 says, "Now at that time Michael, the great prince who stands guard over the sons of your people, will arise. And there will be a time of distress such as never occurred since there was a nation until that time; and at that time your people, everyone who is found written in the book, will be rescued." (NASB) What we see in Zechariah 13 and 14 is a complete breaking of the power of the nation of Israel. For many years now, after defending themselves from their neighbors, Israel has been victorious in every war, so much so that they have begun to trust in their own strength.

Wikipedia lists eighteen wars that Israel has fought since they returned to the land and declared statehood after World War II. Three of those wars were major wars for the very survival of the nation. Israel is viewed as the power in the region, and it takes pride in being a mighty nation. But Daniel 12 tells us that their power will be shattered during the time of the Antichrist. Daniel 12:7 says, "And I heard the man dressed in linen, who was above the waters of the stream, as he raised his right hand and his left toward heaven, and swore by Him who lives forever that it would be for a time, times, and half a time; and as soon as they finish smashing the power of the holy people, all these events will be completed." (NASB) The good news here is that the shattering comes to an end, and all these things are finished. But why is this shattering necessary? Daniel 12:10 gives us the answer, "Many will be purged, cleansed, and refined, but the wicked will act wickedly; and none of the wicked will understand, but those who have insight will understand." (NASB) This coincides with what we read in Zechariah 13:9,

> "And I will bring the third part through the fire, Refine them as silver is refined, And test them as gold is tested. They will call on My name, And I will answer them; I will say, 'They are My people,' And they will say, 'The Lord is my God.'"

Chapter 14 begins by providing details on how Zechariah 13:8 is fulfilled.

> Zechariah 14:1-2 (NASB) Behold, a day is coming for the LORD when the spoils taken from you will be divided among you. 2 For I will gather all the nations against Jerusalem to battle, and the city will be taken, the houses plundered, the women raped, and half of the city exiled, but the rest of the people will not be eliminated from the city.

Thoughts On Zechariah

This is tough to read and imagine. Yes, the LORD is going to deliver His people, but reaching that point will be very tough for the people of Israel, and as we know from Revelation, it will be equally tough for the people of the whole Earth. Amos 5:18-20 tells us it will be like fleeing from a lion only to run straight into a bear. Zechariah 14:2 tells us that it is the LORD bringing the nations against Israel. Unfortunately, Israel has not recognized Jesus as their Messiah, and God is taking drastic measures to ensure that Israel looks to Jesus for their salvation. On October 7, 2023, one of the main attacks upon Israel occurred at a music festival in Southern Israel.

What were the young people dancing around, a statue of Buddha? Not only has Israel rejected their Messiah, but they are worshipping other gods. Please don't misunderstand, I am not saying that Israel deserved to be attacked, never! But God will have to take drastic action to bring His beloved to see Jesus as their Messiah, and to worship the only true God. I love Israel, and even as I write these words, it breaks my heart to know what will happen. I can't imagine what it is like to be Jewish and have people hate you just because you are Jewish, to rape your daughters and your wives, to humiliate them, just because they are Jewish. It is because they are the beloved of the LORD, and the enemy hates them for it.

Since the Holocaust, Israel's slogan is "Never Again," and they are relying on their own strength for their salvation. God is going to make it impossible for them to rely on any god other than the God of Abraham, Issac, and Jacob. He is going to make it impossible for them to see salvation in any other but in Jesus, their Messiah. Israel will be all but lost, the enemy will take their victory lap, and the first thing that we are told is that the enemy will be dividing the possessions of the Jewish people right in front of them. As we saw on October 7, 2023, the women are considered part of the spoil, and the soldiers use the women of the land at their pleasure. Women have the most to fear from an invading army that is victorious. Not only the women, but the children. Joel 3:2-3 says,

> *"I will gather all the nations And bring them down to the Valley of Jehoshaphat. Then I will enter into judgment with them there On behalf of My people and My inheritance, Israel, Whom they have scattered among the nations; And they have divided up My land. They have also cast lots for My people, Traded a boy for a prostitute, And sold a girl for wine so that they may drink." (NASB)*

On that day, the Jewish people will be defeated. There is nothing that they can do; the enemy is taking what they want. As Daniel 12:7 says, their power is shattered. It is broken so that the King of Kings can show them that He is their only salvation. At this point, the people feel helpless and in despair. The nation has been overrun, and everyone except half of Jerusalem has either been taken captive, killed, or is fleeing into the desert to a place prepared for them by God. I'm sure that those remaining would also be taken or destroyed, but this is when Jesus returns. Psalm 121:1-2 says,

"I will raise my eyes to the mountains; From where will my help come? My help comes from the LORD, Who made heaven and earth." (NASB)

Could this Psalm actually be speaking of the people raising their eyes to Mount Zion, looking for salvation from their Messiah?

Zechariah 14:3 (NASB) Then the LORD will go forth and fight against those nations, as when He fights on a day of battle.

I picture the vast majority of Israel is overrun, maybe all of it. Jerusalem has just been taken, and the only thing remaining for the victorious armies is to figure out what to do with the remaining people in Jerusalem. Zechariah 14:3 tells us, "Then the LORD will go forth and fight against those nations, as when He fights on a day of battle." (NASB) This is where Isaiah 63 and the other desert prophecies find their place. This is where the influence of Joel Richardson and his book, Sinia to Zion," helps us understand and see the other scriptures that reveal a Jesus who returns to Egypt and marches through the Sinai desert, freeing the Jewish captives as He marches to Jerusalem.

There is a 30-day discrepancy between Daniel 12:11, which states that Jesus returns after 1,290 days, and Revelation 11:3, which indicates that Jesus returns after 1,260 days. The counting of these days starts at the abomination of desolation, the desecration of the Temple. I believe that the 30-day difference is the time Jesus takes to march through the desert, freeing captives as He makes His way to Jerusalem. For the Church, we will be caught up together in the air with Jesus in 1260 days, and we will join Jesus in His march from Egypt through the Sinai to Jerusalem. For the nation of Israel, Jesus will deliver Jerusalem and stand on the Mount of Olives in 1290 days. Note that this is an educated guess as to why there is a discrepancy in the number of days between the two scriptures. I would like to take credit for this educated guess, but I was led to this thinking while listening to Frontier Alliance International's series on Daniel.

Then in Daniel 12:12 the Scripture says, "Blessed is the one who is patient and attains to the 1,335 days!" (NASB) Is this extra 45 days for the preparation for the Marriage Supper of the Lamb? Basically, the coronation of Jesus Christ as the King over the Earth! Daniel 12:12 says, "Blessed is the one who is patient," and Revelation 19:9 says, "Blessed are those who are invited to the marriage supper of the Lamb." I know that for those theologians who believe in a pre-tribulation rapture, they believe that the marriage supper of the Lamb occurs between the rapture and the second coming.

However, I believe that the rapture and the second coming are one event, and that Israel is an integral part of the bride of Christ and an essential part of the marriage supper of the Lamb. Therefore, the marriage supper of the Lamb cannot happen until Zechariah 14:3-4 occurs. Again, this is my opinion based on what I believe the scriptures are saying. You may argue that Revelation 19:1-10 occurs before Jesus returns in Revelation 19:11-21. However, when reading prophecy, not everything is chronological, especially Revelation. As we see here in Zechariah, the prophet writes about an event, then moves on to another, and finally returns with more detail about the first event.

> *Zechariah 14:4 (NASB) On that day His feet will stand on the Mount of Olives, which is in front of Jerusalem on the east; and the Mount of Olives will be split in its middle from east to west forming a very large valley. Half of the mountain will move toward the north, and the other half toward the south.*

Verse 3 reveals that Jesus will fight against those nations that are coming against Israel. People commonly misconstrue verse 4 as saying that when Jesus returns, He will touch down on the Mount of Olives. However, the Scripture doesn't specifically say that; it says, "On that day His feet will stand on the Mount of Olives." (NASB) Part of the reason that we believe that Jesus is going to return directly to the Mount of Olives is because of Acts 1:11. Two angels tell the disciples, "Men of Galilee, why do you stand looking into the sky? This Jesus, who has been taken up from you into heaven, will come in the same way as you have watched Him go into heaven." (NASB) Since Jesus departed the world from the Mount of Olives, we combine Zechariah 14:4 and Acts 1:11 to assume that He will come down directly from the Mount of Olives when He returns during His second coming. However, Zechariah 14:4 says His feet will "stand", as in He will stand firm.

However, it doesn't just say that He will stand, but when he stands, He will split the mountain in two and form a vast valley between the two halves of the mountain. One half of the mountain will move north, and one half of the mountain will move south. Therefore, the valley will run east-west. Based on what we see and read in this passage, this marks the beginning of the battle for Jerusalem, and the splitting of the Mount of Olives is a sign that Jesus is making a way for the people to escape to safety from a city under enemy control. In my mind, I picture Jesus making his march through the desert, releasing captives as He goes (Deuteronomy 33:1-5; Isaiah 34 & 35; Habakkuk 3; Psalm 68; Isaiah 42; and Isaiah 63), and as He approaches Jerusalem from the east he makes the mountain split as a way of escape for the people of Jerusalem to flee through this valley that He created. He does this before He begins the destruction of the armies of the Antichrist, so the people of Jerusalem will not be caught in the destruction. I believe that this event precedes the large earthquake that will change the topography of Jerusalem and the country. Perhaps He uses the first earthquake to split the mountain, and larger or more earthquakes will follow. We read about an earthquake or a series of earthquakes in Zechariah 14:10, Ezekiel 38:18-19, and Revelation 16:18.

> *Zechariah 14:5 (NASB) And you will flee by the valley of My mountains, for the valley of the mountains will reach to Azel; yes, you will flee just as you fled from the earthquake in the days of Uzziah king of Judah. Then the LORD, my God, will come, and all the holy ones with Him!*

Verse 5 tells us that the people "will flee by the valley of My mountains, for the valley of the mountains will reach to Azel". Concerning the location of Azal, Wikipedia tells us, "In the late 19th century, Cyril of Alexandria stated that Azal was known to be "a town situated at the far point of the mountain". In 1850, geographer Rabbi Schwarz claimed that Azal was modern Azaria, half a mile southeast of the southern most peak of the Mount of Olives. The New Unger's Bible Dictionary states that Azal is "A place, evidently in the neighborhood of Jerusalem and probably east of the Mount of Olives." The point is that Jesus created an escape route for the residents of Jerusalem to retreat behind Him and out of the frontline of the battle.

Jerusalem is about to come under heavy shaking from earthquakes, hail, rain, wind, and every other natural and unnatural phenomenon that the LORD has at His command. Zechariah is picturing this as a similar event that must have been well-known by Jewish people. Zechariah tells us that an earthquake occurred in Jerusalem during the reign of Uzziah, King of Judah. Amos 1:1 confirms that an earthquake happened during the days of Uzziah. This gives us the picture of an earthquake that Jesus uses to split the mountain, providing the Jewish people with a path of escape. Possibly, the earthquake triggers their memory of Zechariah 14:5, and they know then to flee toward the Mount of Olives and into this valley to make their escape to Azel. Or perhaps it is this larger-than-life Jesus standing on the Mount of Olives that encourages them to flee through the valley. Joel 2:32 says,

"And it will come about that everyone who calls on the name of the LORD Will be saved; For on Mount Zion and in Jerusalem There will be those who escape, Just as the LORD has said, Even among the survivors whom the LORD calls." (NASB)

Amen, amen, and amen!!!!!

To bring us to this point in Zechariah, what has taken place? Before the war of Gog and Magog, the Antichrist will go to war with some of Israel's neighbors, principally those nations that were part of the Ptolemaic Kingdom, Egypt, Jordon, and Saudi Arabia, and subdues these nations so that several of these nations are part of the confederation against Israel (Daniel 11:21-45). These nations are known in Daniel as the Kings of the South. In the early part of this war, Israel is left out of the war due to the treaty that they have with the Antichrist. At the midway point of the tribulation, the Antichrist breaks the treaty and commits the abomination of desolation and invades Israel from the north and the south. The forces of Israel experience attrition, and they continue to lose ground.

Eventually, they even lose Jerusalem. I believe that Jesus shows up just as they lose all of Jerusalem. During this war, those Jews who are not killed, or who have not fled to refuge, are placed into concentration-type camps in the desert of Southern Israel and the Sinai. Women, girls, and boys are sold and traded as sex slaves. This is a dire situation, and Israel believes that they are lost; only the Messiah can save them now! Jesus appears, and He leads a march from Egypt through the Sinai, freeing captives as He goes. Some scriptures indicate it is a march, while others say he rides on the clouds, and still others refer to Him riding a chariot/throne. I believe that it could be all three, or some of it could be imagery. He recreates the Exodus scenario, with the Church and His holy angels following Him. Deuteronomy 33 tells us He comes with ten thousand of His holy ones with flaming fire at His right hand.

If we stitch together many of the passages that speak to his march from Egypt through Sinai and the desert south of Jerusalem, we see a picture of what his march to Jerusalem will look like. Just His appearance alone will be scary to the forces of the Antichrist. Revelation 1:13-16 tells us what Jesus looks like. He appears in the form of a man, wearing a long, white robe with a golden sash around His chest. His robe will be white until He begins to defeat His enemies, then it will be stained with the blood of His enemies. The hair of His head is white like wool and snow, His eyes are like a flame of fire, and His feet are like burnished bronze. His face is shining like the sun. His voice is like many waters, strong, deep, and authoritative, and with His voice, He defeats His enemies by just speaking their destruction.

Psalm 68 tells us that the enemy will flee before Him, be blown away like smoke, and melt like wax melts before the fire. Psalm 68 also tells us that the Earth will quake and there will be a downpour of rain in abundance. He leads the prisoners out of the wilderness, and the women sing His praises and divide the spoils. The dogs will lick the blood of God's enemies. Isaiah 34 describes the massive destruction that the LORD shall produce. The mountains will flow with the blood of His enemies. Most likely, all the rain will mix with the blood, resulting in a watery blood mixture. The stench of their corpses will rise as they rot. Isaiah 34:5-7 gives the picture of a total slaughter with the LORD's sword filled with blood and fat. It provides the picture of the total slaughter of His enemies as he works His way from the south, Edom and Bozrah (verses 5 and 6) to Jerusalem. Isaiah 34:9-10 reveals that the LORD will use fire and brimstone, as it says,

> *"Its (Edom's) streams will be turned into pitch, And its loose Earth into brimstone, And its land will become burning pitch. It will not be extinguished night or day; Its smoke will go up forever. From generation to generation it will be desolate; None will pass through it forever and ever." (NASB)*

It also appears that Edom shall be an abode for animals going forward. Isaiah 63 tells us that the LORD is coming from Edom and Bozrah, and that He is splendid in His appearance, mighty to save! His garments are red, splattered with the blood of His enemies. He pours the lifeblood of His enemies on the Earth. Habakkuk 3 tells us that God comes from Teman and Mount Paran, which is likely a reference to the Sinai Peninsula. His radiance is like sunlight, and lightning flashes from His hands. Before Him and after Him are plagues. He causes the whole Earth to shudder. The mountains saw Him and quaked, the downpour of waters swept by, and the sun and the moon stood in their place.

He marched through the whole Earth in fury. He thrashed the nations in anger. He will use every element of nature at His disposal to defeat the army of the Antichrist. The days will be both terrible for the enemy and glorious for the Church and Israel. Swirling around Him will be dark storm clouds with lightning and thunder, hail, and torrential rain. Going before him will be pestilence and sickness, most likely from the seven years of famine and death that preceded His return. Not forgetting that Isaiah 34 tells us he will also use fire and brimstone. It will be like a Marvel comic book or movie where the hero can use all of nature at their will.

There is so much Scripture discussing this event that I feel like I am drinking from a firehose, and my writing is all jumbled. I am in awe reading these scriptures. It is as if the LORD took all these prophets and showed them the same event from different angles, as if different news crews were at various locations filming the same event. What is clear from Scripture is that God will gather the nations against Israel (Zechariah 14:2, Joel 3:2, and Revelation 16:12-16) to both judge the nations and bring Israel back to their God and their Messiah. Revelation 16 tells us the enemy is gathered at a place called Armageddon.

The best estimate is that Armageddon refers to the hill country surrounding the plain of Megiddo, which is approximately 60 miles north of Jerusalem. Joel 3:2 tells us that the Lord is bringing the nations down to the Valley of Jehoshaphat, situated between Jerusalem and the Mount of

Olives. These passages refer to the same event, where the army of the Antichrist will have captured Jerusalem, and they will cover the land like locusts, stretching from Jerusalem northward through the plains of Megiddo, where armies have battled many times in antiquity. Most likely, as the survivors of Jerusalem escape through the valley created by the splitting of the Mount of Olives, the army of the Antichrist moves to block their escape. However, Jesus will not allow the enemy to stop the escape of the Jewish people to Azel.

We read that the LORD gathers the army of the Antichrist for destruction, and we read of their destruction, Habakkuk 3; Joel 3; and Revelation 19:11-21. In Joel 3, the LORD mocks His enemy as being too weak. It is even more than that. He gathers the nations to bring their best against His people, Israel, so that He can once again show Israel that there is no other god but ADONAI in all of creation. He tells us in Habakkuk that He crushes the head of the house of the wicked, laying him bare from thigh to neck. This is a reference to Genesis 3:15, where the LORD says He will crush the head of the serpent. In Revelation 19, He gathers the birds to this place to eat the flesh of kings, captains, mighty men, horses, and their riders. Revelation 14:20 says the carnage shall be so great that the blood will be as high as the horse's bridle (5 or 6 feet) for 180 miles. That would certainly be enough to cover the distance from the Valley of Jehoshaphat back through the plain of Megiddo. It will most likely be a mixture of blood and water from the torrential rains that God brings. The LORD is destroying His enemies and saving Israel in such a mighty way that they will never again worship another god.

Zechariah 14:6 (NASB) On that day there will be no light; the luminaries will die out.

One must read Zechariah 14:6 in the NASB to get closer to the original intent of the verse. The Tree of Life version and the ESV bring cold and frost into the passage, which, in my mind, confuses what the passage is trying to say. When you read the NASB, the passage fits very nicely into other passages that speak of this event. Once again, the Word of God is amazing. We can refer to Joel 3:15, Isaiah 13:10, Matthew 24:29, and Revelation 6:12 to gain more detail and understand what is happening in Zechariah 14:6.

I'm struggling to proceed because these passages, and not just the verses, but each of these chapters tells the same story from a slightly different perspective, watching the event. This is the day of the LORD, He is in all His glory, a refuge to Christians and Jews, a terror to his enemies and sinners. This will be a terrible day; even those who have been waiting on the LORD will feel the terror of the LORD and will fully understand His unlimited power and might. The horrifying events of that time, and in particular that day, will leave no doubt in the believers' minds that God is God, and we are not. We are the creation, and He is the Creator. Although in the process of being saved from the forces of evil, this day will put fear in the hearts of all men, including believers. It will teach us what it is to fear the LORD. It doesn't mean we walk around afraid of Him, because He is also loving and kind, but we understand His ultimate power over everything.

Picture this: the Earth has gone dark, with no sun, no moon, and no stars to provide even a little bit of light. All of nature is attacking mankind: torrential rain, hail, winds, earthquakes, plagues, wild animals, and even fire and brimstone. In the midst of this darkness, there is light coming from Jesus Christ as He rides across the sky and arrives in Jerusalem. His very being is light, just as He was in the cloud of fire by night that led Israel through the desert and out of Egypt. From his hands come lightning, and His voice is like thunder. Isaiah 13:6-8 tells us,

> *"Wail, for the day of the LORD is near! It will come as destruction from the Almighty. Therefore all hands will fall limp, And every human heart will melt. They will be terrified, Pains and anguish will take hold of them; They will writhe like a woman in labor, They will look at one another in astonishment, Their faces aflame." (NASB)*

Revelation 6:15-17 says.
> *"Then the kings of the earth and the eminent people, and the commanders and the wealthy and the strong, and every slave and free person hid themselves in the caves and among the rocks of the mountains; and they said to the mountains and the rocks, "Fall on us and hide us from the sight of Him who sits on the throne, and from the wrath of the Lamb; for the great day of Their wrath has come, and who is able to stand?" (NASB)*

I am trying to convey what a terrible yet glorious day that will be. I am particularly captivated by Isaiah 13. Isaiah 13 leaves no doubt that God's judgment has come. The patience of God has run out, and the love for His people demands justice for them now. No longer will the Jew wonder where ADONAI is when they need salvation, no longer will the Christian wonder how long the LORD will let evil triumph over the righteous. This is the day of reckoning, and all accounts will be tallied and settled. Quoting Isaiah 13 seems appropriate, as it is the passage that most conveys how terrible that day shall be. Zechariah tells us about how terrible this time will be for Israel, but Isaiah tells us how terrible this time will be for the enemies of Israel and the enemies of God. I will pick up in Isaiah 13:9 to reveal God's judgment on those who have rejected Him, fought against Him, and fought against Israel. Isaiah 13:9-13 says,

> *"Behold, the day of the LORD is coming, Cruel, with fury and burning anger, To make the land a desolation; And He will exterminate its sinners from it. For the stars of heaven and their constellations Will not flash their light; The sun will be dark when it rises And the moon will not shed its light. So I will punish the world for its evil And the wicked for their wrongdoing; I will also put an end to the audacity of the proud And humiliate the arrogance of the tyrants. I will make mortal man scarcer than pure gold And mankind than the gold of Ophir. Therefore I will make the heavens tremble, And the Earth will be shaken from its place At the fury of the LORD of armies In the day of His burning anger."*

The patience of the LORD will be at an end, and He will punish those who have not turned to Him for forgiveness of sin. It will be a terrible day for all of mankind, friend and foe alike. If you are on God's side, this day will bring justice and peace, but you will see the power that resides in our God.

This brings us back to Zechariah 14:6, where there will be no light; the luminaries of the sky will cease to exist. We see this event mentioned in numerous passages of the Bible. Jesus tells us in Matthew 24:29-30 that this will be the sign right before the coming of the Son of Man. The darkening of the world and the great earthquake will trumpet His coming. There will also be a sign appearing in the sky. Matthew 24:29-30 says, "But immediately after the tribulation of those days THE SUN WILL BE DARKENED, AND THE MOON WILL NOT GIVE ITS LIGHT, AND THE STARS WILL FALL from the sky, and the powers of the heavens will be shaken. And then the sign of the Son of Man will appear in the sky, and then all the tribes of the Earth will mourn, and they will see the Son of Man coming on the clouds of the sky with power and great glory." (NASB)

I love how the Bible tells the same story repeatedly. When Jesus comes back, He will be literally the "Light of the World." Joel Richardson and Stephen Holmes believe it will be Jesus, appearing as the pillar of cloud by day and fire by night. How spectacular that will be! It will be Jesus giving His light to the pillar of fire by night.

Zechariah 14:7-8 says,

Zechariah 14:7-8 (NASB) For it will be a unique day which is known to the LORD, neither day nor night, but it will come about that at the time of evening there will be light. 8 And on that day living waters will flow out of Jerusalem, half of them toward the eastern sea and the other half toward the western sea; it will be in summer as well as in winter.

Zechariah 14:8 brings us back to the living waters. I wrote extensively about these living waters that will flow out of Jerusalem in Chapter 13. They will originate from the Temple, from the Throne of Christ, and they will flow east and west. I believe that these waters will initially be for the ceremonial cleansing of the people as they come to Jesus and recognize Him as their Messiah and their Savior. Additionally, these living waters will heal everything they come into contact with: the water, the land, and the people.

If people were injured during the tribulation or had a chronic condition or disease, as they fulfill their ceremonial cleansing, they will also be healed. Ezekiel 47:9 states that everything will live and be healed wherever the river flows. Ezekiel 47:12 says every kind of tree will grow beside the river, and its fruit will be for food and its leaf for healing. This will be a very special river, coming from the throne of God here on Earth in the Temple, the Holy of Holies. There will be much healing needed as this Earth will have undergone extreme destruction over the past seven years. As I read about the river and the land next to the river, I can't help but think of the Garden of Eden. If you read Randy Alcorn's book "Heaven," you will be convinced that Jesus intends to restore this Earth to its original designed perfection. The whole Earth will be restored and renewed to its original design, except for several nations mentioned in the following few paragraphs.

God even puts a river of living water in the New Heaven and the New Earth. Revelation 22:1-5 tells us that on either side of the river was a tree of life, and its leaves were used for the healing of the nations.

> *Zechariah 14:9 (NASB) And the LORD will be King over all the Earth; on that day the LORD will be the only one, and His name the only one.*

Zechariah 14:9 leaves no doubt as to the purpose of everything that has happened to bring us to the "Day of the LORD". Zechariah 14:9 says, "And the LORD will be King over all the earth; on that day the LORD will be the only one, and His name the only one." There will be no other gods to try and take His glory; He will destroy them and condemn them all to the pit of hell. Genesis 3:15 tells us that Jesus will crush the head of the serpent, and Habakkuk 3:13-14 says,

> *"You went forth for the salvation of Your people, For the salvation of Your anointed. You smashed the head of the house of evil To uncover him from foot to neck. Selah You pierced with his own arrows The head of his leaders. They stormed in to scatter us; Their arrogance was like those Who devour the oppressed in secret." (NASB)*

No one and no god shall stand before Him. Revelation 20:1-3 tells us that Satan will be bound for 1,000 years, and Revelation 20:7-10 tells us that Satan will be condemned to the lake of fire forever and ever. Satan will be released for a short time after the Millennium, and he will engineer another rebellion, but it will be quickly put down. The point of this rebellion is to demonstrate the wickedness of the heart of man, that even when everything is perfect and Christ is ruling, some of those who live during the Millennium will still have rebellion in their heart. Until you give your all to Christ, you are in rebellion against Him. The point Zechariah makes in verse 9 is that Jesus will rule, and there will be no other gods.

Zechariah is making another point. He is telling us that at this time, the Jewish people will recognize that Jesus and the Father are one! When Jesus was walking on the Earth, he would often say, "I am" and equate himself with the Father, and when He said, "I am", the Jews typically tried to stone Him (John 8:21-59; John 10:22-39). We struggle with understanding the Trinity. Likewise, the Jews could not understand the Trinity, and for them, there was only the Father. Zechariah is saying that on that Day, they will come to understand that Jesus, the Father, and the Holy Spirit are one. Jesus is God!

> Zechariah 14:10 (NASB) All the land will change into a plain from Geba to Rimmon south of Jerusalem; but Jerusalem will rise and remain on its site from Benjamin's Gate as far as the place of the First Gate to the Corner Gate, and from the Tower of Hananel to the King's wine presses.

Zechariah 14:10 does not explicitly state that there will be a great earthquake, but it does describe the result of a great or many great earthquakes. Several passages talk about the darkening of the celestial lights, and each of those passages also contains news of a great trembling of the Earth, or earthquake. Isaiah 13:13 says,

> *"Therefore I will make the heavens tremble, And the earth will be shaken from its place At the fury of the LORD of armies In the day of His burning anger." (NASB)*

Ezekiel 38:19-20 says, "In My zeal and in My blazing wrath I declare that on that day there will certainly be a great earthquake in the land of Israel. The fish of the sea, the birds of the sky, the animals of the field, all the crawling things that crawl on the Earth, and all mankind who are on the face of the Earth will shake at My presence; and the mountains will be thrown down, the steep pathways will collapse, and every wall will fall to the ground." (NASB) In Zechariah 14:10 we see this great earthquake with a few simple words, "All the land will change into a plain from Geba to Rimmon south of Jerusalem; but Jerusalem will rise and remain on its site from Benjamin's Gate as far as the place of the First Gate to the Corner Gate, and from the Tower of Hananel to the king's wine presses." (NASB) While everything else is being flattened, Jerusalem will rise.

The name of the city of Jerusalem is prophetic. Through its name, God is telling us what will happen with Jerusalem. Jeru means "The LORD loosens, God will lift up, Yah (God) exalts". Salem means "Peace". Jerusalem means, "The LORD will lift up the city and it shall be a city of peace", Ken's version. God raises Jerusalem to a place where the whole world will look up to it as the capital of the world, both literally and metaphorically.

> *Zechariah 14:10-11 (NASB) All the land will change into a plain from Geba to Rimmon south of Jerusalem; but Jerusalem will rise and remain on its site from Benjamin's Gate as far as the place of the First Gate to the Corner Gate, and from the Tower of Hananel to the King's wine presses. 11 People will live in it, and there will no longer be a curse, for Jerusalem will live in security.*

Zechariah 14:10-11 tells us that Jerusalem shall be raised and shall forever dwell in safety. On that day, all around Jerusalem shall become a plain, but Jerusalem itself shall be lifted. Amazing! Jerusalem is the apple of God's eye and shall be the place of His throne forever. As I was going through Zechariah, several months before I reached chapters 13 and 14, I became curious about the meaning of the name Jerusalem. I looked it up and it was interesting. I wrote it down, but I didn't understand the reason behind the name. Working through Zechariah 13:1 led me to Zechariah 14:8, which led me to verses 10 and 11. Suddenly, as you read Zechariah 14:10-11, you understand that the name Jerusalem has been prophetic since its origination. With the raising of Jerusalem, we also understand how the water will flow from the Temple both east and west, as it will naturally flow downhill. This is what it meant to find nuggets of gold in the WORD of God. Understanding these prophecies is gold; seeing them all connect is gold. It is also very heavy, understanding that we are living in the days when these things will occur.

Verse 11 tells us that the people living in Jerusalem will live in security and that there will no longer be a curse on the city. Never again will there be a decree of utter destruction for Jerusalem. Throughout history, Jerusalem has always been a target of destruction because it is the capital of the nation. If foreign kings want to conquer Judah, they must conquer Jerusalem. Jerusalem was a symbol of power for the people and for the King. If the LORD wanted to discipline the people with exile, Jerusalem would be invaded and destroyed by the invaders. Never again will Jerusalem be destroyed; Jerusalem will be inhabited by Jesus, the Messiah, and will be protected forever! Never again will the people inhabiting Jerusalem transgress the laws of the LORD and require the discipline of the LORD. Going forward, this shall be God's city, and His throne will dwell there in the Temple!

Zechariah 14:12 (NASB) Now this will be the plague with which the LORD will strike all the peoples who have gone to war against Jerusalem; their flesh will rot while they stand on their feet, and their eyes will rot in their sockets, and their tongue will rot in their mouth.

Verse 12 tells us of a great plague that shall consume the invaders of Israel. As I read the text, it is unclear whether the plague will be limited to the invading army or will also be inflicted upon the people in the countries from which the invaders came. When I read verse 12, my first thought was of atomic weapons that will cause some bodies to vaporize instantly and others to suffer radiation poisoning and just rot away. However, I began to think about the COVID-19 pandemic of 2020 and how quickly the virus spread globally. I believe that COVID was the result of governments developing biological weapons, and it escaped the lab. This plague could be the result of biological weapons used on the battlefield, or it could be the result of the circumstances of death and decay spreading via fleas or other insects on the battlefield.

I looked up "Plagues that cause people's flesh to rot" on Google and found two interesting candidates right away. The Bubonic Plague causes people's flesh to rot, and it is transmitted by fleas that carry the bacteria and bite humans. With all of the dead on the battlefield, there will be plenty of bacteria and pests to spread such a disease. Another possibility is necrotizing fasciitis, commonly referred to as "flesh-eating bacteria." Typically, water helps the bacteria take hold, and as I mentioned earlier, I believe that there will be significant rainfall and flooding, resulting in many dead bodies in the water. These are just two candidates of natural causes, or it could be that God supernaturally sends a plague upon the invading armies and people.

Another point to note is that it appears to infect only the invading armies and possibly the people in the homeland of the invading armies. This, in and of itself, will be a supernatural event. When the 2020 pandemic struck, no one was immune; the virus spread worldwide, affecting both the rich and the poor. For this plague to only touch the people of the invading armies will be due to the hand of God. It will be like the first Passover, when the death angel did not touch the homes with doors marked by the blood, but the homes that did not have the doorposts marked by blood had the firstborn die. God will supernaturally protect Israel from this plague. It will only affect the people who have attacked Jerusalem.

> *Zechariah 14:13-14 (NASB) And it will come about on that day that a great panic from the LORD will fall on them; and they will seize one another's hand, and the hand of one will be raised against the hand of another. 14 Judah also will fight at Jerusalem; and the wealth of all the surrounding nations will be gathered, gold, silver, and garments in great abundance.*

As we see in verses 13 and 14, fighting continues to occur. Therefore, not all of the invading army has been incapacitated by this plague. Skipping over verses 13 and 14 for just a moment, verse 15 tells us that this plague will not just infect the people of the invading armies but will also affect the livestock of the invading armies.

> *Zechariah 14:15 (NASB) And just like this plague, there will be a plague on the horse, the mule, the camel, the donkey, and all the cattle that will be in those camps.*

In the Old Testament, we see that when people set themselves against God and led the nation of Israel astray, God not only commanded that the offenders be put to death, but that their property, including livestock, be put to death (Deuteronomy 13:15; Numbers 16:31-33; and 1 Samuel 15:1-3). God is affecting their livestock, possibly obstructing their ability to wage war or diminishing their food supply. We know that animals and people are not affected by the same diseases. As with COVID, the virus had to be manufactured to transfer from bats to people. What certainly seems like the same plague will infect the animals in the camps of the enemies of God. This could be the result of God's supernatural doing, or it could be the result of man's attempt at biological warfare. It could also be the result of nuclear weapons. Verse 14 tells us that the IDF will still be involved in this fight. Therefore, it is possible it could be nuclear weapons; however, only God knows how this will happen. I leave all possibilities open because I believe that God will cause supernatural events to occur, as well as permit the natural consequences of human actions to affect the world. The supernatural will happen, but so will the natural.

In Zechariah 14:13, we see a tactic that the Lord has used frequently in the defense of Israel. He causes confusion and fear among the forces of the Antichrist, and they begin to fight and kill one another. They panic because they do not quite understand what is happening, they don't know where the enemy is coming from, and the fear is so great that they see the enemy everywhere. We see this happen in multiple places in the Old Testament, particularly with Gideon (Judges 7:19-22), when the King of Syria (Aram) wanted to capture Elisha and laid siege to Samaria (2 Kings 7:3-8), and with Jehoshaphat against the Moabites and Ammonites (2 Chronicles 20:20-25).

The LORD uses the human frailty of our minds against His enemies. Our minds play a crucial role in directing our behavior. In the end times, we see that the Word of God warns us of a great deception coming and to be on guard. The LORD uses the mind of the enemy to throw them into panic to help defeat them. The fear will be so great that the armies of the Antichrist and his people will turn on each other. You have darkness, extreme weather, armies rising when you thought you had defeated Israel, a powerful figure who himself exudes light, and a plague that has infected the army. I don't think my mind can comprehend all that the enemies of God will encounter during this time. An army that was on the cusp of victory suddenly stopped in its tracks and was killed in a myriad of ways, from which it seems there is no defense and no place to hide.

The idea of verse 14 appears to be that part of the IDF has been cut off from helping Jerusalem, and now, with the leadership of Jesus Christ against the enemies of God and His people, the IDF is able to consolidate its forces and join in the fight to destroy the enemy. Very possibly, it is those members of the IDF who had been captured and whom Jesus released on His march through the desert on His way to Jerusalem.

The other event that we see in verse 14 is the reversal of the taking of plunder. Zechariah 14:1-2 tells us that the invaders will take plunder from the people of Israel. With the return of Jesus Christ, the tables have been turned, and the invaders have been defeated. Now it is Israel's turn to take plunder, to take what was taken from them and to take what did not belong to them originally. I wrote about verse 15, saying that in the past, there were instances where God commanded all the property of the enemy to be destroyed.

That is not the case here. Yes, God affected the livestock of the enemy, but God will allow Israel to take the spoils of war. At this point, the land of Israel will be ravaged, much like we see in the photos of Germany after WW II or what we see today in pictures from Gaza. Israel just barely survived this war, and they have very little left of their country; it is damaged beyond belief. The nation and the people will need this plunder to replenish their possessions. Verse 14 says,

> *"and the wealth of all the surrounding nations will be gathered, gold, silver, and garments in great abundance." (NASB)*

In verses 16 through 19, we see that there will be those from nations that fought against Israel and the LORD who live through the great judgment of the LORD.

> *Zechariah 14:16-19 (NASB) Then it will come about that any who are left of all the nations that came against Jerusalem will go up from year to year to worship the King, the LORD of armies, and to celebrate the Feast of Booths. 17 And it will be that whichever of the families of the Earth does not go up to Jerusalem to worship the King, the LORD of armies, there will be no rain on them. 18 And if the family of Egypt does not go up or enter, then no rain will fall on them; it will be the plague with which the LORD strikes the nations that do not go up to celebrate the Feast of Booths. 19 This will be the punishment of Egypt, and the punishment of all the nations that do not go up to celebrate the Feast of Booths.*

These people, for some reason, did not take the mark of the beast and were able to survive this time without being discovered and killed. We know from Revelation 14:9-11 that those who take the mark of the beast will be doomed to hell. Therefore, those who live through this time and enter the Millennial Kingdom will not take the mark of the beast. Those nations that will fight against Israel are the nations that will be aligned with the Antichrist, but there will also be nations that will not fight against Israel, and there will be people from those nations that survive the Tribulation. All survivors who do not take the mark of the beast will enter the Millennial Kingdom. That does not mean that they will all be devoted to Jesus Christ. Not all who enter the Kingdom of God will bow their heart to Jesus Christ, but they will bow their knee. I don't know how significant this number will be at the beginning of the Millennial Kingdom, but we know that at the end of the Millennium, it will be large enough to wage war against the Messiah (Revelation 20:7-10). Most will see the glory of the LORD and will believe, but some will submit only because they know they must.

Zechariah 14:16-19 says, "Then it will come about that any who are left of all the nations that came against Jerusalem will go up from year to year to worship the King, the LORD of armies, and to celebrate the Feast of Booths. And it will be that whichever of the families of the Earth does not go up to Jerusalem to worship the King, the LORD of armies, there will be no rain on them. And if the family of Egypt does not go up or enter, then no rain will fall on them; it will be the plague with which the LORD strikes the nations that do not go up to celebrate the Feast of Booths. This will be the punishment of Egypt, and the punishment of all the nations that do not go up to celebrate the Feast of Booths."

Those who put their faith in Jesus Christ before He returns will be caught up with Him in the air, will receive incorruptible bodies, and will rule and reign with Jesus during the time of the Millennial Kingdom. All people who enter the Millennial Kingdom with their corruptible bodies will be those who did not accept Jesus Christ as their Savior before His return. When Jesus returns, the entire Jewish people will recognize that He is their Messiah and God, and they will give their hearts to Him. All Gentiles entering the Millennial Kingdom will have to come to that same conclusion. However, there will be those whose hearts are not truly devoted to the LORD, and although they shall want to return to the worship of their previous gods, they will hide their belief in their gods to avoid judgment. Yes, the LORD will know, but He is patient and desiring all to repent. Jesus will allow this to show us that the cause of our sin is not Satan but our own wicked hearts. Jeremiah 17:9 says

> *"The heart is more deceitful than all else And is desperately sick; Who can understand it?" (NASB)*

After 1,000 years of the reign of Jesus Christ, when the world has lived in a state of utopia, there will still be people who rebel against His rule.

I find a similarity in the time of the Millennial Kingdom and the way that God treated the nation of Israel during the Old Testament. If they obeyed, they would be blessed, but if they did not obey, they would suffer chastisement. During the Millennium, if the nations do not go up to Jerusalem annually for the Feast of the Booths to worship Jesus, they will not receive the rain they need to grow their crops. Egypt is specifically pointed out in verses 18 and 19. This appears to be a strange singling out of Egypt in Zechariah 14:18, which says, "And if the family of Egypt does not go up or enter, then no rain will fall on them; it will be the plague with which the Lord strikes the nations that do not go up to celebrate the Feast of Booths." (NASB)

I found it odd that God would specifically name Egypt. Ezekiel 29:12-16 says,

> "So I will make the land of Egypt a desolation in the midst of deserted lands. And her cities, in the midst of cities that are laid waste, will be desolate for forty years; and I will scatter the Egyptians among the nations and disperse them among the lands." 'For this is what the LORD God says: "At the end of forty years I will gather the Egyptians from the peoples among whom they were scattered. And I will restore the fortunes of Egypt and bring them back to the land of Pathros, to the land of their origin, and there they will be a lowly kingdom. It will be the lowest of the kingdoms, and it will not raise itself above the nations again. And I will make them small so that they will not rule over the nations. And it will no longer be a kingdom on which the house of Israel relies, bringing to mind the guilt of their having turned to Egypt. Then they will know that I am the LORD GOD."'" (NASB)

Thoughts On Zechariah

Egypt is singled out because Israel looked to them for their salvation on multiple occasions instead of looking to God for their deliverance. While Israel is blessed beyond measure, some nations and lands will feel the judgment of the LORD. Consider what the Scripture says about Babylon and Edom. We see in Joel 3:19 and Isaiah 34 that Edom shall forever be a place of desolation, and it will not be fit for people to live there. We see a similar fate for Babylon. Isaiah 13:19-22 and Jeremiah 50-51 tell us that Babylon will not be inhabited by people again and that God will judge Babylon. While Israel enjoys the favor of the LORD during the Millennium, some countries and lands will feel the judgment of the LORD. Other lands that were destroyed in the war of Gog and Magog will be restored; Israel, Assyria, and Jordan are specifically mentioned. Egypt has even recovered after a period of time.

Zechariah 14:16-19 and the other passages mentioned above reveal that Jesus Christ will rule with a rod of iron and the believers who died before the second coming or were raptured at the second coming will rule with Him (Revelation 2:27; 12:5; and 19:15). Most of the time Christians believe that after the second coming everything will be idyllic, but if everything is idyllic why does Jesus need to rule with a rod of iron? Because the kings of the Earth have not entirely given their hearts to him. They are kings who have been defeated and must give their allegiance to the victorious King, or else they will suffer chastisement. Therefore, some will bide their time and provide false allegiance. There will be death during the Millennium; the first of the rebellious will pass away, but some born during the Millennium will not devote their heart to the LORD. I believe Psalm 2 is a prophetic Psalm that talks about this time during the Millennium. Read Psalm 2 with the understanding that the nations have been subdued by force and Jesus is ruling them with a rod of iron from Jerusalem. God is warning them in Psalm 2. Psalm 2:10-12 says,

> *"Now then, you kings, use insight; Let yourselves be instructed, you judges of the Earth. Serve the LORD with reverence And rejoice with trembling. Kiss the Son, that He not be angry and you perish on the way, For His wrath may be kindled quickly. How blessed are all who take refuge in Him!" (NASB)*

Jesus displays His power, and having shown the world that He is the Creator and King, He will have no patience for rebellion. We know from Revelation 20:7-10 that Satan will be loosed, and He will lead those who have not given their devotion to Jesus Christ in a revolt against the King of kings. In the end, it is a vain attempt at rebellion, for the entire rebellion shall come against and surround Jerusalem, and there they will be consumed by fire (Revelation 20:7-10).

Revelation 21-22 reveals that this period of the Millennial Kingdom is a time of testing for those who have lived through the tribulation. Even with Jesus here to rule on this Earth, some are not entirely devoted to Him, and they have this time to choose Jesus. How do they miss the fact that He is the Creator and LORD of all, He is all-powerful, and all good! This is one reason why God does not bring down the new heaven and new Earth right after Jesus conquers His enemies. He is still giving those who made it through the tribulation more time and opportunity to devote themselves to Jesus Christ. The Millennial Kingdom will be a wonderful period, but it is not eternity. There is still sin and imperfection in those who made it through the tribulation. What sin there is will be hidden, as we saw in Zechariah 13. (It should also be noted that the Millennial Kingdom will be a time when God fulfills his covenantal promises to Israel. See Joel Richardson's teaching on this point in his YouTube series "Fulfilled".)

Now we come to the last two verses in the book of Zechariah, verses 20 and 21.

> *Zechariah 14:20-21 (NASB) On that day there will be inscribed on the bells of the horses, "HOLY TO THE LORD." And the cooking pots in the LORD'S house will be like the bowls before the altar. 21 Every cooking pot in Jerusalem and in Judah will be holy to the LORD of armies; and all who sacrifice will come and take of them and boil in them. And there will no longer be a Canaanite in the house of the LORD of armies on that day.*

These verses tell us that everything belongs to the LORD, and everything is used for His purposes. Once again, I find myself looking at prophetic verses in the Psalms. Psalms 24:1-2 says,

> *"The earth is the LORD's, and all it contains, The world, and those who live in it. For He has founded it upon the seas And established it upon the rivers." (NASB)*

Psalm 24:7-8 goes on to say,

"Lift up your heads, you gates, And be lifted up, you ancient doors, That the King of glory may come in! Who is the King of glory? The LORD strong and mighty, The LORD mighty in battle." (NASB)

This sounds like what we are reading here in Zechariah 14. We've already seen the King of glory in Zechariah 14:3, and now we are seeing that the Earth is the LORD's and everything and everyone in it. (Zechariah 14:20-21).

Zechariah 14:20-21 applies mainly to Israel. Verse 21 tells us, "Every cooking pot in Jerusalem and in Judah will be holy to the LORD of armies". The Millennial Kingdom will be a special time for everyone, but especially so for the nation of Israel. Israel will be the crown jewel in this earthly Kingdom of the LORD Jesus Christ. Reread Zechariah 8 to see the blessings that fall upon Israel from the LORD. Zechariah 8:12-13 says, "For there will be the seed of peace: the vine will yield its fruit, the land will yield its produce, and the heavens will provide their dew; and I will give to the remnant of this people all these things as an inheritance. And it will come about that just as you were a curse among the nations, house of Judah and house of Israel, so I will save you that you may become a blessing. Do not fear; let your hands be strong." (NASB) Zechariah 8:23 says. "The LORD of armies says this: 'In those days ten people from all the nations will grasp the garment of a Jew, saying, "Let us go with you, for we have heard that God is with you."'" (NASB) Isaiah 49:22-23 says,

"This is what the LORD GOD says: "Behold, I will lift up My hand to the nations And set up My flag to the peoples; And they will bring your sons in their arms, And your daughters will be carried on their shoulders. Kings will be your guardians, And their princesses your nurses. They will bow down to you with their faces to the ground And lick the dust from your feet; And you will know that I am the LORD; Those who hopefully wait for Me will not be put to shame. (NASB)

The LORD takes the everyday things in Israel and makes them holy, consecrating them to Him. The bells on horses and the cooking pots in the LORD's house will be holy. The bells on the horses are actual flat metal plates, but there are multiple plates so that when the horse moves, they hit against each other and make the sound of a bell. The inscription on the bells on the horses is interesting; it says, "Holy to the LORD". This is interesting because the inscription upon the mitre (headdress) of the high priest was "Holy to the LORD" (Exodus 28:36). If you read it in the King James Version, it is "Holiness to the LORD."

During the Millennial Reign of Christ, the most common items in Israel will be dedicated to the LORD. Verse 20 tells us that these cooking pots will be sacred, like the bowls that hold the blood before the altar. I'm not sure if my mind can comprehend what this truly means. My corrupted and fallen mind can't comprehend a time when everything will be set aside and used for the purposes of the LORD. The LORD's physical presence here on this Earth with us will make all things about Him and His reign. Common things will have "Holy to the LORD" written on them. We will look to bring Him glory and honor in the everyday things that we do. What was once inscribed only on the mitre of the High Priest will now be inscribed on many common everyday items, and it will be done out of devotion to the LORD. Verse 21 tells us that in Jerusalem and Judah, but I can't help but think that there will be items consecrated to the LORD throughout the Earth.

I first took notice of the phrase "Holy to the LORD" when I heard about the revival on the Asbury College campus, which began on February 8, 2023. My wife and I visited the campus to catch a little bit of what God was doing. Inscribed on the front wall of Hughes Auditorium is "Holiness unto the LORD". Hughes Auditorium was built in 1929, and I am unsure if the exact phrase was inscribed on the front wall of the building, which previously served as their chapel. A Google search tells you that there have been nine revivals on the campus of Asbury College: 1905, 1908, 1921, 1950, 1958, 1970, 1992, 2006, and 2023. I don't know why the LORD chooses to visit Asbury College with revivals over these many years. Still, I can't help but wonder if the phrase on the wall of that Chapel has special significance to the LORD and moved Him to bless Asbury College with revival.

Verse 21 tells us that all the cooking pots in Judah and Jerusalem will be holy to the LORD and can be used in sacrifices to the LORD. Here is an issue that we have not addressed: the sacrifices to the LORD. Why? They are not needed for the remission of sin; the King himself has already paid the cost of redemption. Is it a reminder of what the King has done for us? Is it to help us remember that there is a cost to sin, because those who survive the tribulation and go into the Millennial Kingdom will still sin? J Vernon McGee states that these sacrifices are like a memorial that points back to the cross. Just as the sacrifices in the Old Testament foreshadowed the cross, the sacrifices in the Millennial Kingdom are to serve as a memorial that points back to the cross and reminds the people of the cost of sin.

All of the people who survived the tribulation and entered the Millennial Kingdom had the opportunity to accept Jesus as their Savior before His second coming, but they rejected Him. Now, I believe that they must make their faith in Him public with works of faith. Those of us who trust in Christ today must make our faith public with works of righteousness; these works that we do are not tied to ceremony. In a sense, the works that Jesus Christ requires from believers today are stricter than the works He asks of those in the Millennial Kingdom.

Today, we should be listening to His voice and giving our bodies as a living sacrifice. During the Millennial Kingdom, He will require the people to follow many, if not all, of the Old Testament feasts and sacrifices. James 2:14-26 tells us that faith without works is dead. I believe that today, a significant portion of the American Church overlooks this point. However, during the Millennial Kingdom, there will be requirements for people to sacrifice and celebrate the feasts. If they do not, there will be consequences from the King, specifically the lack of rain on their land. These are just outward signs, and people will be able to perform these activities without a genuine heart transformation, and Jesus will know. He is the discerner of hearts.

Most likely, there are more reasons behind the requirement of the sacrifices and feasts. I look forward to the day when we can ask Him, and He will tell us. As far as the Millennial Kingdom is concerned, I see three reasons for it; 1) to fulfill the promises made to Israel and for God to shower His favor on His people; 2) to reveal rebellion is in the heart of man even when God provides near perfect conditions, man chooses to rebel; and 3) to give those who did not put their faith in Jesus before the Tribulation the opportunity to put their faith in Him. When the Millennial Kingdom is over, Satan will be loosed from the pit and will go forth to deceive the nations. He will gather a great multitude that will march against Jerusalem. As they surround Jerusalem, they will all be destroyed by fire from heaven (Revelation 20:7-10). There is rebellion in the heart of man, I feel it in my own heart, and only abiding in Him keeps me in check.

The last phrase of the previous verse piqued my curiosity. Zechariah 14:21b says,

"And there will no longer be a Canaanite in the house of the LORD of armies on that day." (NASB)

It could be referring to the fact that Israel will be for the Jewish people and that those people who are Canaanites are required to live outside of Israel. However, Biblehub.com provides this from Strong's Exhaustive Concordance, "Patrial from Kna'an; a Kenaanite or inhabitant of Kenaan; by implication, a pedlar (the Canaanites standing for their neighbors the Ishmaelites, who conducted mercantile caravans) -- Canaanite, merchant, trafficker." The passage is likely referring to Jesus' casting out the money changers from the Temple. What this last sentence is telling us is that there will be no merchants, no money changers, on the Temple grounds during Jesus Christ's reign here on Earth.

Zechariah is a call to bow to the King before it is too late. Jesus is King, and He will take His throne in Jerusalem. He will punish those who rebel against Him and reward those who put their faith in Him. Which are you? As stated in this Book, He is calling both Jews and Gentiles into His family. Those who reject His call will find His wrath, and those who accept His call will become a co-heir with Christ. I pray this book helps you decide to follow Jesus Christ.

If you have already put your faith in Jesus as the Christ, I pray that this book brings you closer to Him as you read it. I pray that this book inspires you to make Him and His kingdom your priority, to recognize that He is the King and He deserves your love and obedience.

About The Author

Ken Giesman was born into a Christian family and raised in the Baptist Church, which played a significant role in shaping his early beliefs and values. For eight years, during his primary and secondary education, he attended a Christian school, which further deepened his faith-based upbringing. Ken later pursued higher education at Cedarville University, where he earned a degree in accounting with an emphasis in finance and completed a minor in biblical studies.

Although Ken hasn't worked in full-time Christian ministry, he has made meaningful contributions through various volunteer positions within several churches. He served as an Elder and as a member of the finance committee, providing leadership and financial oversight. Additionally, Ken taught adult classes and dedicated fifteen years as a volunteer youth leader across two different student ministries, impacting the lives of many young people.

Ken has been married to his wife since June 1991. Together, they raised three children who are now adults.

For the past thirty-eight years, Ken has built a successful career in the banking industry. He began his professional journey with the Federal Deposit Insurance Corporation (FDIC) before spending the next thirty-four years in various roles within the commercial lending field. Ken continues to work in this sector, bringing decades of experience and expertise to his profession.